THERE HAS NEVER BEEN AN AUTOBIOGRAPHY AS JOLTING, AS DEEPLY MOVING, AS SHATTERING AS *WILL THERE REALLY BE A MORNING?*

WILL THERE REALLY BE A MORNING?

AN AUTOBIOGRAPHY BY
FRANCES FARMER

A DELL BOOK

Published by
DELL PUBLISHING CO., INC.
1 Dag Hammarskjold Plaza
New York, New York 10017

Dell ® TM 681510, Dell Publishing Co., Inc.

ISBN: 0-440-19068-1

The poem "Will There Really Be a Morning?"
is from *The Complete Poems of Emily Dickinson*,
edited by Thomas H. Johnson and published by
Little, Brown and Company.

Reprinted by arrangement with
G. P. Putnam's Sons
New York, New York 10016
Printed in the United States of America
First Dell printing—July 1973

Second Dell printing—September 1973

New Dell printing—May 1979

TO JEAN RATCLIFFE

Will there really be a morning?
Is there such a thing as day?
Could I see it from the mountains
If I were as tall as they?

Has it feet like water-lilies?
Has it feathers like a bird?
Does it come from famous places
Of which I have never heard?

Oh, some scholar! Oh, some sailor!
Oh, some wise man from the skies!
Please to tell this little pilgrim
Where the place called morning lies.

EMILY DICKINSON

1

For eight years I was an inmate in a state asylum for the insane. During those years I passed through such unbearable terror that I deteriorated into a wild, frightened creature intent only on survival.

And I survived.

I was raped by orderlies, gnawed on by rats, and poisoned by tainted food.

And I survived.

I was chained in padded cells, strapped into straitjackets, and half drowned in ice baths.

And I survived.

The asylum itself was a steel trap, and I was not released from its jaws alive and victorious. I crawled out mutilated, whimpering and terribly alone.

But I did survive.

The three thousand and forty days I spent as an inmate inflicted wounds to my spirit that could never heal. They remain, raw-edged and festering, for I learned there is no victory in survival—only grief.

I can recall the twisting circumstances that eventually locked me into a world devoid of all hope, but I cannot rationalize why it happened. All that is left is the painful memory that it did occur and that somehow I managed to live through it.

My life never brimmed with pleasant memories, for I was born into a disturbed environment. I was born too late in the lives of my mother and father, always to be the last of a long and bitter series of encounters between them.

Childhood was a desperate span of years, and I emerged from it never having known the comfort of feeling loved, or even wanted. Security, of any kind, was unknown, and most of my life was spent in this isolation.

Who was responsible for the pain? Certainly I contributed to my agonies, but there was another villain.

Even in the beginning, I knew that God was not the culprit, for in my mind He was too distant and too disinterested to have singled me out in particular and set his universal forces against me.

There is a Jewish saying, "God could not be everywhere and therefore He made mothers," and whether I was justified or not, I held mine accountable as the main root of my despair.

No matter how hard we thought we tried, there was never a day when we were able really to understand each other. From childhood on our relationship was strained and torn by strife. Every encounter between us ended in screaming hysteria and slamming doors.

My mother was a determined, hard-willed woman, and her eccentricities created humiliating circumstances that nearly destroyed my life.

But, on the other hand, I was not a docile offspring, and I fought back as long as I could and with any weapon available. It was a long and bitter battle that eventually led me into the grimmest encounter that any human can face.

Between the ages of twenty-one and twenty-eight I made nineteen motion pictures and appeared in three Broadway shows, as well as seven stock productions. I had the lead in more than thirty major dramatic shows on radio and went on countless personal appearances. My career was fast-paced, but I was torn with inner conflicts. I had never been able to adjust to the pressures of Hollywood, and I realized too well that I was one of the most unpopular stars within the industry.

I was a difficult and high-strung actress and had made enemies in high places. I remember reading an article in which one of my directors said, "The nicest thing I can say about Frances Farmer is that she is utterly unbearable." He was no doubt correct, for I found Hollywood and the motion picture industry equally unbearable.

During this unhappy period my marriage came disastrously to an end, and in the fall of 1943, a frightened, overworked and embittered young woman, I collapsed.

My life reached a frightening climax when I was arrested on a minor charge of driving in a dimout zone with my lights on. From this seemingly simple wartime arrest, charges against me snowballed into a nation-wide scandal and a six months' probationary jail sentence. When I failed to report to the parole officer as ordered, a warrant was issued for my rearrest.

I was living at the Knickerbocker Hotel in Hollywood, and late one night, after I had retired, three policemen disturbed the whole floor by pounding on my door. When I would not admit them, they forcibly entered, shoved a warrant in my hand, and hauled me off to the Santa Monica jail.

My reaction was violent! Everything exploded! The court finally released me to the Screen Actors Sanitarium for rest, so I was, at least, spared a jail sentence. Perhaps if I had been left alone during that period of confinement, I would have reconciled the problems in my life, but my father, who was an attorney, secured a court order and had me extradited to my

home state of Washington with my mother as my legal
guardian.

When I returned home, although my career and personal life were a shambles, I still had hope of gathering the shattered pieces and somehow fitting them together again.

From the moment I was placed under my mother's
legal control, I was shoved headlong into a deep abyss
from which there was no escape. It was only a short
time before she had me committed to the state hospital near our home in Seattle, where I remained for
three months and was then released as "completely
cured." Unfortunately, I did not know enough to have
her guardianship set aside, and I was chained to a
woman who, perhaps subconsciously, seemed determined to destroy my life. The asylum released me into
her custody, and for the next seven years her power
and control was unlimited.

There was nowhere to go but home with her, and
although my career and personal life were a shambles,
I still had a frayed idea of gathering up the pieces
and somehow fitting them together again.

But in my thirtieth year all my hopes came to an
abrupt and frightening halt. On the morning of May
22, 1945, I reached the point of no return.

2

I was living at my mother's home in Seattle, and relations between us were strained and difficult. We were both on guard and explosive. I had been released from the state hospital for nearly a year, but isolated alone with her in a crumbling house, I became more unhinged. I was restless and rebellious at the restrictions she enforced, but I was helpless to do anything about them.

At the time of my arrest, I was found to be completely without funds. Curiously, one day it seemed that I was a productive, well-paid actress, and the next I was a penniless, incompetent woman.

Since the time of my release, Mamma and I had fought, argued, threatened, and screamed until it had finally come down to a climax of two exhausted women sitting across from each other in a small, cluttered kitchen. We were enemies who had grown tired of pretending. We were strangers pathetically bound by the invisible cord that lashes parent to child and child to parent.

It was midmorning and we were at breakfast. The kitchen table wobbled under the weight of my elbow and the coffee splashed from my cup and ran over the oilcloth.

"Goddamnit," I shouted. "What the hell did you do with all the money I sent you?"

"Money?" she replied vaguely.

"You're damn right," I spat back. "M-O-N-E-Y! You bitched about this goddamned table for years and I've sent you enough to buy a truckload. So what did you do with it? You sure as hell didn't spend any of it around here."

The room was disgusting. Neither of us had ever been much of a housekeeper, but now we had abandoned any pretense of tidiness. The floor was dirty. Trash was piled under the sink and dust was on top of everything.

So this is the house of a movie star's mother, I thought bitterly. Not at all like the fan magazines would picture it . . . but then, what was?

I had sent money home since my first job in Hollywood, and although it had not been a fortune, I felt it had surely been enough to have improved her life. It irritated me to see things in such a mess.

"What did you do with the money?" I asked again.

She peered at me over her glasses. "Don't work yourself up. You know what happens when you get all worked up."

"For Christ's sake!" I said.

"You've got a rotten mouth," she mumbled. "Rotten! Rotten! And I never thought I'd raise a child, let alone a daughter, who would spit out filth like a deckhand."

"Shit!" I said.

She smacked the table with the palm of her hand, rattling the dishes that cluttered it. "I won't listen to any more of this," she warned. "So you just better keep your mouth shut!"

She rummaged through the pocket of her bathrobe for a cigarette but was able to retrieve only a grimy kitchen match from it. I tossed my pack across to her, and without taking her eyes off me she pulled out one, raised the edge of the cloth, and scratched the match across the bottom of the table. She lit the cigarette, held the match in front of her for a moment, then dropped it, still burning, onto her breakfast plate.

"For God's sake, Mamma!" I said. "That's a disgusting habit."

"Finish your breakfast," she ordered. "And keep your mouth shut."

We sat in silence until she pushed herself back from the table and went to the stove. She was an old lady, in her seventies, wrapped in a faded bathrobe. Her nightgown hung around her ankles in uneven scallops, her hair was thin and uncombed. She was stooped and shuffled when she walked, but her face was strong and determined. She was old, but age had never forced her to relinquish her powerful spirit, and everything about her was dominant and positive.

She picked up the coffee pot and looked at me over her shoulder.

"More coffee?" she asked.

"No," I said. "No more."

She carried the pot back with her and stood over me.

"Have some more coffee," she urged. "It'll settle your nerves."

"Mamma," I said irritably, "I don't want any more!"

"Don't be silly," she said. "Here, I'll just warm your cup."

"Jesus Christ!" I yelled. "Leave me alone."

She stood there for a moment, then very deliberately filled the cup to the brim, shuffled arrogantly back to the stove, slapped the pot on the burner, and spun around to face me. She was flushed and angry.

"I'm just about at the end of my rope with you," she warned. "I've just about had all I can take. I've put up with you for years and what do I get for it? Nothing! Absolutely nothing! But you're my daughter and you're going to do exactly as I say, or back you go. Do you understand me? Back you go! And this time . . . for keeps."

I lit a cigarette as she spoke and studied the curling smoke.

"Answer me!" she shouted.

"Okay, Mamma," I retorted. "What do you want me to say? Do you want me to promise to be a good little girl and mind what you tell me? Is that what you want to hear? Is that it, Mamma? Well, you can go to hell!"

"You're a disgusting brat!" she spat contemptuously.

"I'm a thirty-year-old woman," I answered bitterly. "And I know damn good and well that you'll send me back the first chance you get."

I began to dance around in front of her, jiggling and waving my arms in a wild sort of way, making idiotic faces.

"Let's send little sister back to the asylum," I babbled over and over.

"Don't use that word!" she screamed.

I stopped in front of her defiantly.

"Oh, does it bother you, Mamma? Would you be more comfortable with 'sanitarium' or 'hospital'? Which would you prefer?"

She tried to slap me, but I ducked, laughing at her.

"It's an asylum. A nut house. A loony bin. Full of crazy people like me . . . so don't try to dress it up."

"Then you better understand what I'm saying," she said, not backing down.

"You'd do it, too, wouldn't you, Mamma?"

She dropped her cigarette into a dirty glass. God, what an ugly room, I thought. What an ugly house. What a goddamned ugly world.

"Yes," she said sternly. "If you force me, I'll do it.

But it'll be your fault because you won't do a thing to help yourself. Just look at you. You've wrecked everything you've touched. You've ruined a big career and a fine marriage . . . and you've hung around with every no good pink in this country until right here, in my own neighborhood, I can't show my face."

She turned her back abruptly and began stacking dishes in the sink. Her hands were trembling. Oh, God, I thought, I'm so tired of fighting with her. I'm so tired of being on the prod. I'm so scared.

I went to her and wrapped my arms around her waist.

"Mamma, please don't let it be like this."

I felt her stiffen against me and I slowly took my arms away, for I knew then that reconciliation was so hopeless.

"I'll clean up in here," I said, surprised at my lifeless voice.

The storm between us was over. It had been brief and flashing, finished almost before it started. Now we would pretend, for a while, that nothing had happened, but the pretense was the thing that was destroying me.

"Why don't you finish your coffee on the porch?" I said.

Without looking at me, she dried her hands on a towel draped over a spike nail, which had been carelessly driven into the plaster, and walked from the kitchen, letting the screen door slam hard behind her.

The sink was old and hung under a narrow window that looked out over the backyard. She had planted her vegetables early, and now the tiny shoots of her garden were showing bright and healthy.

The flowers she had started in seedbeds would be vivid, but there was no grass. She never concerned herself with such trimmings, and the dirt was packed hard and brown around the house.

I often wondered why she bothered to plant flowers, for they were never picked or brought into the house. I'll do that this afternoon, I thought. I'll pick the early roses and make a bouquet for the table. And then I looked around the kitchen, with the yellow walls that needed washing, the old wooden chairs with the paint chipped and peeled, and I knew I would not bother.

I wondered how much longer I could stand it. I had to get away from her . . . just for a little while. I had to take a walk or talk to somebody else. If I didn't, I'd go crazy.

That thought came bitter. Maybe she was right. I was getting worked up, and I knew that if things got really bad, she'd send me back. But before the final break came, I had to get away from her.

I finished the dishes halfheartedly, hung the towel on the nail, and went out to join her on the porch. I sat down on the steps and locked my arms around my knees.

"Mamma," I said thoughtfully. "Do you think I'm able to go back to work?"

"They said you could," she answered.

I looked at her questioningly. "They?" I asked.

"The hospital," she explained.

"Well, maybe that's what I better do. When Arthur called the other day, he said the studio had been putting out feelers about me. He said, with a little negotiation, I could have a picture."

"I know," she said. "I talked to him."

"When?" I asked in surprise.

Arthur Blair had been my manager, and I was puzzled as to why he would be talking over my personal business with her. He knew how I felt about such things.

"Well," she hedged.

"When did you talk to him?" I repeated. The very

thought of her doing it behind my back infuriated me.

"Well," she said again. "After he called, you didn't bother to tell me a word he said, and I could see from the look on your face that something was up. So I called him back to find out what was going on."

"But that's my business, Mamma," I said angrily. "You've got no right to pry into my business."

Defending herself, she said, "I have every right in the world to know and find out what you're up to. You're just like your father. Always a big secret. Always a big secret. That's your trouble."

"Oh, God," I groaned. "Don't start that again."

"Well, how else am I supposed to know what's going on?" she said, her voice rising. "What did you plan to do, sneak out in the middle of the night? Well, just try it, young lady, and I'll have the police pick you up. I've done it before and I'll do it again, so don't get it into your head that you can go anywhere or do anything unless I say so!"

"Jesus Christ," I shouted. "Can't we just talk without getting into a goddamned free-for-all?"

Then, remorsefully, I stretched out my hand and rested it gingerly on her knee. "Look, Mamma," I said pleadingly. "Let's just talk. We're in a bad way, I haven't worked for a year, and if I can go back, maybe that's what I should do. I can make three or four more pictures, and if we're careful with the money, we can get by on it for a long time."

"Why must you always put a limit on things, Frances?" she said, moving my hand away. "That's one of your big problems. You're always putting a limit on things."

"I don't like making movies, Mamma," I said through my teeth. "I've told you that over and over. I hate everything about it, and if I go back, it's for one thing—money!"

"And then what?" she asked.

"Who cares?" I shrugged. "Maybe we'll buy a car and just roam about the country. Or maybe I'll get a job in a library. Who cares?"

"You're talking nonsense," she said, dismissing the thought. Then added, "He said it was a good role. A real challenge."

"Challenge?" I said bitterly. "Challenge?"

"They're casting Cary Grant in it," she said enticingly.

"So?" I said.

"Well," she said. "It wouldn't hurt you, that's for sure." Then added, "And he's such a nice man."

"Who?" I asked.

"Cary Grant!" she said in exasperation.

"Oh, for God's sake," I said. "How the hell do you know what kind of a man he is? And what's that got to do with it, anyway?"

"That's the trouble with you, Frances," she said accusingly. "You never took up with anyone who could help you. Oh, no! Not you. You were never satisfied unless you were hanging around with all those freaks."

"Okay," I said. "Okay. So Cary Grant is a nice man."

This admission seemed to satisfy her. She had loved being a star's mother. She had devoured the Hollywood scene with the appetite of a piranha. Grant and I had made one picture together, and Mamma saw to it that she visited the set often, but I was neither impressed nor repelled by him.

He was an aloof, remote person, intent on being Cary Grant playing Cary Grant playing Cary Grant. I considered him a personality, not an actor, and I loathed the picture we had made together.

Paramount had loaned me out to RKO to costar with him in *The Toast of New York*. At first, I was rather excited about it, for it was the story of Jim Fisk and his mistress, Josie Mansfield. Together they had all but ruled Wall Street in the eighteen sixties.

My role posed an interesting acting challenge, or so I thought! Josie Mansfield had been a designing harlot, it's true, but she was also a woman of pathos in her desire for respectability. If honestly portrayed, it could have been a real acting experience, but the Hollywood frosting of the forties changed it into a sugar-coated distortion. Instead of a cheap vixen, they wanted an ingenue fresh from Sunnybrook.

So I rebelled. I argued with the producer. I fought with the director, and got into verbal knockdown drag-out battles with the writers. I gave out interviews that sent the studio heads into angry shock, and I made it extremely difficult for everyone on the set by belittling the whole procedure.

But they won, and I ended up beautifully costumed, and Josie Mansfield was safely tucked into a chastity belt.

The picture, as could be expected, was a hit, and Grant was obviously undisturbed and unaffected by my outbursts. Our love scenes in the picture had been mutually detached and were void of any emotional kickbacks. He remained polite but impersonal, and the prospects of another film with him created no interest for me, one way or another. What did concern me was the money I needed.

As I studied Mamma's face, I could see that she was wistfully reliving the Hollywood days, and an ingenious scheme began to germinate in my mind.

"Mamma," I said, my voice saccharin. "Why don't you talk to Arthur and tell him you think I'm able to work again? I'm afraid I wasn't too nice when he called."

"He understands," she said patiently.

She had always been impressed with Hollywood, and the slightest chance that I might agree to go back changed her attitude toward me almost immediately.

She went on, "He only wants to help you out, Frances."

"He only wants his ten percent," I said.

"Now, Arthur is a good friend," she said defensively. "And he's earned every cent you've paid him."

"Maybe so, Mamma," I said. "Maybe so. But why don't you sound him out? Only don't be too anxious. Find out what kind of a deal you can set up, and then I can talk to him in a day or two. Will you do that for me, Mamma?"

I threw out a tempting bait and she nibbled.

"You know I'll help any way I can," she said, so condescendingly that I wanted to laugh at her. "I only want what makes you happy. That's the only thing any of us wants. Surely you know that."

"I know," I said.

I stood up and stretched my arms high above my head. I felt good.

"Why don't you go in and call Arthur now?" I suggested. "And I'll go down to the market and get something for lunch. I'd rather not be here when you call him. That way you can talk more freely."

She liked the idea, and things were working out just as I had planned. After all, I knew this woman.

"I'll give you three dollars," she said agreeably. "And you can pick out something very special."

Involved with her new project, she did not stop to consider that, for the first time since my release from the asylum, she was agreeing to let me out of her sight, and she was trusting me with money, as well.

We had not been separated, except to sleep, since my return, and any errands were farmed out to the neighborhood children. We had not so much as left the house during the last five weeks, and even though I had been released as cured a year ago, she was still suspect and watched me like a hawk.

I needed to be away from her. But other things were gnawing me as well. I had not had a drink in almost a year, and the pressure of my thirst was foremost in my mind. I had become increasingly on edge and was convinced that a drink would help ease the tension. I was feeling better physically, but anxiety lay just below the surface, and my mother knew it.

But now she chattered away as we went into the house. I didn't know where she kept the money, and I interrupted her chirping by reminding her that I needed it to go to the market.

She reached down the neck of her robe, pulled out a small roll of bills, and carefully handed me three ones. I could still feel the warmth of her body on the soiled, damp paper.

"Now you run along, little sister, and surprise me with something nice," she cooed. "I'll call Arthur while you're gone and we'll see if we can't work out something."

As I left the house, I could hear her talking to the operator and I was satisfied, for I knew she would be kept busy with her plans.

I was free! I was free!

At the market four blocks away, I selected an excellent cut of meat, some fresh vegetables, milk, bread and three packages of cigarettes, spending all but thirty-five cents. On the way I had used all my willpower not to stop at a bar before buying the groceries, but now, with them safe in a small bag, and the leftover change in my purse, I almost ran back down the street.

I wanted a drink. Although I fully realized that liquor had contributed to my problems, I still wanted to feel that initial shockwave of confidence it gave me.

I was not a good drinker . . . and drinking too much was like pointing a loaded gun at my temple. It unleashed all the stifled bitterness and contempt that lay fermenting in me.

I was never the life of the party. Most often I ended up angry at everyone and sometimes violent, with an uncontrollable need to retaliate against everyone and everything that surrounded me. Liquor set free the fury.

I was not a social drinker; neither was I an alcoholic. Rather, I should say that I was emotionally allergic, for everything about me changed with the first drink. I could feel it, and others could see it, for anger spewed out of me like an erupting volcano.

I can't remember a time when I was pleasantly high, and there were many instances when one drink sent me into vehement orbit. But, within me, there was a strange paradoxical escape hatch that preserved me. In contradiction, it nearly destroyed me. Perhaps all actresses rely on it to some degree, but in me it attained life-and-death proportions.

As an actress I had always been able to submerge myself in a role so that a part of me actually became the character. Another part of me was able to stand in the wings, so to speak, and observe the performance.

I first became aware of this while rehearsing for a college play. My role was extremely demanding for an inexperienced actress, and I had a great deal of difficulty separating my own personality from that of the character. During this period I began to sense a mysterious dual faculty within me. The prospect of this schizoid condition was fascinating, but it also left me uneasy and frightened.

The role was that of Else Brandt in Sidney Howard's *Alien Corn*. As rehearsals progressed, and throughout the run of the play, I was as much Else Brandt as I was Frances Farmer. I could actually sense the two distinct beings, and while Else was onstage, Frances was in the audience watching the performance. I was two separate beings, and the separation was well defined.

After that, when things became intolerable at home, and later, when any condition became unbearable, I simply stepped aside and watched another part of me perform in a role under specific conditions. However I was always aware of this split, and although it created indescribable tensions in my life, it later became my greatest strength. During my bleakest years in the asylum I survived solely because of this strange separation. In the violent ward, a part of me stood apart from the frantic woman all but devoid of her senses and watched, with detachment, the horrendous nightmare that all but destroyed her.

Drinking, of course, was an aggravation, and I knew it. I knew that I always took a risk with that first drink, but now I wanted one, and I had saved thirty-five cents to buy it.

The bar was a run-down neighborhood joint like ten thousand others across the country, and since it was still quite early, only two hard-core drinkers were in it. It smelled musty from the night before, and the darkness, after coming in from the morning sun, was blinding.

I stood at the bar and a thick-necked Greek leaned across and grinned at me.

"Wod you wand, gurlee?" he said. His accent was halting and very difficult to understand.

I dumped the coins on the counter and mumbled, "How much wine will this get me?"

"We talk about it," he said, grinning. "But how 'bout one on house, gurlee?"

Crummy little bastard, I thought, but said, "Sure, why not?"

He put a shot glass in front of me, and I watched as he filled it with the pale amber of scotch. I drank it quickly and shuddered as that old familiar fire flowed down my throat. He filled the glass again and set the bottle in front of me, keeping his fingers wrapped around the neck.

That's better, I thought. Already my body was eased and my mind seemed sharper. I sat down on the stool and toyed with the empty glass while the Greek slowly wiped the countertop, making no attempt to hide the fact that he was ogling me.

But I was feeling better. It was good to relax. He set up a third drink, and I took it in one swallow, then looked around the room, finally returning to his open stare. He filled my glass again, and this time I toyed with it for a moment, sipping, letting it roll around in my mouth, liking the taste of it stinging my tongue. It was cheap and raw, but it was good.

I pushed the change toward him. "Gimme the wine," I mumbled.

He shrugged and sacked a half pint, twisting the paper tight around the neck of the bottle. I snatched it from him, defiantly tore off the sack, unscrewed the cap, and drained it, slapping it down hard on the bar.

Very carefully I picked up my groceries and staggered through the front door. I was drunk, and I knew it.

The sun was blinding, and for a few seconds I was baffled as to which direction led home. My legs were weak and I was beginning to feel sick to my stomach. Then that old familiar panic began to swell up within me—the panic that told me everyone was my enemy, that they would hurt me, that they were after me, that they wanted me dead.

Then came the fierce angry-hate, so deep rooted that I could not remember when it had been born.

Jesus! She'll send me back! She hates me! She's always hated me! Run! Faster! Get away from her! Oh, God! I hate her! Hate her! They'll get you! Be still! Don't let them hear! Act! God damn you, act! Act sick! Don't let her know! A new Garbo, they said! Run! No! Steady! Walk! Easy! Easy! Smile big for Mamma!

I wanted to lie down. My legs were giving out, but somehow I held on. And then slowly my mind came into focus and I knew where I was and who I was.

Then, almost clearly, I watched a woman who looked like me, but who was nothing more than a remote and disgusting stranger staggering down the street.

I leaned weakly against the side of a storeroom and waited for the calm to settle over me.

There would be no pretending to Mamma that I was sick. I was. But gradually, as it had so often happened before, my equilibrium returned, and I was frighteningly sober.

I looked up and saw my reflection in the store window and was startled to see, looking back at me, a calm, rather beautiful young woman.

It doesn't show, I thought. My God, it doesn't show.

I managed to get home. I cautiously opened the front door and put the groceries in the kitchen. From the back window, I saw her weeding the garden.

"Mamma," I called. "I'm back."

She looked up, shielding her eyes from the sun with her hand, and waved.

"I've put the groceries away," I told her. "But I'm not feeling very well. I think I'll lie down for a while."

She started toward the house.

"I'm all right," I called, stopping her.

"Are you sure?" she asked.

"Don't worry," I assured her. "It's nothing. I'll just lie down till lunch."

"All right, Frances," she said. Then added, "I spoke with Arthur and he's calling back later today. Everything is going to be just fine."

"That's good," I said.

"Are you certain you don't want anything?" she added.

"No. No," I said quickly. "I'll be fine."

Satisfied, she resumed her weeding. I watched for a long moment, then went up to my room and stretched out across my bed.

The room was dark when I awoke. The streetlight glowed faintly through my window and I was grateful but puzzled that she had let me sleep undisturbed.

I tried to turn on my lamp, but it did not work, and the overhead light was off as well. Our bedrooms were directly across from each other, with a stairway and small landing separating us. I tried the hall light, but still nothing happened.

Everything was dark. I felt my way across to her room and found the door open. I knew this meant that she was not in it, but, all the same, I called "Mamma?" There was no answer.

I found my way down to the landing in the living room. The streetlight was pale through the window and by it I saw the outline of her figure on the couch.

"Why are you sitting down here in the dark?"

She was fumbling around for a cigarette, and I listened as the match scratched against the sole of her shoe. When she held it up before her face, I could tell by the set of her head that she was angry.

"What's wrong with you, Mamma?" I said. "Do you know all the lights are out?"

"Sit down," she ordered.

I started toward the couch but her voice stopped

me. "Don't you dare come near me. Sit in the chair."

I felt a sudden chill and I was frightened of her, of the dark, of everything. I sat down and waited.

"How do you feel?" she asked in an icy voice.

"Better. I guess I needed the rest."

"You needed to sleep it off, you mean," she snapped.

"What are you talking about?"

"Damn you, Frances!" she shouted. "Don't you sit there and play dumb with me. You were drunk! Drunk! So don't try to lie out of it!"

She knew! Somehow she knew! But how? She had not seen me, so how could she know?

"I don't know what you're talking about," I said. "What's wrong with you? What's this all about? Why are you sitting down here in the dark? Jesus Christ, Mamma, you're acting crazy."

"The lights won't work because I've pulled the switch," she hissed. "The thought of having to look at your face makes me want to vomit. I wish I never had to see your face again."

"Oh, God," I groaned and slumped back in the chair.

"Are you ready to talk?" she demanded, and her tone was insulting and imperious.

I was silent.

"Where did you get it?"

"Get what?" I mumbled.

Then it exploded.

"Where did you get the liquor?" she screamed.

"You're nuts," I screamed back. "You're a crazy goddamned old woman and I don't know what you're talking about."

"Don't you lie to me! The whole neighborhood saw you staggering down the street. Now, where did you get it?"

"I don't know what you're talking about."

She moved quickly across the room and I felt her hand slap hard across my cheek.

"Don't lie to me!" she shrieked and slapped me again.

I put out my hand to ward off another blow.

"You rotten tramp! You filthy whore! Where did you get it?"

I pushed her away and she stumbled back.

"Don't you ever lay a hand on me again," I warned her.

"I should have beaten you a long time ago."

"Maybe you should have," I agreed hotly. "But it's too late to try it now. So don't. Ever!"

She slumped on the couch, sobbing hysterically. I began to pace the room. I could not cope with another fight.

"I'm going back to bed," I said flatly. "This whole thing is absurd."

I started up the stairs, but her reply stopped me short. "I'm sending you back, Frances." I was chilled by her sudden calm. "And this time," she went on, "I'll see that you stay."

I stood on the landing with my hands clamped over my ears and screamed at her. "All right, goddamnit, you do that. Do anything you want to do. But do you know something? An asylum would be better than this. Anything would be better than this. Hell would be better than this."

Suddenly all expression drained from my voice. It was without tone or life. "And you're probably right, Mamma. Maybe I am crazy. I don't know. There must be something wrong with me. Something bad. Maybe it's like they say, Frances Farmer is crazy. But do you know something else, Mamma? I don't care anymore. I really don't care. So you do what you must. But remember this, you'll never destroy me. God as my judge, I'll survive! Somehow, I'll survive."

I left her sitting in the darkness, and as I climbed the stairs, I heard the sound of her weeping. "It's too late, Mamma," I said to myself. "It's too late."

My room was dark and cool, and as I lay on my bed, I felt the moist night wind blow across me, and for the first time since childhood, I wanted to pray.

I wanted desperately to believe in something. I wanted to feel that somewhere there was surely a God who knew and cared, for I had reached a point in life where I could not reason with one who set the universe in order yet left His likeness to writhe in chaos.

I was frightened by the unfamiliar spirit that lived within me, and I could find no comfort in a distant God. I also knew the dark world of madness could encase me unless I found a strength outside myself and a faith in something beyond myself.

"Peace" was an unfamiliar impersonal word, for I had never known it, and I could not imagine it as a part of me. But war I understood. I had been nurtured on it from birth. I was accustomed to dreams that became twisted and deformed.

I had hammered my way for thirty years and had lifted myself to the pinnacle, then, without realizing why, I had let go.

My senses had been stunned by success and my mind numbed by shock. My body had known the touch of a caress and the brutality of an assault. Life had carried me on a tidal wave, and I was exhausted . . . but I did not want to die.

I was now vulnerable, and I knew that I would spend the rest of my life walking under a deep and tormented shadow. My career lay crumbled and there was no way ever to regain it. Everything I had worked for was lost forever. I was labeled as surely as though the "Mark of the Beast" had been stamped on my forehead.

I was alone, and I was confused, but was I insane? Was this uncommon reality in which I lived insanity? Had my mind exploded beyond reality or repair, or was I, instead, the result of some dreadful caricature? Had I demanded too much from life, and had I, when the demands were not met, built my own crucifix?

I knew these questions would follow me to the brink of my grave, but I pledged that I would search until I found the answers.

I was the betrayer and the betrayed. Like a twisted nun, I was corroded by the flesh. But deep within me moved the powerful force of hope . . . a force so strong that I almost willingly accepted the hell I would enter, for I knew I would survive it all.

That night, desperately alone in that small dark room, I realized that even though my spirit was tormented almost beyond reason, my soul was in safe-keeping and beyond the reach of any devil or any hell.

I heard my mother's footsteps dragging up the stairs. She's tired, I thought, and so full of pain. She had wanted so much and I had given so little. I listened as her door closed softly, and though we were only a room apart, we were separated by a universe.

Throughout the night I lay quiet and I watched till the sun cleared my window, and for the last time for many years to come I heard the sounds of morning break the darkness undisturbed.

Never before had I known such calm. Never before had I felt such momentary peace. Ahead of me, I knew, lay mortal torment, but that one brief respite gave me comfort and drew me to my final destiny.

It was morning, and I heard my mother rise. It startled me when she knocked softly at my door.

"Frances," she said calmly. "I'd like you to get dressed and come down stairs. There are some people here who want to meet you."

It was almost as if nothing had happened between us—almost as if I were a child again, being called for school.

"I'll be right down, Mamma," I promised. And I thought, with a half-hope, maybe I'm wrong, maybe everything will be all right.

"Frances," she then added. "Please try to look your prettiest."

I smiled.

"All right, Mamma. I won't be long."

I wondered who had come to visit. Certainly she felt they were important, at least to her. So I washed quickly, slipped on a soft cotton dress, and took a little extra care with my makeup and hair. Satisfied that I was presentable and hoping to please her, I went downstairs.

My mother was in the living room with two uniformed men . . . and I knew!

I began to scream and tried to run, but they grabbed me. I fought like a cornered animal but was easily overpowered and wrestled to the floor. They straddled me, and I felt the rough canvas of the straitjacket wrap around me and buckle into place. My arms were nearly stretched from their sockets as I was locked into it.

I screamed! I screamed in pain and fright. The buckle chewed into my back, and I flopped on the floor like a dying chicken.

I screamed every filthy word I knew at my mother, and then, in consuming fear, I was reduced to begging her to help me.

"Oh, God, Mamma, don't do this. Don't do this to me."

She turned away, and as the men pulled me to my

feet, I began to kick. They each grabbed a leg, jerked off my shoes and clamped heavy leather manacles around my ankles, trussing me up like a pig on the slaughter line. A thick roll of gauze, stuffed in my mouth, silenced me, and I thought I would vomit from the gag.

Sweat poured into my eyes and burned like liquid fire. I twisted my head searching blindly for my mother, but I did not see her.

I was carried from the house by the two men. They hauled me to a gray panel truck parked in front, and on the door, in bold scarlet letters, I saw the word EMERGENCY.

The street was full of neighbors. Curious. Huddled together. Staring. Some of the women had their children with them, and in their young innocence they giggled and mocked "the funny lady."

Inside the truck, suspended in the center, was a canvas hammock or swing. I was held on it by one man while the other buckled straps across my chest, waist and legs.

I heard the door slam, and when the lock turned, I was imprisoned in a jet blackness, for a solid padded partition separated me from the front of the truck.

I heard the grind of the motor, and the blackness that surrounded me began to move, throwing me into a violent whirlwind of motion. A siren screamed, just before I fainted.

3

The asylum was about thirty-five miles south of Seattle, and somewhere along that frightening drive, I regained consciousness.

There was no ventilation in the truck, and the close air was rancid with the stench of sweat and stale urine. How many others had been hauled into hell . . . lashed to that same hammock? Straining their flesh against the straps. Wetting on themselves. Befouling their bodies. Feeling chunks of vomit and sour bile fill their mouths. Helpless. Terrified. Alone. Some, perhaps, mad beyond reason but still alive. Still able to feel. Still able to care.

And so it was, on May 22, 1945, at 3:25 in the afternoon, that I was delivered bound and gagged to the state asylum like a dog gone mad.

From the truck, they carried me to a small admitting ward, and despite my thrashing, three orderlies finally succeeded in strapping me into an armless wooden chair that was bolted to the floor.

I tried to fight myself free, but belts were strapped across my chest and lap, and my ankles were tied to the legs of the chair. The straitjacket was still on me, but, mercifully, they pulled the gag from my mouth.

My saliva tasted thick and sour, and I tried to twist my shoulders up and bend my head to the side in order to wipe my mouth, but when I could not, I simply spat on the floor.

After the orderlies left, I looked around the room and studied the other five people in it: three men and two women barefoot and in straitjackets, but only one, a balding, heavy-jowled man, was strapped in a chair as I was.

But he was quiet in the jacket. For that matter, he seemed detached and unaware of his surroundings. His chin rested on his chest, and only an occasional twitching of his shoulders showed any life.

The other four people were wandering around the room, tottering like deformed gnomes. Chattering. Crying. Screaming. Cursing. Pleading. Occasionally, a male orderly would bang on the door, push his face against the wire-covered peephole in it, and growl, "Shut up in there! Shut up, or I'll take the belt to you."

The smell of my body was sickening, and nausea brought on icy waves of sweat. Vomit belched from me, bitter and rank, hanging onto my chin, staining the front of the straitjacket, lying in my lap, curdled and vile. My stomach muscles contracted and knotted into dry spasms until finally the retching ceased and I slumped forward exhausted.

A woman of about my age screamed and loped across the room, pumping her jacketed shoulders up and down as she approached me.

"Stop that! Stop that!" she shrieked, and began kicking my leg with her bare feet. "Stop that! Dirty! Dirty!" She jumped on my feet, hammering on my toes with her heels.

"You goddamned bitch," I screamed. "You goddamned crazy bitch. If I get out of this, I'll kill you."

She stopped abruptly, then began batting her eyes

furiously, cocking her head to one side as though listening to someone. Then in a sudden, wild movement she ran to the door and began beating on it with her head.

"You've turned the Devil loose on us," she screamed. "He's in here. He's here. He's going to kill me. Let me out. Let me out."

A quiet skinny young man of perhaps twenty, reacting to the new commotion, suddenly leaped in the air, jumped on the seat of his chair, stretched his long thin neck back like a howling wolf and started rolling his eyes around and around in his head. Strings of black oily hair hung in his face. His straitjacket was loose, and he wiggled in it like a fish. In a shrill voice he began his high-pitched babbling. "Hear me! Hear me! I will save you. I am the begotten son. Fear not, for I am with you. I will deliver you from evil."

I was fascinated at the workings of his Adam's apple, for it stuck out like a broken knuckle and bobbed up and down like a yo-yo on a loose string.

A toothless old man hopped up and down in front of the young man, first on one leg, then the other, jerking his head vigorously from side to side, cackling, "Glory! Glory! I've seen Jesus! I've seen Jesus!"

The woman who had stomped my feet began running back and forth across the room, bouncing her body against the wall, and then the old man marched around and around in a tight little circle, shouting until the veins on his neck stood out like blue worms. "I've seen Him! Jesus! Jesus! Bless His name! I've seen Him!"

The woman stopped running and screamed, "Where? Where is He?"

"Jesus" was still standing on the chair but had wet his pants in the excitement. Undaunted and unaware, his voice rose higher and higher until it rang above the clatter around him. "I am the Lord. Be saved and kneel before the Lord."

The old man fell to his knees, and the woman screeched at him in wild fury and kicked him.

"You crazy old coot! You said it was Jesus! That ain't Jesus! You old coot."

The old man rolled himself into a tight bony knot and pulled his knees up as high as the straitjacket would allow. Seemingly impervious to her, he rocked and gabbled. "I've seen Jesus! Glory! Glory!"

She began stomping on him, cursing, spitting, screaming. "Devil! Devil! Devil!"

The other woman in the room, who was about sixty, had huddled quietly in a chair, lost in her own world. But on seeing the attack on the old man, she cautiously slid around the wall until she reached the cell door. In a trembling timid voice she pleaded through the window, "Please! Somebody! Help us in here! She's trying to kill the old man! Somebody! Help!"

The door swung open, almost knocking her down, as three men rushed into the room, swinging coiled wet towels above their heads. They whipped the air with them, making clean whistling sounds, and the woman who had called for help ran away and cowered in a corner.

The old man still lay in a huddle on the floor and "Jesus" was jumping up and down on his chair, letting out ear-piercing screams. Two attendants wrestled with the younger woman, struggling to drag her out of the room. She twisted free and headed toward me.

"Get that crazy bitch out of here," I screamed. "You goddamned mother-fuckers, get that crazy bitch out of here."

A short, pale-skinned attendant angrily swung his

towel at me, and I felt my head snap back as it struck me full across the face. The end of the towel seared my face like a hot branding iron. Blood spurted from my nose, and my head shattered in splitting pain.

"You filthy rotten son of a bitch," I screamed, spitting blood from my mouth. "You lousy filthy son of a bitch!"

He drew back the towel again. "I'll show you who's a mother-fucker. I'll knock your damned head off."

At that moment, the other two attendants, still wrestling with the woman, yelled for him to open the door and help them. He stomped across the room, stepping over the old man, and held it open while they carried her out, babbling and kicking. More attendants rushed into the room, and "Jesus" was pulled from his throne, unceremoniously, but offered no resistance and went peacefully.

The room was then awkwardly still except for the attendant who had hit me; eyeing each of us, he walked menacingly around, slapping the towel across the palm of his hand.

Suddenly the old man, who was still huddled on the floor, began passing wind, and then his bowels started to run. The attendant stood over him and groaned, "Oh, for Christ sake." He nudged him with the toe of his shoe, and as the old man stirred, the room was filled with the foul odor that squirted from him and stained his pants.

The man who was strapped to his chair reacted for the first time. "When are you going to let us out of here?" he begged. "When are you going to let us out of here?"

The attendant picked the old man up by the back buckles of his straitjacket and dragged him along the floor like a sack. He kicked on the door, yelling for someone to open it. The last I saw of the old man he was half-dangling, slobber running out of his toothless mouth, still uttering, "I've seen Him! I've seen Jesus!"

When the bolt on the door dropped heavily into place, it locked the three of us in a deep vacant silence. The other woman was hunched in a corner, her face against the wall. The man tied in the chair grinned at me idiotically and whispered, "Are you hurt?"

I shook my head.

"This is a bad day. It's bad of them to treat pretty women like this. I'd never treat pretty women like this. I like pretty women."

His face had a weird, wild cast, but it made me aware of how I must have looked. My hair was wet and soured from perspiration, and it hung in limp strings. Blood and vomit soiled my face and clothes. My nose was swelling and full of blood, and I felt it dripping down into my mouth. Until then I had not realized that I was drenched in my own urine.

In the struggle of strapping me to the chair, my dress had been pulled up, and with my ankles tied to the two front legs of the chair, I sat spraddled and exposed. When I realized he was trying to see up my dress, I clamped my knees together.

"You rotten freak," I snarled. "When I get out of here, I'll poke your goddamned eyes out."

His leering expression remained, but he turned his face away from me and began squirming in the chair in a constricted sexual spasm.

But in the midst of his total despair, my stomach rolled and rumbled, making me know that I was hungry. I had not eaten in nearly two days. From far off I heard a hyena laughing . . . then lost control when I realized it was me. I had to pull myself back.

The room, lighted only by a bare bulb hanging from

the ceiling, was growing dark. I managed to quiet myself by staring at the raw light; then, for want of a
better thing to do, I began to concentrate on localizing
the pain that racked my body.

I felt the itching dampness of my armpits. I felt the
soggy wetness of my underpants that stuck offensively
between my legs. I felt the hard, gritty floor with my
bare feet and flinched at the pain in my toes. I sniffed
the mucus and blood up through my nostrils until it
lumped and fell down into my throat. I coughed it out
onto my lap. My eyes were raw, and my face ached
from the whip of the wet towel.

My mother! My mother had sent me into this hell.
My own personal Judas. And the thought of it drowned
me in hatred.

I would nurture this passion. I would live on it.
Feed on it. Keep it alive. I would not be weakened or
coddled into accepting her power over me. I would be
ruthless in my search for truth and reality, cutting
away any fragments or sentiments that could impede
me. I knew I could only find reality clamped within the
steel jaws of hate. I would purge myself in the surrounding violence and lay bare the infection that
smoldered within me. I would look nowhere but to myself for survival.

I was trapped and filled with fear, but I knew that
as long as I could focus my hatred on those who had
been merciless in their drive to defeat me, an arrogant
courage would provide me with the determination to
stay alive.

I was worn out, but my mind was alert and every
faculty was on guard. I whispered to myself, "You
are strong, Frances, and no matter what they do to you,
don't let them win. Don't let them win."

I lifted my head and sat straight and stiff in the

chair, and my mind grew still and assured. The other two people had fallen asleep. I breathed a long painful sigh and soon joined them.

Much later a nurse and two women attendants came for me. I was sleeping soundly, and when they untied me from the chair, I was unable to stand. My legs crumpled under my weight. I slumped to the floor and began to sob uncontrollably as needlelike pains shot up my legs and my calf muscles knotted in spasms.

The women dumped me back in the chair, but the nurse knelt in front of me and massaged my legs until I gradually felt my muscles relaxing, and I was able to stand.

They took me to a small infirmary, where the nurse washed off my face and swabbed and sprayed my nose with a medication that gagged me. She was impersonal but efficient.

I asked for a drink of water, and since I was still in the straitjacket, one of the women held a paper cup to my mouth while I greedily gulped down the tepid water. I wanted more, but she refused me a second cup.

The nurse made notes on a report sheet, stuffed it into a folder, and handed it to one of the women. From the infirmary I walked between them down a long dim corridor. We stopped before a double door with the words ISOLATION WARD stenciled across it.

One of the women pushed a buzzer, and the door was unlocked from the inside by a nurse. I was guided into a large ward which resembled an underground cave.

The main corridor was perhaps ten feet wide and stretched out into a dim darkness. Just inside the door there was a small room, rather like a cage, that served as a nurses' station. A wire-covered window and door permitted a view of the ward.

We stood in the hall while the nurse went into her office and studied my folder, and while we waited, I listened to the muffled rumblings and groans that came from behind the row of doors that lined both sides of the corridor.

The restlessness. The fetid odors. The unreal sounds all blended together in this gray tomb to form an eerie and discordant symphony.

The nurse was a tall, lean woman whose hair looked like thick cotton pasted on her head. It was cut blunt and short and held back over her ears by black bobby pins that stood out like ebony spears.

The attendants shuffled impatiently while she fumbled through my record. She read a few lines, then peered curiously at me. Then read on. Finally she said, "Take her to the toilet, then we'll put her in seven."

From the steel cabinet in her office, she took out a short blue cotton gown and handed it to one of the women. "Leave the jacket on her until she's back in the cell."

She studied me again, then asked them curiously, "What happened to her face?"

"She was that way when we got her," one of the women grumbled. "She probably fell. She's been raising a lot of hell from what they say."

"Accidents happen." The nurse shrugged indifferently. "Go ahead and take her to the toilet and leave her on the stool. Use the strap and then come on back and have a smoke with me."

They took me to a small room a short distance down the hall. It was about ten feet long and not more than six feet wide. When the door was pushed open, a hideous, deathlike odor streamed out with such force that I began coughing.

"You think this is bad?" One of the attendants

laughed. "Just stick around, honey . . . you ain't seen nothin'."

A dirty washstand, an ancient bathtub and two stools cramped the closetlike quarters. The room was filthy. Rusty iron rings were bolted to the floor on either side of each stool. From an unlocked wall cabinet one of the attendants took out a dark-stained canvas strap with hooks on either end and an adjusting buckle in the middle.

The other woman stood me in front of one of the toilets, reached up under my dress, and pulled down my pants. They were soiled and damp, and I felt a wave of embarrassment as they fell around my ankles.

"Well," she ordered, "step out of them."

Then she pulled up my dress and held it around my waist as I sat down. The other woman hooked the strap to one ring on the floor, pulled it across my lap, and hooked the other end to the ring on the opposite side. She pulled the adjusting buckle, and my body was jackknifed into the bare toilet bowl, the water touching my flesh. Then they left.

My pants lay on the floor, and I strained until I was able to clamp my toes around the ugly, soiled material. I scooted my filthy foot back toward me and kicked them behind the stool and out of my sight.

I waited until every muscle in my body spasmed, and I started screaming and kept it up until the three of them came charging into the toilet. One of the attendants slapped me hard across the face and my nose started to bleed again.

"You'd better learn to keep your mouth shut 'cause there ain't nobody gonna hear you but us, and we ain't gonna listen."

"Ignorant bastard," I snarled, spitting out a flow of obscenities at her until she tried to shut me up by rapping the palm of her hand back and forth across my face with the rhythmic rat-a-tat of a machine gun.

"Leave her alone," the nurse ordered. "For Lord's sake, we'll wake up the whole ward." The woman eyed me hatefully, shaking her hand from the sting of slapping me, then shrugged.

"Did you have a bowel movement?" the nurse asked me, and the thought of this absurd and ironic solicitude made me want to laugh or scream or cry, but I merely grumbled, "Yeah."

When the other attendant stooped to unlock the strap, I started to get up, but the woman who had struck me pushed hard on my shoulders and shoved me back on the toilet. She leaned on me until my buttocks swam in the dirty water.

"Hold your horses, big shot, and spread your legs apart."

She had several sheets of toilet paper balled up in her hand and proceeded to grind the paper into me until I was begging her to stop. She stood up and with one hand clamped her fingers around my chin in a steel grip and pinched my jaws until my mouth was held open involuntarily. I was terrified at the look on her face, and when I saw her lifting the wad of wet paper toward my mouth, I tried to scream, but her fingers slipped down and clutched my throat in a painful vise.

I knew, perhaps for the first time, pure fright, but I was unable to speak. Only groans and whimpers came from me. I looked at the nurse, begging her with my eyes to help me, but she seemed busy at the wall cupboard. She was aware of what was going on, and I knew it, but she was removing herself from the episode. The other attendant looked away, and I caught a fleeting shade of sympathy cross her face.

"Open wide, big shot," the woman said. "You might as well learn now, 'cause in here sooner or later everybody eats their own shit."

I knew she was enjoying her power, for her eyes were burning and her words panted out almost sexually. Her fingers tightened around my throat and I smelled her breath hot on my face. Then the paper, dripping and stained, was shoved into my mouth.

Determined not to let her win, I fought down every normal reaction. Very deliberately I relaxed on the stool, stared her straight in the eyes, and began to chew. I had foiled her pleasure, and she was furious. She doubled her fist and hammered it straight into my face.

"Let her alone," the nurse interrupted. "Unbuckle her and let's get out of here. I'm worn out."

Because it is difficult to keep balanced or to maneuver normally in a straitjacket, I had to lunge up from the toilet. I tried again to wipe my nose by hunching up my shoulders and twisting my head around, but once more all I could do was sniff it into my throat and spit it out.

The three of them took me to a cell near the center of the ward. Its only furnishing was an iron cot anchored to the wall. On the cot was a thin mattress, with a sheet but no blanket or pillow. The barred window was closed and the smell was as rank as the toilet, musty and rotten.

One attendant unbuckled the straitjacket and my arms fell limply to my sides. The other attendant, the one who had hit me, leaned against the door and frowned at me. When the straitjacket was removed, I tried to flex my shoulder muscles but flinched at the pain and stiffness. I had lost track of the hours I had been in it.

The nurse told me to take off my clothes, but when I could not raise my arms above my head or even make my fingers work, the attendant offered to help me. She undressed me and then dropped the nightgown over my head.

"You can go now," the nurse said to them. "I've signed the receiving slip for her—it's on my desk. And take her clothes and give the stuff to Admitting. It's their responsibility."

I made a quick move and grabbed my dress. I blew my nose on it before anyone could stop me, getting rid of the blood that was beginning to cake, then rolled it up and handed it to the woman who had helped me.

The two attendants left, and I sat down on the cot and pivoted my head, trying to work out the stiffness in my neck. My body luxuriated in its freedom and I stretched out on the cot and groaned in relief.

The nurse, watching me, abruptly said, "You're Frances Farmer, aren't you? I've seen all your pictures." She went on, "Why, it looks to me like you'd be in one of those fancy places. I can't imagine why a big movie star would end up here. No indeed, I just can't imagine."

I covered my eyes with the back of my hand and yawned.

She stood over me and furtively said, "Could I have your autograph?"

I cocked open one eye, not quite believing my ears.

"Here, you can write on this." She stuck out a yellow pad and offered me a stub of a pencil.

I sat up, gave one of my warmest smiles, and said, with controlled charm, "Why, aren't you nice."

I took the pad and pencil, smiled at her again, and she responded in typical fan fashion, embarrassed but pleased.

"What's your name?" I asked sweetly.

"Foster. Marion Foster."

I wrote with a great flourish and handed it to her. She snatched it and anxiously began to read, but as she did, her face caught fire. She pulled her lips together and stomped from the cell, slamming the door behind her. I heard the bolt fall into place with a loud clang, and I was in darkness. As I heard the leather soles of her shoes slapping angrily down the hall, I squealed with delight.

I was pleased with myself and sat on the cot and giggled, for I had written, "Dear Marion Foster. Fuck you. Sincerely, Frances Farmer."

I lay back, rollicking over my last word, and laughed until I was choking back the tears. My mind was alert and racing. The absurd comedy I had just gone through peppered my thoughts with Hollywood and the power it exerted—a power so frightening that its influence was felt even in the solitary cell of an asylum.

Get out of your straitjacket, Miss Farmer, and give me your autograph.

My God. What kind of help could I expect? None!

I would have to help myself. Talk to myself. Administer to myself. I would have to become my own physician. My own counselor. I would have to find my own answers, for I was surrounded by weird and insane creatures. Some were in violent wards, and some carried the keys to these wards, but they all were torn from the same cloth. The caged and the keepers of the caged were soul-mates.

I paced back and forth and began to build a plan of personal therapy. I fully realized that I was at their disposal, but I would never submit to it. Let them judge me insane. Let my mother paper the universe with court orders proving it. Whatever, I would never play their game.

It was my singular and solitary task to force out the tigers that lurked deep in my mental jungle. I realized, perhaps more than anyone, that they were there, but I would trust the hunt to no one else. I would drive them out into the open, one by one, and when I could see them clearly, I would shoot to kill.

Insanity, legal term that it is, cannot prevent the mind from functioning. In many cases, thoughts flash like white streaks across the memory screen. At other times the mind is almost halted in its march, yet it creeps on. Those who sit in stupors, staring into nothingness, are perhaps remembering times long past when things were better for them . . . when their lives were not complicated or harmed. And those who thrash in violence are at war with the injustices that finally became too bitter to bear. Those who scream incoherent challenges at unseen enemies perhaps were too gentle to slash out and destroy their real and intimate foes.

By the standards set by the majority, to be insane is to be different, and those who are uncontrollably different are "locked away in crazy houses," to exist through years of intolerable misery and perpetual nightmares.

It is not possible for the conscious mind to remain unimpassioned when confronted with personal brutality, nor can the ego become so deadened that it does not flinch when mocked or degraded.

It is not insanity to have mental demons or periods of dementia, but let these demons rise to the surface and run amok, let the nerves collapse, let the spirit be so wounded that it limps and falters, and a commitment results.

The world is proud and arrogant, and fineries have been added to these miseries, perhaps in the hope that they will lessen or even go away. A drunkard is now an alcoholic. A dope fiend is an addict, and the insane are no longer crazy but mentally disturbed. But whatever label is attached, the horrors still exist and still breed the same misunderstanding and destruction. The victimized still cringe under the weight of the oppression. Nothing is really done to diminish the disgrace. It still clings, like an eternal fungus.

"Asylum" is not a contemporary word. The words "state hospital," "psychiatric clinic," "sanitarium" are easier to say. But to those inside the walls, it is still an asylum of squalor and inhuman treatment.

At the age of thirty, I realized that perhaps I had been wounded beyond hope of healing. I knew that my spirit was anemic and that my soul was hiding in a deep thicket . . . almost afraid to show its existence.

And I was well aware of my unique position. What was it the nurse had said? "I can't imagine why a big movie star would end up here."

I had to think it all out while it was fresh in my mind. I had to recall before the ability to remember was knocked out of me. It was quiet, and the cell clothed me in a strange but private dungeon.

My plight, I decided, was my own concern, and the causes that had brought me screaming to an asylum were also my personal affair. Nothing could make me bare these events with any nurse or doctor. The causes were my own personal possession. That was all I had left and no one could tamper with it. I would never give up this secret privacy, for I considered everyone a contributor to malicious gossip.

They would go home at night and say, "Guess who they brought in today? Frances Farmer." Or "Guess who I rapped across the mouth today? Frances Farmer." Or "Guess who's gone crazy? Frances Farmer."

My pride would prevent me from ever again trusting anyone, and I would never risk becoming involved in any form of therapy. My hope now lay, not in prestige or money, but in my ability still to think. Still to function. My earthly goods were these intangible faculties, and I would not give them up.

It was now up to me to work out my own salvation, and to do so I would have to retaste each day of the past, finding the frailties. The errors. The virtues. And however the past revealed itself in my mind, I would find the courage to meet it and dissect it, until I alone was satisfied that it was true and meaningful.

The future loomed before me like an open crematorium, and I was frightened. Unless I guarded myself carefully, I could be pushed into it, and what little hope that was left me would be consumed.

Life is sprinkled with many beginnings linked together in some mysterious chain, and my mind flowed back to Hollywood. The nurse, asking for my autograph, had triggered these particular thoughts, and I let the images swim in front of my closed eyes, going back until I was able to pinpoint the events that had brought me to Hollywood.

It all began in 1931, the year I entered the University of Washington. I knew that I would have to work my way through college, for there was never any extra money in the family. But jobs were scarce during those Depression years, and the pay was low. However I was willing and anxious to work at anything to secure my education, and during the next four years I waited tables, worked in a perfume factory, posed for art students, ushered in a downtown theater, and acted as a summer camp counselor. Most of the jobs were unexciting and taken only out of desperation, but during my sophomore summer I had a job as a singing waitress at Mount Rainier National Park, and this was the most pleasant experience of the lot.

As a freshman, I enrolled in the School of Journalism and worked on the campus paper as a reporter. Whenever there was extra space and no one had any ideas for fillers, I managed to insert some of my own poetry. But even though it pleased me to see my words in print, I was dissatisfied with my cub reporter status. When I was assigned to cover the infirmary, I felt it insulted my somewhat inflated opinion of my literary talents and basic intelligence.

Before the semester was half over, I was restless and impatient for some literary challenge. My journalism courses provided scant inspiration, assignments became a chore, a mere imitation of some other writer's style or thought. I would labor over a story, letting my ideas soar like eagles, but my professor would shoot them down like helpless sparrows with his brutal analysis and pointed criticism.

One bright spot in an otherwise dismal atmosphere was the girl reporter from the Drama Department. I found her offbeat personality intriguing. She wore her severely tailored clothes with a special flair and her straight hair was cropped in what was then called a boy's bob. She moved like a stalking lioness, and everything about her was a theatrical exaggeration. I later discovered she was involved with a strikingly feminine drama student. I innocently thought then that all lesbians tried to look and act like men, and I was puzzled that someone so completely feminine could be queer. The reporter looked the part, but the actress confused me.

One night the two of them invited me to a Black and Tan spot, and there I met one of the most commanding women I have ever known.

Sophie Rosenstein was a young drama instructor at the university, with a fleet of disciples who followed her as she cooed, moaned and screamed about "The Art."

For two or three weeks after our first meeting, I stopped by their hangout almost every night, and I became a part of the strange and exciting world over which Sophie reigned.

But I was still an outsider. A listener. Yet I knew that I had to belong. My only concern was how to wedge my way in. Late one night seven or eight of us crowded around a table listening to Sophie or, rather, hanging onto every word she uttered, when she suddenly leveled her finger at me accusingly and said, "Farmer, you're a phony. Why don't you get up off your ass, throw away that goddamned reporter's badge, and come with us where you belong?"

"But I can't act," I argued.

"So look at our new critic. How do you know what you can do?"

"I can write," I defended, halfheartedly.

"From what I hear you're not setting the world on fire," she chided. "What do you want to do?" she went on. "Spend the next four years ducking in and out of the infirmary, writing about who has the flu? Or would you rather come with us and learn how to be alive?"

She reached across the table and picked up my hand, pressing it hard against her cheek. She was an affectionate woman given to impulsive and occasionally embarrassing demonstrations, and this movement made me blush and feel conspicuous.

"Let me tell you something," she cooed. "You've

got everything you'll ever need. Look at you. You're beautiful."

She twisted my face back and forth, studying me intently. I wanted to sink through the floor, but none of the others took notice of my embarrassment. They were absorbed in Sophie.

"Yes," she said decisively. "You're beautiful. Such bone structure. Such color. Let me tell you something. We're doing theater like nowhere else in the country, and if you really want to sharpen your teeth on something, bite off a piece and come in with us."

"But I don't know the first thing about acting," I said weakly.

"To hell with what you don't know. I'll teach you. You've got a voice, a fabulous instrument. Use it. Make it come alive. Make it sing. Send it out from your heart. Capture with it. Love with it. Live with it."

I was already hooked, and all Sophie had to do was reel me in. From that day on, I carried the theater like a flaming standard. I, at last, belonged.

I met little resistance when I applied for a transfer to the Drama Department, and I buried myself in the study of theater history and literature. Of speech. Of movement. Of techniques. Of play reading.

I was consumed, and I was also not fit to live with, or so Mamma said, for anything or anyone interfering with my studies provoked a tantrum.

I had quickly picked up the habits and mannerisms of my fellow actors. Once I had merely thought four-letter words, now I spewed them out, all to Mamma's horror.

I learned to drink straight without choking. I learned to argue a point, not debate an issue. I learned to go without sleep. And I became acutely aware of the power and responsibility the theater has in forming social and political attitudes. I was living in an all-consuming world, and it was a well-fitting mantle. I was confident, and I was revoltingly aggressive. I challenged and probed . . . and, at last, I acted.

Helen in *Helen of Troy* was my first role, and from that experience on, there was no turning back, especially after a local drama critic gave me a review that kept my head in the clouds for days:

> The name of Frances Farmer, who has the divine intangible maturity to her acting, is destined for the lights of Broadway. She has that mysterious something that separates the actress from the hack.

With this kind of review, I became the important personage in the Drama Department. I was Sophie's find. I was her godchild. I was her light.

When *Alien Corn* was presented, we played fourteen consecutive weekends, an unprecedented run for the university's players.

My review in this role exceeded my first, and when I read it, I could think of nothing else except our next play. Writing faded quickly into a vague past. Let others write the words, I would bring them power and meaning.

It was an exciting and rewarding time for me, and life was going well while I was on campus, but my home life was growing extremely difficult. Mamma was in a constant turmoil over my choice of friends, my late hours, my arty ways, my disrespect, my flippant attitudes, my vulgarities.

She tried to force me into a different pattern, but the struggle was useless, for I was eaten alive with ambition. I was going to the top, and no one could stand in my way. The rest of the world, Mamma included, could go to hell, but Frances Farmer was going to act.

I was impossible to live with, and I knew it, but I didn't care. I had catching up to do. Living to do. And Mamma bored me with what I considered dull, insignificant nagging. In fact everyone bored me who was not in my tight little circle.

I was alive for the first time in my life and functioning in a world that was young and intent on experimentation, whether in a scene on stage or in a bed. For the very first time, I was involved, and every fiber responded. I was madly in love with the theater and with all the people who contributed to it.

To many of my generation, as in succeeding ones, the theories of Konstantin Stanislavski, known as the Method, stood for total, meaningful theater. The real core of the Method was reality and absolute involvement. It ripped aside the frills and brought to the footlights the torn sweat shirt and the worn strumpet. It had to be real, and according to the standards, you had to feel and experience it before you could act it.

We were young, and we took the Method to heart, and if our characters were sleeping together, we slept together. If homosexuality was involved in a characterization, we were likewise involved, for how could you act what you had not experienced?

The Method became a moving force in the theater, but we were the first in its throes on a university level. We were the newborn. We were not afraid. We acted and reacted. We had nothing to live up to, for we were the embryos. Within a walled city, we were alive, bringing everything else to life. But we went too far. We were too enraptured. Too concerned. And we lost control. It was a raw and dangerously uninhibited world, and to some it became a deadly game of self-destruction.

I studied people. How they walked. Their faces. I looked for their fears. Their joys. I searched the eyes of the old and sought for the lilt in the young. It became more than a serious game to me. It grew into a devoted effort, and I tried to project myself into every conceivable circumstance.

One particular incident stands out in my memory and it should have served as a stoplight, but I ignored the warning.

During my sophomore year in high school I made friends with Lottie Stevens, a strange, brooding girl who lived alone with her mother. We shared a great deal in common, Lottie and I. Although I had an on-and-off father, both our homes existed without any real help or benefit of a father. Yet any similarity ended there, for even though her family was probably as poor, if not poorer, than we were, there was, nonetheless, a gracious attitude in their home. It was a quiet, intelligent and well-run house, and I never heard Mrs. Stevens raise her voice or criticize Lottie. She was as gentle as Mamma was flamboyant.

Lottie was my only friend, and we remained close throughout high school and both enrolled at the university. During our first term we made a point of being together as much as possible, but after I transferred to the Drama Department, I saw less and less of her. But whenever we would run across each other on campus, she was always with a giant brooding Indian. He was overpowering in his build and was openly rude and sullen to everyone.

I had heard that he treated her like a punching bag, and it was obviously true, for she looked drawn and haggard. I was curious about her, not because she was a friend, but because I could use her as a potential character study.

I could not imagine allowing oneself to become so

victimized by passion, especially that brought forth from a bedroom. It was disgusting to see her with a black eye, still hanging onto his arm. As an actress, I had to find out why she tolerated it and try to learn what motivated her.

She had a one-room efficiency apartment off campus, and I decided to drop by to probe and observe her firsthand. There was no answer to my knocking, and I tried the door. It was unlocked, and as I opened it, gas fumes poured into the hall. I found Lottie with her head stuck in the oven.

She was unconscious, but I managed to keep calm, open the window and lug her to it, shouting for help. In seconds the room was filled with people, and an ambulance took her to the hospital.

Everyone was praising me for my quick thinking, telling me I had saved her life, but I felt a temporary guilt in lapping up their congratulations. I knew that my motive had not been lofty, for at the time I found her, and even during the pandemonium that followed, I had kept one eye on the scene, so to speak. I had studied the faces of the people crowding into the room hovering over her. I had watched her body as it was laid on the stretcher and tried, within myself, to mimic the way her mouth hung limp and distorted. I looked at the intern and noticed that his hands were dirty and his nails were chewed to the quick. I picked out one woman who kept peering over heads in the hope of getting a closer look.

This is the real thing, I thought. This is it. I followed Lottie down to the ambulance, and as soon as it had pulled away, I went directly to Sophie and acted out the scene. I spoke not about a friend who had tried to kill herself, but about the powerful impact of witnessing something horribly real.

A few days later I visited the hospital, expecting Lottie to shower me with tears of remorse and gratitude. Instead, her eyes were hostile, and she flung a shocking accusation at me.

"How could you?" she said, sobbing. "Why didn't you leave me alone?"

I stumbled from the room confused. I had yet to know that life can reach unbearable limits. I had saved her life, and she repaid me by never speaking to me again. Later she married her Indian and sometime afterward killed herself.

I felt no sympathy for her or anyone else who would allow themselves such utter defeat, and in my most desperate hours I never once contemplated suicide. As a college senior I was sympathetic to only one thing, my craft, and I had but one goal, to reach New York.

I wanted to work, in any capacity, with the Group Theatre. The storm center of theatrical creativity in the 1930's, it had defied every tradition, and, though short-lived, it dreamed a dream that still haunts Broadway.

The Group, as it was called, was a collection of talents and based its methods of acting, direction and production on the Stanislavski Method, to which I had been conditioned.

It molded some brilliant, if confused, talents. Leading the pack was playwright Clifford Odets, a radical genius. There was also Harold Clurman, who imagined he shared a similar genius. Some of the acting talents to emerge from the ranks were Sylvia Sidney, Lee J. Cobb, John Garfield, Karl Malden, Franchot Tone, and Elia Kazan.

I knew if I was to belong to the theater, it was imperative that I also belong to the Group, and my one single aim was to reach New York. I told Sophie that if

I had to, I would walk there, and she kept pressing me on.

"Don't ever give up," she said. "Climb. Knock down anyone who stands in your way. But climb."

By the end of my final semester I was frantic. I had no money. Whatever I earned went for tuition and expenses. I was beginning to tire under the academic load, my extracurricular work as an actress, and my full-time job as an usher at the Paramount Theater. I was exhausted, but I was young and the strain would not show for a few more years.

During my job as an usher I first felt a growing contempt for motion pictures, and Sophie fanned it with her mockery of the "hack talents and artistic anemia" churned out by the "factory." She infected us all with her opinion. Compared to the live theater, we felt movies were little more than unskilled abortions. Hollywood was an ugly yardstick, and we were taught to mock it.

I scoffed at the industry's products, and yet the thirties were years of gloom, and perhaps Americans with empty bellies and thin wallets needed the escape provided by Hollywood's unreal world of song and dance and horse-kissing cowboys.

But I was of a new generation enraged by the deplorable economic and political conditions brought on by the Depression, angry at having to do without and bored by hearing about the good old days—days that we could not even recall. We had lost our appetite for promises. We were aggressive and impatient.

Seattle, the scene of bitter labor disputes and immigration riots, had had a hearty share of far-left activity. Jobs were scarce, workers underpaid, and many laborers and intellectuals alike looked for quick answers in revolutionary political doctrines. I could not agree with the university's more radical students that life would become less complicated and more desirable if we all reached one great Marxist level. The only thing I wanted was an equal chance to use my own bootstraps.

To say that I had a natural sympathy for the underdog is oversimplification, but I did feel sadness for the girls I had worked with in the factory. For the most part, they were unschooled, and imprisoned in a dull, drab world. They were also brazen, lusty and pitifully uncomplicated. Receptive to any farflung promise, they became victims of their own innocence.

I was the outsider, the strange one who spent all her money on books, and this made a barrier between their world and mine, even though we were bound together in similar want. By the same token, the affluent, soft-spoken sorority girls, with their bright-colored roadsters, were cut off from this world as surely as the factory girls were severed from mine.

But reaching New York, not social problems, was my major concern. I knew that it was impossible for me to earn enough to get there, and I had had no success in talking any of my friends into hitchhiking cross-country with me. I had almost decided to attempt it alone when Sophie came up with a possible solution.

After an evening rehearsal, she kept the cast and crew together for a meeting, which she began head on with her usual pointed bluntness.

"Most of you," she said, "have gained a scrap or two from your drama studies here, but there is only one who can go beyond the university level, and that is Frances Farmer."

The class interrupted her with a warm applause directed at me, but she impatiently hushed them.

"Let's face it," she continued. "We've got to get her

to New York. I've made arrangements to introduce her to people in the Group, and if I know her, she'll take off from there. But first, she must get to New York."

I had no idea that she had contacts within the Group, and the very thought of it filled me with excitement.

She held up a copy of *The Voice of Action* and said, "We'd all like to feel that we had a part in your career, Farmer, for that's probably as close to glory as any of us will get, and here's the way we can do it."

The Voice of Action was a radical Seattle newspaper that did nothing to disguise its efforts to promote the growth of Communism. It was openly read among the students and not so openly read among a large percentage of the working class. I knew because I had seen dog-eared copies tucked in lunch bags at the factory.

She explained that the *Voice* was conducting a subscription contest, with the winner receiving an all-expense-paid round trip to Moscow, via New York. The trip was to coincide with the Russian May Day celebration, and there was an added cash bonus of one hundred dollars for the winner.

"Here's our answer," she said, waving the paper. "If we all pitch in, we can win this trip for Farmer. Think of it. She can go to the very heart of the theater and observe the Method in its original environment. But more than anything else, she'll be in New York."

Everyone went overboard for the idea, but I did not allow myself to contemplate winning. It seemed too simple, too easy. Although I could not bring myself to sell any, thinking it would be like voting for oneself, my reserve had no dampening effect on my fellow students. Within a month I was given the incredible news that I had won by a margin of two subscriptions.

The Drama Department went wild. We got high on

success and some very raw whiskey. I was kissed, hugged and toasted. It was unreal. It couldn't be happening to me. I couldn't wait to tell Mamma.

Sophie stuffed as many of us as she could into her car, and we drove up in front of my house laughing and singing "The Volga Boatman" at the top of our voices. I had never been happier, but before I could get out of the car, Mamma came tearing through the front door, whirling a broom over her head, screeching like a wounded witch.

"Get away from my house," she screamed, and began pounding on Sophie's car with her broom. "Get away from here. Don't you dare stop in front of my house, you . . . you . . . Red devils. Get off my street."

Mamma had been given the news by a reporter from the Seattle *Post,* and it had not set well. He had called and faced her with the query "How do you feel about your daughter going to Russia for the Communist Party?" He then proceeded to editorialize for his right-wing newspaper . . . and all hell broke loose.

I had never seen her angrier or heard her more vocal. Using her broom as a club she beat on Sophie's car and ran down the street after it, still swinging her broom, until they turned the corner on two wheels. I watched stupefied, for I had no way of knowing what had come over her.

She came panting back down the street and grabbed me by the ear, painfully pulling me into the house. I didn't resist, but I was so humiliated by her attack on my friends that the moment we were inside, I started screaming.

"What the goddamned hell do you think you're doing?"

"Don't you smart off to me, you . . . you Red menace."

"Red what?"

"I told your father you'd come to no good end. Oh, yes. Over and over I've said it."

"Now you wait a minute. I come home to tell you that something wonderful has happened to me, and you attack my friends like a goddamned crazy woman."

"That's it. That's what I mean. You've let those Russian spies turn you against your own mother. I saw it coming. I've said it all along. But they'll never lay another hand on a daughter of mine. Never! Never! Never!"

"What are you talking about?"

"Don't pretend. It will be spread all over the front pages, so don't play little miss innocent with me. I've heard all about it. You can't pull the wool over my eyes any longer. And understand this, young lady, you're going to confess everything. I'm going to see to it, even if I have to beat it out of you. No daughter of mine will ever betray her country."

"Jesus Christ."

"There! That's what I mean. You see, already you're making fun of our Saviour."

"Of our what? Good God, Mamma, where did you come up with that one?"

"You think I don't know what you're up to? I know very well what's going on."

"Mamma, what are you talking about?"

"A spy. That's what you are. A spy. So don't try and pretend to me. Hanging around with all those no good pinks. I told your father this would happen. Over and over I told him, but would he listen to me? Not him. And now, look at the shame and disgrace you've brought down upon us."

I threw up my hands and started to my room, but she grabbed me halfway up the stairs.

"You're a spy," she screamed. "A sneaking low-down spy. They've got you in their clutches and they've turned you against me."

I jerked away from her and stomped to my room, with her still on my heels. "Mamma, I'm telling you, leave me alone. Why do you have to spoil everything?"

"Well, if spoiling everything is uncovering their plot, then I'm proud."

She hotfooted it down the stairs, calling back, "Don't think you've heard the last of this. You're not going anywhere, let alone to THAT place. If you think you can get away with this, you're badly mistaken."

She spent the rest of the afternoon shouting dire predictions of disgrace and ruin, until she was finally reduced to a heart-rending appeal to my patriotism. There was no chance for me to give her a reasonable explanation, and it shocked me to realize that she was placing me in a position of having to deny subversive plans to overthrow the government.

The Seattle *Post* had been waging a serious battle against any hue of pink, and a left-wing paper awarding a trip to Russia to an American coed was new ammunition.

Mamma became their most devoted ally. She rolled up her sleeves and waded into the thick of battle. Her fuse was short, and when she exploded, the air reverberated for days. Pictures of her appeared daily, posed like an enraged battle-ax, and one lurid headline followed the other. Reporters hounded the house, quoting her verbatim, for no one could possibly add a gloss to Mamma's dialogue. Responding to the clarion call of outraged motherhood, she declared, "If I must be the one to sacrifice my baby girl to Communism, I hope other mothers can save their children before they, too, are turned into radicals in our schools. I shall devote my life to purging our Red-ridden corridors of learning.

The Soviet dagger has struck deep into the hearts of America."

Headline: MOTHER WARNS AGAINST RED TEACHERS.

And she said more. "My daughter is lost. She does not know about Red trickery. She will be presented to the Russian audiences as a Communist representative from an American university."

Headline: COED TO ACT FOR REDS.

. . . And more. "The Communists will even use my daughter to solicit funds to spread their propaganda in the United States. She will cut the throat of her own country. She is a beautiful girl and they will misuse her. We have all read of white slavery. Let us fear, instead, Red slavery."

Headline: MOTHER UNCOVERS RED VICE RING.

These stories were picked up by the national wire services, and bundles of letters arrived daily. For the most part, foul and threatening. Heartsick and embarrassed, I stayed away from campus. My college days were over. The stories became so distorted that the university newspaper finally entered the melee and printed an editorial.

"There was a time," it read, "when the ethics of the American press forbade dragging family quarrels, no matter how spicy or entertaining, into the public limelight. But those days seem to be gone. A breakfast table quarrel doesn't even have to be interesting any more, it only need be concerned with communism, or some other phobia, to become page one stuff. Thus we witness the spectacle of a Seattle mother's attempt to prevent her daughter, a university coed, from going to Russia under the auspices of a communist newspaper because she fears her daughter may be converted to the Russian way of life during her brief stay in the Soviet.

"But snooping reporters brought back even more than sordid details of the quarrel. They got 'A Seattle mother's warning against Red teachers.' We have long wondered how low the press would stoop in its Red baiting campaign. We have seen professors branded as 'Reds' because they spoke out against war. We have seen students crucified because they dared to parade on Armistice day, for peace. We have seen high school teachers fired because they told their students that capitalism had not been completely successful. And now, we see the sanctity and privacy of a whole family sacrificed so that the public may be warned against 'Red school teachers.' Is there no limit?"

I assured my friends in the Drama Department, who were grieved and upset by the outcome of their efforts, that nothing or no one would or could prevent me from accepting the trip.

I repeated this one last time to Mamma and then never argued the point again. I quit speaking to everyone. I would not talk to any reporters or anyone else, except Papa. I had made my decision and I could not be swayed from it.

Papa had remained much in the background, but his advice gave me the courage I needed. He was understanding and made every effort, of course without Mamma's knowledge, to confirm his trust in me. He also promised that after I returned to New York, if I decided to stay, he would send me five dollars a week until I found a job. Like most of his other sincere intentions, this fell by the wayside. Yet before I left, he gave me twenty dollars and suggested that I might use it for some new clothes. Sophie's husband was a hat salesman and they gave me a new hat, so with that, I was generally prepared.

The *Voice* had scheduled a banquet at the YMCA

auditorium to present me with the prize ticket, but reservations were canceled two hours before the affair was to start on the ground that it was against their policy to allow controversial meetings at the center. I accepted my prize at the newspaper office and returned home to find Mamma in a state of near collapse.

But however weak she seemed to be, she gathered her strength for one last dramatic effort. When the *Post* reporters came to get her comments on my accepting the prize, she was in tears and sobbed, "I still have two weapons left. I will appeal to the city prosecutor and attempt to restrain her by legal means. But if all else fails, I shall lay myself under the wheels of the bus and let it drive over my prostrate body. She will never go."

Headline: MOTHER THREATENS SUICIDE IF DAUGHTER DEPARTS.

The city prosecutor could offer her no solution. I was twenty-one and, contrary to her declarations, no longer a "baby." However, I lived in constant fear that on the day of my departure she might very well carry out her final threat.

On the tenth day of April, 1935, I left Seattle by bus, and up to and including the last minute, Mamma still threatened me with the police and God's wrath.

Sophie and my friends saw me off, and as the bus pulled away, I was filled with a deepening sense of sadness. I would return to Seattle many times in the future, but I knew that I could never really go home again.

The cross-country trip was tiring and monotonous. The nights were lonely and I often wondered if I had done wrong. Mamma's last words, "You have broken my heart," rang in my ears, and it was difficult to turn away from so plaintive a cry. I carried this thread of guilt for many years to come, and no matter how high I was to rise or how low I was to fall, this clung to me and filled me with sorrow.

When I left home, I did not dare think of myself as being unfeeling or defiant. I had been taught by Mamma to think and act for myself. She had told me, almost daily, that I had the right, even the obligation to decide for myself what I must be and what I must do. Her teachings were deeply embedded. So much so that I was probably too self-preoccupied. This self-preoccupation may have led me down some bleak corridors, but it also proved, many times over, to be my greatest strength.

Although because of Mamma's accusation I was always suspect, I was not nor have I ever been a member or an active supporter of the Communist Party. I was probably a prime target for their subtleties, but it never occurred to me to involve myself seriously with any doctrine further left than the Democratic Party of the Roosevelt era.

Circumstances and bedfellows indicated otherwise, but when I accepted the trip, it was nothing more than a convenient step up a dedicated and ambitious ladder. I took it willingly and with appreciation. I was an actress and I was making my way by whatever opportunity fate offered.

4

Exhausted from the five-day bus ride, I was grateful for the three-day layover in New York, prior to the ship's sailing.

The *Voice* had given me the address of a hotel in Manhattan, assuring me that I would have reservations. It turned out to be a run-down boardinghouse in a shoddy district. I had just checked in when a representative of a sister paper to the *Voice* knocked on my door.

He was a squat, rumpled man, and despite my protests, he insisted on taking me to dinner. To him, dinner meant a nearby sandwich shop. He was my first introduction to someone who openly admitted to being a card carrier, and I was appalled as I listened to his outlandish ideologies.

According to him, I had a responsibility to act as a contributing correspondent during my stay in Russia. The Seattle editor of the *Voice* had casually mentioned this but had not pressed the fact; but the New Yorker made it clear that I was expected to write a favorable account of what I saw.

I was too exhausted to argue, and the longer I listened to his fanatic ramblings, the more irritated I became. He planned for me to spend my layover at their newspaper office, during which time I was to acquaint myself with my Russian schedule. Since I had

had quite enough of him and his orders, I emphatically refused, and a tirade of "What kind of party worker are you?" followed.

When I informed him that I was nobody's comrade, he was outraged that the *Voice* would have allowed someone with questionable loyalty to win the contest. It pleased me to know that, despite the paper's radical connections, the contest had been honest, but I did not intend to spend any more time around this dreadful, dull man.

I left the sandwich shop thinking that my trip would surely be canceled, and had it been, I think I would have felt relieved, for despite my brave front at home, I was apprehensive about going halfway around the world alone. I had reached New York, and no one could take that away from me. The Moscow trip was simply a side bonus that I could do without, if necessary. But plans were not altered, and I went by the newspaper office the next morning to pick up my itinerary. He shoved it across his desk with no harsher reprimand than a frigid glare.

Sophie had kept her word and given me a letter of introduction to J. Edward Bromberg, an actor whom she knew working with the Group. I called him and was pleased to hear a cordial voice. After inquiring politely about Sophie and congratulating me on my trip to Russia, Bromberg invited me to join him the next night at what he called a "hard-time party" at the Group's rehearsal hall. I could hardly wait, but I used the rest of the time walking Manhattan streets, as only a first-time visitor can.

I was nervous about the party, aware that I lacked even social graces, and, too, I had never been around professionals. I would mean nothing to the Group, but even with these qualms, my excitement was unbounded. The party was for scene designer Max Gorelik, and when I arrived, on the dot of nine, I entered a small, dirty room overstuffed with people. I finally found someone who could stop drinking or shouting long enough to point out Mr. Bromberg, and when I introduced myself, he made an offhand effort at introducing me to a wide assortment of people whose names I hardly heard and whose faces did little more than flash before me.

But I met one man in particular, Percy Elias, an editor with the Emerson Publishing Company, who eagerly relieved Bromberg of the chore of keeping tabs on me. My first night with the Group was made bearable because of his consideration and attention. He seemed out of place in such a desperate and arty world, and he took the trouble to find out who I was and where I was going.

It was Percy who introduced me to Clifford Odets, and I was immediately attracted to the playwright. He was brittle and snapping, and even though our conversation was brief, a little more than a curt nod in fact, just meeting him had a deep effect on me. I managed to stand within earshot of his voice most of the evening hoping to pick up the crumbs of his opinions on art, music, and, especially, the theater.

He was a brilliant playwright, surrounded by a fascinating conglomerate of skilled professionals. Very quickly I realized that this party was much like ours had been at the university. The people were, of course, more confident, more exaggerated, and certainly more theatrical, but the same forces propelled us, and I felt comfortable with them.

I'm sure I went unnoticed that evening, especially to Clifford, for during our later intimate relationship, he claimed no recollection of having met me. That night, it was Percy who made me feel an attractive and an integral part of the atmosphere, and when the party finally broke up, he took me back to my rooming-house and made a date to see me to the ship the following day.

Before I boarded the boat, we had coffee together and I was relieved that no one from the Communist Party was at the dock to see me off—at least no one identified himself as such.

My shipboard accommodation was, literally, in steerage. The cabin was suffocatingly small and occupied by five other women of varied nationalities. No sooner had we left the harbor than one aging German lady was stricken with a dreadful case of seasickness. *"Mein Gott. Mein Gott,"* she groaned over and over and then began to vomit. With that, I went out in search of fresh air and returned to the cabin only to sleep.

Our deck was little more than a walkway, but the April weather was brisk and clear, and standing at the crowded rail, looking out over the ocean, brought into quick focus the reality that I was on my way. I had never been the type to pinch myself to see if it was all real, but I was bemused to consider that I, Frances Farmer, through no effort of my own, was crossing the Atlantic.

It was still too early in the season for students or teachers to be traveling, and the deck was a crowded mob of Poles, Germans, Italians, Slavs, and Irish going back to the old country. There was no room to move about freely, and I had to push and shove my way through the sweating, screeching herd. I spent most of my days at sea perched on an iron stairway leading to the off-limits upper decks. From it I was able to watch the milling hive without being involved. It was a compelling sight. Earthy. Base. And violent.

Life in Seattle had been raw and poor, but it contained guidelines of behavior. For instance, I had never

seen women bare their breasts and suckle their babies
or men urinate in public before. And at night, when
the cabins became too stuffy, the steerage passengers
lay about the deck like animals in heat. No shipboard
romances, only the vulgar, public exchange of bodies.
Rolling. Grunting. Ejecting. Receiving. Women were
taken without a thought of tenderness or modesty. I
saw men humping them like bulls, while they lay be-
neath, chattering like neighbors with other women, also mounted. Also unconcerned.

These were people who had no choice but to strang-
gle life before it strangled them. Sturdy. Illiterate.
Hopeful. Impure.

As the days passed, the crowded conditions created
even more havoc, and all restraints were abandoned.
Wherever I looked, my eyes fell on sex. Children of
seven or eight copied the adult behavior around them
and added more repulsion to an already nauseating
sight.

Witnessing all this, I realized that our so-called
search for reality at the university had been infantile.
How could we, as mere actors conveying a given
scene, create within ourselves the inherited lust of
these people? How could we begin to reason with their
logic? How could we, smug and secure in our intellect,
assume to pursue the base motivations of others? It
was then I knew that I had far to go and much to
learn before I could give life and truth to my work.

Early one morning I saw a young girl of perhaps
seventeen lying under a hulking mustached man who
bore his weight down upon her like a pile driver, and
she shrieked with each thrust, clawing at his back, pulling him deeper into her. When he was spent, she rolled
on top of him, straddling his body, and churned herself against him until he could take her again. Still it
was not enough. He rolled off and two other men

boarded her. One sat upon her breast and she grappled for him with her mouth while the other entered her like a grunting boar. An old man was asleep beside them. A baby crawled around underfoot and picked trash off the deck and stuffed it in his mouth. A gnarled, wrinkled woman squinted at them and grinned, letting tobacco-stained saliva dribble out of her hollow mouth.

When I was seventeen, I had lived in a world without church or spiritual obligations; nevertheless I was morally aware and restrained by this morality. In comparison, the girl I watched on the deck probably had all the Old World beliefs and devotion to God. No doubt she sincerely sought His eternal reward and trembled under the prospects of His promised punishments, and yet she lay there quivering in a guiltless lust that left her nothing more than a soiled barbarian.

I wondered: If I were ever faced with creating such a role, could I do it? Could I understand? And, if I understood, could I possibly convey it?

In my confusion, I hated her. Hated her needs. Hated her means of fulfilling them. And yet, if I were to act, I knew I could never withdraw from any facet of life. Still, these people sickened me and I was unsympathetic to the fact that they had been born into a world stripped of privacy. They were birthed in public and died in the middle of a multitude. Solitude was unknown, for they were confined in a primitive and crowded universe that raped their hopes and deformed their spirits.

When I thought of this, I felt a deep, intense pain. I wanted to run to the girl and pull the men away. I wanted her to experience with her mind. Not her body. I wanted to save her. To lift her up. To protect her. I wanted, alas, to help where no help was wanted.

The two men finally left her, and as she lay face up,

her dress pulled awkwardly above her waist and her breast bared, I saw a frail girl with sperm smeared over her flesh.

Her eyes were rolled back and her teeth chattered while her own hands continued to explore and excite her body, and I asked myself: How could one help that which was helpless? How could one save that which was lost? I could find no answer and I wept at the futility.

On the voyage my inexperience struck me like a steel-tipped arrow and I no longer hated that which I could not understand. I feared it, and felt superior to it, and withdrew from it, but I no longer hated it. What was left to me was the youthful hope that someday I would surely come to understand the world around me.

I saw the lonely Russian wastelands. I walked the drab streets of Moscow. On May Day I watched the endless parade of lead soldiers and iron cannons and sweating horses and silk banners. Russia was a land crawling and half-dead, but determined to live.

I saw the bleak squares of Warsaw, which would soon crumble. I saw the fiercely vibrating commerce of Berlin. I saw the wide boulevards of Paris and the gentle French countryside. I saw the mists of England and the purple waters of the North Sea.

I saw people, and I grew. My emotions took on firm flesh and my curiosity reached beyond myself. It was a new experience, and yet, despite all this remarkable sense of bursting forth, I still viewed life with a single eye. I reacted to conditions only as, and if, they affected me. I still did not consider their effects on others.

In reality, my world remained narrow and populated by one: Frances Farmer. My compassion was sharpened, but my interest dulled if it did not benefit my growth as an actress. This, I suppose, is ambition. Selfish. Brutal. Determined. Lonely. Creative.

Finally my tour brought me to Southampton, where I sailed for America on the *President Harding*. I was ecstatic to find I had third-class, not steerage accommodations. It was all behind me. I had suffered the pangs of homesickness and had traveled by every cheap conveyance available. I had been shocked and gleaned from it. It was the only time I was ever to go abroad, so I still cherish the memories and the experience it offered me.

I met a young doctor named George Gladsman on the ship. We were drawn together as friends and spent most of our time sharing our individual hopes and ambitions. He told me that he personally knew nothing about the theater, but he had a college friend in New York who was "in the business" and could surely help my career. He insisted that as soon as we arrived, he wanted to arrange for us to meet.

But when the *Harding* docked and we said our good-byes, I was faced with the critical problem of where to go and how to live. Although I had been very frugal with my hundred-dollar prize money, I arrived back in the States with only seven dollars left. A refund on my bus ticket home added twenty-five dollars. From the YWCA, where I got a temporary room, I called Jane Rose, a college classmate who was living in New York, trying for the theater. She had a small apartment on West Seventy-fourth Street, which she offered to share with me. I saw a means of stretching my thirty-two dollars, and I moved in that evening.

As soon as I was settled, I wrote Papa that I intended to stay on in the East, and with that die cast, I buckled down to the daily grind of going from one casting office to another.

My contact with the Group was frustrating and

futile. None of them had the time or interest in auditioning me. Bromberg acted as if he had never heard of me and brushed aside my attempts to have him follow through with Sophie's introduction. Finally, I called Percy Elias, and although he was sympathetic, he could not help me penetrate the "sacred realm."

He took Jane and me out from time to time and would show up at the apartment with groceries just when our larder was almost bare. He also extended personal help by giving me a temporary job reading manuscripts for him.

Papa answered my letter immediately and wrote that the newspaper campaign had continued after I left home and that he and Mamma were still being hounded. I felt low about it, but I had not deliberately created the situation. It had crept up on me. Whether it was to pacify myself or console him, I wrote back and told him that it was my ambition to erase someday the stigma and make them proud of me.

Papa replied lovingly that I should not burden myself with their problems and urged me to concentrate on my own life.

I heard nothing from Mamma.

I finally called George, not really thinking that his shipboard promise would be carried through. But he had been waiting to hear from me in order to set up the meeting with his friend, Shepard Traube.

I met Traube on June 25, 1935, and he immediately signed me to a personal contract. I had no way of knowing that later he would use the contract to instigate a bitter lawsuit against me.

Since Broadway was floundering in the summer doldrums, Traube decided the obvious thing for me was to try for motion pictures. He insisted that I trim off several pounds and encouraged me to be more clothes-conscious.

I went on a dedicated diet and filled the hunger hours with play reading, but I was neither optimistic nor excited about the possibility of a screen test. I was greatly surprised when Traube called to say I had an interview with Oscar Serlin, who was then New York talent chief for Paramount Pictures.

When I met Mr. Serlin, I was trim and relatively well groomed, but he was not a man to waste time or words. He looked me up and down, fired a few inconsequential questions, then had me read a brief scene, only to cut me off in the middle of it.

"Okay," he said. "We'll arrange a test." He dismissed me with a curt nod of his head.

After meeting him I had even less faith in the prospects of the test and I was not really too concerned about it, for working in motion pictures had never entered my mind. In contrast, Traube was enthusiastic. The test did serve our purpose for me: I saw a way of breaking the ice with Mamma, and I wrote her about the coming screen test. She answered me immediately, never mentioning the breach between us, but writing at length about her daughter, the movie star.

Jane and Percy were strong emotional helpmates during the time I had to wait for the shooting date, but I was still not able to work up any personal excitement, though I was assigned to do a scene from *The Lake* in the role originally created by Katharine Hepburn. Then, late in July, the test date was scheduled. Everyone was unnerved and kept trying to reassure me, but strange as it seems, I really wasn't worried.

I reported to the makeup department, where Eddie Senz was assigned to prepare me. I was in his chair for hours, during which time my hair was hacked off and my eyebrows shaved off. I was furious and ready to walk out, but they kept telling me I would be happy with the finished product. Finally, I was curled and powdered to their satisfaction, and they allowed me to look at myself in the mirror.

A strange, sleek creature stared back at me, and I was horrified. Nothing was left of Frances Farmer, and I exploded. Warned that nobody except Mr. Serlin "threw a shoe" when he was around, I quieted down and went through the test, doing a good job. When it was finished, I looked at Mr. Serlin questioningly. He left the studio with a single curt comment. "We'll let you know."

Angrily I scrubbed my face until it was raw, and I burst into tears when I saw the wide hairless span above my eyes. I returned to the apartment in a state of blind fury. The whole impersonal business grated on me. "They'll not make a goddamned wampus baby out of me," I stormed.

Except on stage, I had never worn any cosmetics other than lipstick, but now I had to labor with a pencil to draw on my eyebrows.

All the while Traube kept calling me, saying that I was "in," but I was also hungry and broke. While we waited for word from the West Coast, I took whatever work I could find. I took a fifteen-dollar modeling job for Chesterfield cigarettes, and a sprinkling of other assignments followed. Life was sparse, but I lived.

August came and went, and there was no word. Traube retained his enthusiasm and Jane was still encouraging, but the silence only confirmed my original doubts. Then, early in September, Mr. Serlin called Traube and offered me a seven-year contract with Paramount Pictures. I was to start at a hundred dollars a week with a six-month option. That meant that my salary would be advanced every six months if the studio picked up the option. If they did not, I was out of luck and on my own.

For the first time in my life I learned that money talks. I felt like an heiress and I wrote Mamma about the incredible outcome of the test. "Dear, dear Mamma. At long last life seems to be reaping a small reward. I will be leaving for Hollywood this week, with a contract. I have signed with Paramount Pictures, and although I can never consider movies as my life's work, I can use it as a stepping stone. Then, there is the money to consider, and they are starting me off at a good salary with the prospects of more. I remember enough about what the lack of money has done to your life, and I could never be satisfied with art and life in a dusty garret. There is nothing to poverty except spiritual disintegration, and so with every ounce of strength I have, I'll spend my days getting myself and my family out of it. I feel so many ways that I'm a great deal like you, and I know how you've felt all these years of a makeshift existence. So hold on, Mamma, and God willing, things will be different someday."

Hollywood was a golden trinket dangling in front of me, and I wanted to reach out and take it, for no matter how disturbed I was in having to lay aside the legitimate theater, the movie contract did offer me the first real security I ever had. I kept telling myself that I could always come back to New York.

Jane and Percy were thrilled at my good fortune and scoffed at my skepticism, and there were parties in the apartment almost every night. People I didn't know would show up and greet me like a long-lost friend. I was suddenly everyone's darling, and at this initial burst of familiarity, I automatically withdrew from them.

On my twenty-first birthday, September 19, 1935, I signed the Paramount contract. I was given a two-week advance in salary and told, rather pointedly, that I would have to pay more attention to my clothes.

I wasn't about to spend all that money on a wardrobe, but I did buy two modest oufits and an inexpensive raincoat.

I boarded the train for Hollywood on September 29, and Eddie Senz, the makeup artist, showed up with a gift for me, an eight-week-old puppy. The little fellow was beguiling, and perhaps Eddie thought it would give me an added dash when I landed in Hollywood. It seemed to me too intimate and untimely a gift, but, I tucked the dog under my arm and waved good-bye.

5

I rose from the asylum cot, stretched my bruised arms stiffly above my head, and stumbled the three short paces that took me to the window. A gray morning mist lay in thin sheets between the dim buildings. It looked cold outside, and the leaves moved silently in a listless morning breeze.

I turned from the window and went to my cell door. Through the wire-covered porthole in the door I studied the sullen and colorless hall, littered with waste and debris. I could hear voices and make out other faces also peering from their cages. I wanted to scream —and so I did. It was not a scream of pain or fear, but of hot violent anger. I listened to myself as I let it die in my throat.

"Hey. Somebody out there. What time do you feed the animals?" I yelled over and over.

The woman in the cell across from mine whimpered and nervously stuck her fingers through the wire window.

"You crazy damn fool," I shouted. "You crazy God-forsaken fool. Anything I hate is sniveling . . . so shut up. You bore me. This whole stinking place bores me."

My tirade only provoked more whimpering and I turned away in disgust. I felt miserable, and although my physical activity had been limited, I was dizzy and staggered back to the cot. Weak with hunger, I was drained by any movement, and I held back the nausea as I lay back. Then, despite the turmoil within me, I fell asleep.

The sound of keys unlocking my cell door jarred me awake, and a woman wearing a filthy cotton dress told me to line up in the hall. She wore a bright-red rag tied around her upper arm, and I later learned this was a trustee's badge. She was a limp, ugly woman, and as I staggered sleepily past her, I managed a loud belch in her face. It had no effect.

In the hall, standing in front of each cell, were women of all ages in every manner of personal disarray. Many of them were crying. Others stared blankly. Some hid their faces in their hands and refused to look up. Others babbled to themselves or talked to some invisible presence.

A day nurse, with a squat, round body, stood outside her cage at the head of the hall, and when I saw her looking at me, I made a face, which she ignored.

"Ladies," she said. "Quiet down. I want your attention."

She had a horn of a voice that immediately halted all crying and muttering.

"This is the isolation ward. You're to be kept here until we can schedule your physicals. After that, you will have your interviews with the staff doctors. But until then, you will remain in isolation, except during your toilet periods. Now, I want you to understand that I demand full cooperation from each of you." Then, looking directly at me, she continued, "Any one who decides to make trouble will be dealt with."

I thumbed my nose at her, but again she ignored it.

"You will be taken to the toilet four times a day," she went on. "After each meal and before lights out. And you will go to the toilet only during these peri-

ods. I don't want any of you messing up your rooms. If
you do, you'll be punished. It's that simple. We have
very little help here and we can't waste our time cleaning up your messes. Do you all understand?"

I stuck my thumbs in my ears and wiggled my fingers but still could not get any reaction from her.

"This is Mrs. Clemments, our ward supervisor, and I
want you to follow her to the toilet. Now, line up in
single file and hurry up with it."

Mrs. Clemments was a stout woman with elephan-
tine ankles that sagged over her corrective shoes. Her
back was broad and rounded, and a mat of thick steel
hair was tossed carelessly on her head. Her breathing
was heavy, and as she chugged along, she sounded like
a distant locomotive churning uphill. But she gathered
us up in a haphazard line and did so without any
screaming or shoving. This made her more human
than anyone I had met.

Helping her was a squadron of trustees. Trustees
were patients considered well enough to be assigned
ward duties, and in this case it was their job to take us
to the toilet.

When this weird, frightened procession reached the
toilet room, we each were pointed to a stool and then
strapped to it. We were left undisturbed for about
fifteen minutes while some of the trustees stood
around and watched. They seemed as "sick" as any of
us. Some slobbered. Others played with themselves.
Others sang or yelled at the top of their lungs. The
whole room clattered, and then Mrs. Clemments came
back and the trustees began handing out a few thin
sheets of toilet paper. Some of the women used the
skimpy ration. Others held the paper in trembling
hands with no idea what to do with it. A few stuffed it
in their mouths and tried to eat it. Then, one by one we
were unbuckled and guided back to our cells.

While we had been in the toilet, trustees had opened most of the windows in the cells and a fresh morning wind cleansed the air. But before I was halfway down the hall, I became dizzy again and staggered against the wall. Mrs. Clemments took my arm and asked, "Is there something wrong?"

I jerked away from her and snarled, "What the hell kind of question is that?"

"Try not to cause any trouble," she cautioned under her breath. "It can go hard on you."

"You take care of your side of the street, sister, and I'll take care of mine."

She moved on with no comment. Suddenly everything was in confusion. The women were lost or beginning to fight with each other or standing blankly with their faces to the wall. I pushed my way through and stumbled weakly into my cell. I had never been so hungry. I lay on my cot fighting to keep from screaming or pulling my hair in anguish.

Finally a food cart rattling in the hall stopped in front of my cell. I was handed a tin can with oatmeal in it and a wooden spoon. Another trustee gave me a tin can with coffee in it. No milk or sugar for the cereal, but I ate it like a starved rat and washed it down with the cold rank coffee.

But rather than satisfying me, it made me even hungrier. I went out in the hall and beat the coffee can against the wall.

"Come on back here," I shouted. "Come on. Let's have some more."

The nurse stormed out of her cage and charged toward me.

"You listen to me," she said. "You'll get no special treatment here. You'll eat what everyone else eats and there are no seconds. We're not running a hotel, so get back in your room and stay there."

I glared at her and kept beating my tin can on the wall. She snapped her fingers and motioned for a trustee. I threw the cans and spoon on the floor, then marched back to my cell and plopped down on my cot like a pouting child.

"You get back out here and pick this stuff up," she ordered. "And you'd better be quick about it."

I fluttered my eyes weakly and mocked, "Oh, nursie, I'm too sick. Can't you see I'm too sick?"

She stomped over and jerked me to my feet. I drew back to hit her, but she pushed me into the hall and pointed to the can on the floor.

"Now pick it up." I felt her fingers dig into my shoulder. "Pick it up," she repeated.

I tossed my head. "If that's all it takes to make you happy, sister, then who am I to screw up your day?"

I picked up the can and spoon, and then crawled down the hall on my hands and knees to where the coffee can had rolled. I crawled back and groveled before her, dangling my tongue out of the corner of my mouth. She grabbed my hair and yanked me to my feet. "Now put them on the cart," she directed.

I tried to pull away, but she tightened her grip on my hair.

"Who the hell do you think you are?" I began screaming.

"I'm boss." She yanked my hair again. "And the sooner you realize it, the better off you'll be."

She turned to the patients watching us. "Let this be a good lesson to you. This woman wants to cause trouble, and you can see how far it's getting her." They scurried back to the safety of their cells like frightened mice.

She let go of my hair and I rubbed my painful head. "Okay, sister," I retorted harshly, "so you're really big time. Well, you might run this sideshow, and maybe you can scare hell out of the rest of these loonies, but as for me, you're as important as a pimple on a whore's ass. You don't scare me one bit."

Mrs. Clemments was standing behind her and gave me a warning shake of her head. The nurse spun on her heels and shouted a direct order to her. "Put this woman in total restraint. Put her in a jacket and no food until tomorrow."

In the heart of an asylum, I saw a move of pure diplomacy come from Mrs. Clemments.

"I don't blame you," she said softly. "But, oh, dear, we're so short of help and I hear we're getting more patients this afternoon. And you know how much extra work restraint takes. Maybe she'll settle down. Maybe she's really hungry. If she takes sick, it won't look too good on her physical report. She's already had to have infirmary treatment, and it's hard telling how long she's been without food. Maybe if we give her another bowl, she'll quiet down. There's a little left over." Looking at me, Mrs. Clemments asked, "Are you still hungry?"

"No," I snapped.

Turning to the nurse, she almost cooed, "Bless your heart, you're so overworked. Why don't you let me try and settle this with her?"

The nurse studied me, then shrugged, "All right. But keep her quiet. I'm not going to put up with any more outbursts. Do you understand?"

Mrs. Clemments nodded and, tucking her hand under my elbow, guided me back to my cell.

"You sit down," she said quietly. "And I'll get you some more oatmeal and another cup of coffee. But don't cause any more trouble. She'll not be talked out of it again."

She puffed out of the cell and I slumped back on the cot. The last thing I wanted to do was to accept defeat, but I was ravenous, and when she returned, I gulped the oatmeal down in big heaping spoonfuls . . . washing my mouth with the vile coffee.

While I was eating, she sat on the cot beside me and rubbed her swollen ankles. I handed her the oatmeal can and asked, "Could I have some more?"

She shook her head. "I scraped the bottom. But I think there might be a little more coffee. I'll see." She shuffled out again and returned with the can half full. As I drank it, she dug in her pocket and pulled out a Hershey bar. She carefully peeled off the wrapper and broke off four squares.

"Something sweet always makes things taste a little better, you know. She'd have a fit if she found out, but I like to do what I can to help you girls."

I grabbed the candy and stuffed it in my mouth, not chewing, but letting it melt and run sweetly down my throat. She gave me a quick pat on my shoulder and left, locking the door behind her.

I was still hungry, but the chocolate had satisfied me to some extent. I stretched out on the cot, and for the first time since I had been taken from home, I felt a sense of inner quiet.

My nightlong memories had troubled and challenged me well into the dawn, and I was sleepy. I was also at ease. Perhaps it had been that one glimmer of personal contact with Mrs. Clemments. I had to admit, grudgingly, that she had handled the nurse well. And I could still taste the sweet residue of candy in my mouth. I felt myself softening toward her, then I remembered the promise I had made to myself. The promise not to weaken. I would not be coddled or threatened into submission. I brought to the surface the steel of my convictions. I knew I could not survive if I allowed even a tinge of sentiment to penetrate my defenses. Was my strength so frail that it could be tempted by a piece of candy? "No," I screamed aloud. "No."

I began pacing up and down the small cell. Back and forth. Back and forth. Hitting the walls with my fist. Pounding on the thin mattress. Tearing the sheet from it and stomping it with my feet. I ripped my gown down the front, tore it to shreds, and threw it on the floor.

Standing naked, I screamed, "You'll not win. Not ever."

I slept for several hours until the noise of the food cart in the hall jolted me awake. When my cell was unlocked, I started through the door and then realized that I was naked. My gown lay in shreds where I had thrown it. I wrapped the sheet around me and stood in the hall, waiting passsively for my lunch. A trustee handed me a can of brown beans with a thin slab of corn bread floating on top. It tasted like mucilage, but I ate it. There was nothing to drink with the noon meal.

When the cart came back, I put the can on it carefully and asked the trustee for a gown. She merely stared at me blankly and moved on. I went back in my cell, and when an attendant came to lock the door, I asked her to get me a gown. She too looked at me blankly and, for an answer, slammed the door.

I sat on the cot mumbling to myself for an hour. When the door was unlocked for our march to the toilet, I wrapped the sheet around me and was startled to see several other naked women in the lineup. But they had not been as ingenious as I; they had not thought of wearing their sheets.

I felt quite superior, but when we got to the toilet a trustee took my sheet away. As she was strapping me down, I asked her, very politely, to get me a gown, but in reply she only giggled and stared curiously at my body.

There was more noise and confusion on this trip, with all the patients either screaming or singing. Some tried to reach between their legs and get their hands into the stool water. It was a naked, animal nightmare filled with every imaginable offensive sound.

Finally, when they came to unstrap us, I began screaming for my sheet. "You stinking bags. If I can't have a gown, then by Christ, give me back my sheet." It was mine and I wanted it back.

A trustee grabbed my arm and spun me around, forcing me back in line. "Get your fucking hands off me," I screamed, swinging my fists. Two trustees put a stranglehold on me and forced me to the floor. They began beating on my head and stomach with their fists, and instinctively I screamed for Mrs. Clemments, but she was not on the ward. I was dragged back to my cell and tossed into it with such force I splashed against the wall and ended up spraddled on the floor. The door was slammed and locked, but I ran to it and hammered my fists against the wire porthole.

I heard myself shouting startling obscenities, but I kept on screaming until my throat was on fire. I went back to my cot exhausted but violently angry.

"Bastards," I hissed. "Rotten dirty bastards."

Every part of my body hurt. I spit on my hands to wipe my scraped knees and elbows. My hands were filthy, and it was then I realized that I had not washed since the morning I had been taken from home. And so I sat. Naked. Filthy. My body reeking. My teeth coated. My mouth sour. My hair matted.

I crossed to my window and peered out at the sky. The sun was weak, but I looked toward heaven thoughtfully, and after a while I thumbed my nose.

I stretched out on my side and made a pillow with the crook of my arm. Half awake, I listened to the amplified cacophonous sounds coming from the ward. I could hear screaming and fighting. I could hear moans and cries for help. It went on and on, until the air vibrated with it. Monotony was setting in. The solitude of isolation was taking hold. The asylum was reality.

Each woman responded to her fears in an individual way. We each fought our particular battle with our own private, primitive weapons, and the sounds of grief and rebellion swelled until the walls seemed to shudder and cave in.

Then, somehow, I fell into a fitful sleep, a sleep that was penetrated by screams—some of them mine.

By nightfall the ward was sundered by a noise so intense that I curled up in a naked ball and covered my ears with my hands. A trustee unlocked my door, hastily put a tin can of stew and a can of coffee on the floor, and relocked the door.

While I ate, the noise and commotion in the ward continued to swell in great garbled, deafening waves. After I finished, I began pacing up and down my cell, reciting childhood poems that my mother had taught me, projecting at the top of my voice in order to drown out the clamor.

I was interrupted by an attendant and a trustee with a slop jar.

"You use this tonight," the attendant said. "So be quick about it."

"No trips to the can?" I smirked.

"Come on, we can't stand here all night."

I looked at the slop jar and saw that it was already half full, and the sight and smell of it made me sick. I made a move toward them. "Get the hell out of here. Go on . . . get out."

The trustee grabbed me by the hair and twisted my head around, and then the attendant said, "Sit down and pee."

The trustee let go of my hair and pushed me onto the

jar. Indifferently, I relieved myself, and almost as though she was reading my mind, the attendant warned, "Don't you try to kick it over, or so help me God, I'll push your face in it."

From the looks of her, I knew she would, so when I was finished, I raised myself daintily and tiptoed back to my bunk.

All through the night, the ward seethed in painful restlessness. And on through the next day and the next night. Confined to our cells, the toilet routine with the slop jar was repeated in each cubicle four times a day.

With every passing hour, I could feel my nerves tightening, and to combat the tensions I tried to fill my mind with unrelated thoughts—thoughts of other times and other places. But always I returned to the confining misery to which I was bound.

On the second night of restriction, rain beat through the open window and flooded my cell. It was never mopped up. The weather turned cold, and since I was still without a gown or bed sheet, I curled up and shivered myself to sleep.

Then, all reality gave way to bedlam. I screamed. I talked to myself. I sang. I quoted from the plays I had done, taking all parts. Improvising. Exaggerating. I beat the walls. I cursed. I rolled around on the wet floor. I begged for mercy. I threatened. I wept. And by the third day I lay exhausted, hardly aware that the ward had also quieted down. It had been strangled and stilled. A soundless world, except for the slamming of cell doors and the routine of feeding and elimination.

Then, on the morning of the fourth day, when my cell door was unlocked, I recognized Mrs. Clemments. I wanted to throw myself into her arms and cling to her. Yet even in this great despair, I curbed myself and prevented any show of weakness.

"How are you, Mrs. Anderson?" she said.

I curled up tighter on the cot and pulled my arms over my head.

"You'll have to get up, Mrs. Anderson," she said. "You ladies are going to get a shower, and then you'll be going down for your physicals. You'll be meeting before the staff doctors today."

Firmly, but gently, she pulled me to my feet and steadied me. Then, when she led me out into the hall, I was horrified by the tattered lineup of human remnants. I looked down at my own body and shuddered. Every woman had been reduced to a cowering, exhausted animal. We shook and trembled and cried as we were led to the toilet. There was no need for straps that day; we sat there limp, humped over, numb and, without exception, naked.

The ward was alive with trustees, who got us up from the toilets and herded us into a long open shower stall. As we stood in a row, liquid soap was squirted over our bodies and into our hair. It was strong and harsh, but when the water began to pepper me, the luxury of it was stimulating. I licked some of the lather off my body and washed it around in my mouth, using my finger as a toothbrush. Then I held my head back and let the water rain on my face. I had not had a drink of water since my first night in the infirmary.

Some of the women stood blank and motionless even when the lather from their hair poured white stinging foam into their eyes. They were beyond feeling. But I responded quickly and heard myself singing as I washed my body. The water was comforting, and when it was turned off, I grabbed at the small towel handed to me and scrubbed it over my body and briskly massaged my hair. Those too dulled to dry themselves were left unattended.

Still naked, we were taken back to our cells, and I

was amazed that so simple a thing as a shower could rejuvenate me. I was hungry, and when breakfast came, even the familiar serving of oatmeal and coffee tasted better.

After breakfast, we were led out into the hall and given big, shapeless gray cotton wraparounds and a pair of cotton scuffs. Marion Foster, the nurse on duty during my first night in isolation, stood outside her cage and waited for us to finish dressing.

"Now, ladies," she said impatiently. "Settle down. I want to give each of you a little advice. You're going to have your physical and staff meeting today, so take my word and be on your best behavior. Don't cause any trouble.

"You'll not be returning to this ward. After your meeting with staff you'll be assigned your regular quarters, and you'll start the treatment set up for you. And try to remember that you're in a hospital. You're here because you need help and you can make it easier if you cooperate with the people who are trying to help you. If you do not, you'll suffer the consequences."

She looked directly at me and added, "No matter who you are." Then, turning to Mrs. Clemments, she said, "All right, take them out."

Like mechanical toys, we shuffled through long and unfamiliar corridors, flanked on both sides by trustees, with Mrs. Clemments leading the column. The days of neglect and isolation had turned us into a wild, frayed-looking lot. I tried to comb my hair by raking my fingers through it, but it was too matted.

The physical was public and crudely done. Shy, confused women were stripped naked and laid out on worn-leather examination tables. With their heels forced into the iron stirrups, they spread their legs while an intern probed into them. The breasts were pinched, the stomach punched, and blood taken for tests. Then each woman was rolled over, and a thermometer was pushed into the rectum. When one is classed as insane, one cannot be trusted with an oral thermometer. Then the dreaded canvas straps appeared again and were buckled in place. Tied down and terrified, I felt the needle inch its way deep into the spine, strike home and suck out the fluid, throwing my body into a pool of swelling pain.

No semblance of dignity was left to us. We waited for our staff interviews defeated, sickened, and for the most part, senseless.

But as I looked around at the physical ugliness of the institution, I was again able to dig deep into the recesses of my spirit and call forth the belligerent, rebellious energy that I believed was my only saving grace. It gave me hardness and strength.

When the trustee called my name, I squared my shoulders and swaggered into the hearing room. I smirked at the six people seated at a long narrow conference table. A man at the head, obviously the chairman, motioned me to a chair at the end. He was a huge, flabby man of about sixty, and the folds of his chins rippled in layers over his collar. His bald head was a glittering pink, but thick white bunches of hair overgrew his brows and shaded his eyes. He rolled a pencil in his fat fingers as we studied each other.

"Sit down," he said.

"Maybe I'd rather stand."

"You'll do as I say. Sit down."

I shrugged and sat in the chair.

"I'm Dr. Raymond McQuinn," he said. Then, indicating with his head he went around the table: "Dr. Edward Conway. Dr. Ralph Masterson. Dr. Evelyn Browning. Dr. Henry Daniels. And Dr. Albert Rocky. Now, will you introduce yourself to us, please?"

"My name is Claudine Monroe and I'm from Elks Ass, Montana."

"That will be enough," McQuinn interrupted. "We know who you are."

"Then what the hell is this tea party all about?" I snapped. "For Christ's sakes, I don't give a damn who you are, and since you know me, they why this stupid preliminary?"

"Why do you insist on using the name Frances Anderson?" Rocky asked.

"Because that's my name."

"You're Frances Farmer."

"My name is Frances Anderson."

"That was your married name. You're divorced."

"So what? It's still my name."

"Why do you try to avoid the name that made you famous?"

"Jesus! Not you too."

"What does that mean?"

"What the hell do you think it means?"

Dr. Browning interrupted. She was a tiny woman with fiercely curled red-orange hair and bright-crimson lipstick. Her voice was shrill and her speech clipped and prim.

"Mrs. Anderson," she said. "You have a very complicated record and your difficulties are, in my opinion, quite serious. Do you know why you are here?"

"How should I know? You're the doctor. You tell me."

"Do you feel you are mentally ill?"

I threw back my head and bellowed.

"Will you answer Dr. Browning?" McQuinn asked impatiently.

"I won't even bother, and you can't make me."

"At this point we will not try, Mrs. Anderson," he

said. "But you have caused a great deal of difficulty since your admission. Your report shows that you have been vulgar, insulting, and uncooperative in every way. It also shows that these same traits and conditions finally forced your mother to commit you."

"Yeah!" I snarled. "I'm a bad girl. A real bad girl."

Dr. Conway pushed back his chair and locked his hands behind his head. "Do you realize," he mused, "that it was your mother who obtained the court order for your commitment and that she has already appeared before this board and given her testimony?"

He tapped a folder on the table in front of him. "From what we have here, she has not painted a very pretty picture, Mrs. Anderson, and I'm of the opinion that you are entitled to know the major charges she has brought out in her testimony."

"You listen to me, big boy. I couldn't care less what she says. So don't waste your breath. And don't ever mention her name to me again."

"Now, Mrs. Anderson," Dr. Browning interrupted, "you must admit that it isn't normal for a mature person to be so antagonistic toward one's mother."

"You silly woman," I blurted. "You absurd, silly woman. You lock me up in a crazy house and then tell me that I'm not acting normal. Jesus Christ!"

"Mrs. Anderson, you'll have to control yourself," Dr. McQuinn ordered.

"Fatso, if you think this is out of control, I could sure show you a few things."

"Take my advice and answer the questions sensibly," he said.

I slouched back in my chair and watched him shuffle through the papers before him. "We'll discuss the testimony on page four, paragraph three. Dr. Rocky, will you handle the questioning?"

Rocky was a slight, middle-aged man, who chomped

vigorously on the stem of an unlit pipe.

"Mrs. Anderson," he began, "Dr. Conway told you that your mother has brought some very serious charges against you. She was informed, by this board, prior to her testimony that whatever she said would be included in your records so please understand that she was well aware of the critical consequences of her charges.

"Now, we have no reason to doubt her, for she seems deeply concerned about your welfare. According to her, you were out of control and she therefore found it necessary to petition the court for a permanent commitment.

"Also, as your legal guardian, she has given us permission to prescribe whatever treatment we consider necessary to assist in your possible recovery.

"Furthermore, your mother has given testimony which indicates that you are dangerous to yourself and others. Therefore, it is no longer safe for you to be at large. She has testified that you have made violent attacks against her person, and she gave further evidence relating to your mistreatment of your dog."

"Wait a minute," I interrupted, stunned. "Go over that last part again."

"Your mother states that you have a pet dog. Is that correct?"

"Yes. But I wouldn't say the dog is especially mine. She belongs to the family. I've taken care of her, of course, but what does that have to do with it?"

"According to your mother, you have repeatedly and cruelly mistreated, beaten and tortured the animal to such an extent that the beast trembles at the sight of you and tries to run away."

"That's a goddamned lie," I shouted. "A goddamned lie! And if my mother told you that, she's a goddamned liar."

"Settle down, Mrs. Anderson," McQuinn warned. "We must proceed calmly."

"Calmly," I screamed. "For Christ's sakes. My mother has accused me of a filthy act and you sit there and expect me to take it."

"Mrs. Anderson," McQuinn warned again. "Now, you sit down and be quiet or we'll restrain you."

Surely it was a mistake. It had to be. How could she accuse me of such a thing?

Dr. Rocky's voice droned on. "Also, Mrs. Anderson, your mother states that you attacked a neighbor's child without provocation and threatened to 'kill the brat.' Do you recall that incident?"

I shook my head numbly.

"She also testified that you have threatened to kill her repeatedly and that she is afraid of you. She further contends that you have been keeping company, and these are her words, with 'weird and unwholesome characters.' "

The room was silent until I finally raised my head. "Is it true?" I asked. "Is that my mother's testimony against me? You're not lying? She said all those things?"

McQuinn nodded. Then, closing the folder, he said, "Mrs. Anderson, in view of your mother's testimony and upon considering your behavior since you were brought here, the board feels that, in all probability, your mother has given an accurate and truthful account of your actions."

Looking around at the other doctors for agreement, he said, "I think you doctors will concur with me that this patient should not be given open-ward privileges." They all nodded.

Then to me he said, "You will be placed under observation until we can further study your behavior patterns. There will be no body restraint unless you make it necessary. But, understand this, Mrs. Anderson, we will not put up with the attitude you've shown these past four days. Our people are here to help you, but we do not require them to tolerate either physical or verbal abuse. Your language has been foul and your manner vulgar. You have been arrogant and insulting to everyone, and we will not have it."

The more he talked, the angrier he became. "The way you have conducted yourself in this staff meeting is uncalled for and intolerable. You are a disagreeable young woman who finds obvious delight in alienating others. You have created a hostile world for yourself, Mrs. Anderson, and the price you are paying for this hostility is high indeed."

The other doctors were as startled as I at his outburst, and Conway finally broke in.

"Dr. McQuinn," he said, "we can't help this patient by meeting insult with insult. She's denied her mother's charges, and there is always the possibility that she is justified in her denial."

McQuinn exploded. "Dr. Conway," he roared. "May I remind you that I am chairman of this board and I conduct the hearings?"

"Dr. McQuinn," Dr. Browning interrupted, "may I ask the patient a question?" McQuinn grumbled but nodded his permission.

"Mrs. Anderson," she said, "you have reacted in a most hostile manner toward your mother, and you have made it quite obvious to each of us that you do not like her."

"Really?" I quipped.

Twisting her curls around two fingers, she continued, "I would like for you to tell me what you think of mothers, in general. If you will, just tell me what motherhood means to you."

I shook my head in disbelief, then mimicking her

shrill voice and twining my fingers in my matted hair, I said thoughtfully, "Well, Doctor, after careful consideration, it is my opinion that the world is not full of mother fuckers—it is full of fucking mothers."

Her fingers froze in her curls and she muttered something like "Well, I never. Really."

Conway chuckled and Rocky chomped harder on his pipestem. I stood up, took particular pain in straightening my wrapper, then said to her, "Anything else you'd like to know, sweetie?"

McQuinn shouted, "That's enough. Quite enough."

Eyeing her up and down contemptuously, I said, "You certainly should do something about the way you look. Really, I should think anyone knows you never wear pearls with polka dots. And that hair. You look like a redheaded porcupine with a cheap permanent."

She covered her mouth with her hand as if to press back a squeal. I winked broadly at the other doctors and blew her a kiss.

McQuinn was furious. "I am assigning this patient to you, Dr. Conway, and I suggest you put her under immediate treatment."

Dr. Conway had the sleek narrow head of a greyhound, with thin pale hair glued to the scalp. He was at least fifty but ignored it by wearing a wild-plaid sport coat and a brilliant-green tie.

Cute, I thought to myself. Damn if he doesn't think he's cute.

"I'll have an orderly take you over to the ward and you'll soon be settled."

He stood back to let me pass through the door, and when I felt his hand on my arm, I instinctively pulled away from him.

"Don't ever touch me," I hissed. "Don't you ever put your hands on me."

"Now. Now," he whispered. "Don't get excited. Just relax, Frances, and between the two of us we'll have long talks. Before you know it, you'll be back in Hollywood."

He cupped his fingers around my arm again, pressing them firmly into my flesh. I pulled away, violently, and screamed, "Don't you try copping a feel. Keep away from me. Do you hear? Keep away from me."

We were in the hall and he motioned for a male orderly. I tried to duck between them, but the orderly tackled me around the waist and held me in a firm experienced grip.

Patting his hair in place, Conway ignored my struggling with the orderly and said, "You'll see, Frances, we'll get along just fine."

He reached over to pat my cheek and I tried to bite his finger.

"What kind of a freak are you?" I screamed at his disappearing back. Then, conscious of the orderly's arms holding me around the waist, I quit struggling.

"Okay," I demanded. "Take your hands off me."

Instead, he grinned and pulled me closer to him. I could smell his body as he pressed himself against me. My wrapper had come untied during the scuffle, and feeling his hardness against my bare flesh, I began to scream. Conway came back through the door and shouted, "What are you trying to do to that woman?"

The orderly, holding me less personally, stammered. "She tried to get away again. What do you expect me to do, Doc? Let her go?"

"He's a rotten liar," I screamed. "Get him away from me."

The commotion brought McQuinn out into the hall. "Is she causing more trouble?" he asked in disgust.

Conway assured him that he could handle the situation, but McQuinn insisted that I be put in restraint. He went back into the staff room, and in moments two women attendants came running toward us with a straitjacket. Another scuffle ensued and the two women and the orderly finally wrestled me to the floor, and I was once more locked into a canvas prison.

McQuinn was reprimanding Conway seriously. "This woman is not capable of handling herself and yet you turn her loose with one orderly."

"Quit chewing out his ass," I shouted. "And fire that goddamned orderly. What are you running here, a whorehouse?"

One of the women wrapped her arm across my shoulder and said, "Listen, honey, this kind of talk ain't gonna getcha nowhere. Why doncha just calm down? You're only makin' it tougher on yourself. If you'll stand still a minute, honey, I'll tie your wrapper back in place." Not until I felt her hands go up under the straitjacket and struggle to pull the wrapper across the front of me did I realize I was exposed.

"That's the best I can do, for now," she said. "But if you just take it easy things will be all right. This here ain't such a bad place, kid, if you learn the ropes. Just play ball and you'll make it okay."

With Conway and McQuinn out of sight, the orderly grinned and sauntered over to us. "Sure, honey, you just play ball and every little thing's gonna be okey-dokey. I'll even let you teach me some of them Hollywood tricks."

"Leave her alone," the woman said firmly. "You just get back over there and leave her alone."

He shrugged and leaned back against the wall, still grinning.

"Christ almighty," I groaned. "Jesus Christ almighty."

The woman tried to push my hair back out of my face, but I jerked my head away. "Don't you touch me."

"Look, honey, we're only tryin' to help you. Everybody knows who you are, and you don't want to go around lookin' all messed up, now, do ya?"

I began to laugh a wild, sobbing laugh. It was an unbelievable farce. Some sort of hideous nightmare. I felt one of the women gather me into her arms. "Now, you just cry it out, honey," she cooed. "Nobody wants to hurt you. Just you go on and cry."

She was a tall, lean woman, and for some unknown reason I responded to the clumsy offer of comfort. I slumped against her and wept, letting her stroke my hair and rock me. "Go on and cry, honey. It'll do you good."

Then the old fire flamed up within me and I pulled roughly away from her. "I'm all right. I'm all right."

She studied me with soft, probing innocent eyes, and, despite myself, I smiled and said, "Really, it's okay. I'm all right now."

Jerking her head toward the orderly, she said, "He'll have to take you to the other building, but I'll ask the doctor if we can go along. He won't try to bother you with us along."

She held a rough handkerchief to my nose and directed me to blow. Then Conway came out into the hall again and she hurried over and talked to him under her breath. I saw him give a quick look at the orderly, who was engrossed in the toes of his shoes. Then he nodded his head and came toward me.

"These two ladies will go with you to the new ward, Frances. Now, I won't put this incident on your report, providing you behave yourself in the future. I think you can do that, can't you?"

I answered him in a cold, level voice. "Look, you brokendown sawbones, you and I both know goddamned well why there won't be any report so don't think I'm taken in by your ass-kissing concern."

He shook his head, dismally, then, with the idea of a new approach, said, "Look, here, Frances. I've made a special request to have you placed under my care because I think I'll be able to help you. You see, I'm not entirely unfamilar with your profession. I've done a lot of acting with little theater groups around here, and I felt you would be more responsive to someone who could understand your work. Why, before long we'll have you back in Hollywood."

I let out an ear-piercing laugh, ending with "Great God, an amateur."

My mockery embarrassed him and he briskly ordered the women to take me to my ward.

"Can she be let out of the jacket after she gets checked in?"

He tapped his lips thoughtfully and said, "I suppose so. I'll call the ward, but make sure it's understood she's to have no outside ward privileges. Absolutely none."

He turned swiftly and closed the staff door behind him, and I walked between the two women until we came to an exit leading to the outside. The orderly tagged sullenly behind us.

Fresh air was a marvelous change from the stuffy, odor-filled corridors. The sun was warm against my face, but I was chilled when I looked at the buildings around me. They were crumbling with decay and their dark forms defiantly blotted out the sky. Every window was barred, leaving a lasting impression of giant cages.

I began to tremble. We turned into a crumbling, trash-littered building and climbed two flights of wide worn stairs. I clamped my teeth together to stop their chattering.

Inside, the air smelled of dust and mold. Great hunks of plaster were knocked out along the walls, remnants of other struggles. As we climbed the stairs, the women tucked their hands under my elbows to steady me. On the second floor landing we came to a door stenciled in the wide letters: WARD-O. FEMALE.

"Let's take the jacket off her," one of the women said. "There ain't no reason why she has to go in there like this."

"Will you promise to act right and not cause any trouble?" the other one asked me.

I nodded and was relieved when they unbuckled the jacket and let the harsh canvas drop away from me.

"Now, then," one said. "Let's just fix you up a little bit. You'll find some nice ladies in here."

The other one, trying to infect me with some enthusiasm, urged, "Honey, fix up your wrapper and straighten up your hair. You're such a pretty little thing."

I shrugged and halfheartedly did the best I could to comply with their suggestions. The orderly was standing behind us on the stairway, snickering. I whirled around and very calmly said, "You ever try anything with me, and if it's the last thing I do, I'll kill you."

His insolent grin spread. "Wait till I tell the old doc that one."

"You shut your mouth and leave her alone," one of the women warned. "And I mean it. You keep on the way you're going and you'll find yourself in a peck of trouble."

She patted my shoulder. "Come on, honey, we'll get you checked in." Then, to the orderly, she snapped, "And as for you, you just go on about your business. You ain't needed here no more."

He cocked his head to one side and, looking at me, made obscene motions between his legs. He went giggling down the stairs and called back over his shoulder, "I'll be seeing you, honey."

"I declare," one of the women clucked. "That's the filthiest man I've ever seen. He makes me sick. Always trying to carry on with these poor souls. You know how he is, Gert."

Gert, the other attendant, nodded silently and said, "The world sure is full of trash, but so long as they don't throw it on my front porch, it don't bother me none."

The other one shook her head in despairing agreement and pushed the buzzer on the door. "All the same," she said, "it just seems to me they keep gettin' worse and worse. These no-account men around here are terrible."

The door was unlocked by a nurse who peeked her head out and asked, "Is this Dr. Conway's new patient?" but without waiting for an answer, she took my arm and drew me into the ward. The door was shut abruptly on the two attendants and I looked back with the fleeting thought of thanking them, but it was too late.

The nurse introduced herself. "I'm Mrs. Lambert," she said, "Lorraine Lambert, but you call me Lorraine like the rest of the girls do, and I'll call you Frances. It's so much nicer that way, don't you think?"

She hooked her arm through mine and chattered on in a flutterly manner. She was small, at least fifty, and very neat and crisp. Her white well-starched uniform stood out like a banner of purity in the midst of the absolute filth in the ward. She reminded me of a bird, nervous and twittery, with a slight high squeak to her voice. At times, she almost chirped.

"This is a large ward, you know. We have over a hundred ladies here, and before long you'll get to know every one of them and make friends. It's so much nicer that way, don't you think?"

"Do you keep this place locked?" I asked.

"Why, yes," she fluttered.

I jerked my arm away from her slight grasp. "Then keep your goddamned hands off me. Understand?"

"Why, Miss Farmer . . . Anderson . . . I mean, Frances."

"Just keep your hands off me. You got this outhouse locked up so I can't get out, can I?"

"No. No," she stammered.

"Okay. Let's understand each other. I don't like silly women holding onto me. I don't go for broads. Understand? And if I did, I wouldn't pick you. I'd want one with bigger tits. Is that clear?"

Her face burned pink and she straightened the front of her uniform, self-consciously aware of her pitifully flat chest.

"We . . . well . . . we mustn't get off on the wrong foot," she stuttered. "We all get along here, Miss Farmer . . . Frances."

I swaggered before her. "Just stick to your side of the street and we'll get along."

I wondered why I had deliberately insulted her. Why without any provocation had I twisted her simple gesture into something dirty and mocked her in such a cruel way?

She managed to dismiss the insult, and raising her birdlike voice to a high chirp, she tried to get the attention of the patients scattered throughout the ward. "Ladies. Ladies. Look here just a moment."

No one paid any attention, and she desperately clapped her hands together, trying to round them up.

Then, a massive deep-throated woman, wearing the red armband of a trustee, boomed, "Hey, everybody. Shut up. Lorraine wants to talk." Immediately the ward quieted down.

"Thank you, Clara," the nurse said, smiling weakly at the woman. And Clara strutted up and stood beside us, rocking back and forth on her heels, grinning. It was apparent she made the nurse ill at ease, but she said again, "Thank you."

"That's okay, Lorraine," the trustee answered. "Any time. Any time."

The nurse was flushed and seemed overpowered by the giant of a woman, but she turned meekly to the ward and said, "Ladies, I want you to meet a wonderful new friend. I think you'll all recognize her . . . and aren't we fortunate to have someone like her living with us?"

The women stared at me blankly as she went on. "This is Frances Farmer, ladies. The movie star. Now, what do you think of that?"

They began to giggle. Some of them pointed their fingers at me or clapped their hands together. Others began to bounce up and down on their cots like excited children.

It was a long, wide room with standard cots lining the walls. In the middle was a space filled with several large tables and straight-back chairs. Obviously the lounging and eating area.

Each cot was haphazardly made up with faded cotton blankets that had, at one time, probably been army green. Barred windows broke up the walls about every fifteen feet. Just inside the door where we were standing was the nurses' office, similar to the one in isolation, only larger. In it were three desks, several four-drawer filing cabinets, a typewriter, five chairs and a locked medicine cabinet. Straitjackets and belts hung over coat hooks. Across from the station were two private cells—private in the sense that they had doors on them.

"Oh, Frances," Lorraine said, beaming. "Just look. They're so thrilled. So thrilled."

Clara nudged me in the ribs with her elbow. "Well, whatcha know. Frances Farmer."

"Now, ladies," Lorraine went on gaily. "I want you to make our Frances feel at home. And make her comfortable. Maybe, if we're real nice to her, maybe she'll tell us all about Hollywood."

She had breathed the magic word and pandemonium broke loose. The women swept toward us in a great wave, chattering and shouting. I ran to the door, tugging on it with all my strength. The nurse was shoved out of the way, and I felt the women pressing in upon me, turning me around, pulling and grabbing.

"Get me out of here," I screamed. "Somebody get me out of here."

They were pulling my hair and had torn my wrapper off my body. I could not stop screaming. I was pressed against the door with such force that the handle ground painfully into my back. I was sinking to the floor and knew I would be trampled when I felt the wave being pulled away from me. I had my head locked protectively in my arms, and when I peeked out, I saw Clara steamrolling the women roughly back down the ward. My scuffs were gone and my wrapper was in fragments.

I huddled against the door and watched the trustee shove and pound them with brute force. Shortly she had the ward as calm as when I entered. Some of the women stretched out on their cots. Some sat at the tables and looked through magazines, and only a few dared slip curious glances at me. Everything seemed quiet, but I knew it was a coerced calmness that could easily erupt again.

Lorraine came toward me ringing her hands and straightening her prim white cap. "Oh, dear. Oh, I'm so sorry. I had no idea they'd respond in such a way. I guess they just got excited over the thought of you. They don't have much to amuse them, you know."

I crawled over to the corner and began to shake.

"I think I'd better call Dr. Conway," she said. "I just don't know what to do."

Clara came back and hovered over us like a shadow.

"You stay here with Frances," the nurse said, then changed her mind. "No, maybe you'd both better come with me to the office while I call the doctor. I just don't know what to do about all this."

Clara stuck out her hand and pulled me to my feet as Lorraine fumbled for her keys and unlocked the wire-covered door to the office. She motioned for us to follow her, and once inside I heard the latch fall into place. It was an ugly room, but I had a feeling of great safety in being locked in a cage within a cage.

Lorraine motioned me to a chair as she nervously dialed the phone. She left a message for Conway to call her back. "Yes. Yes," she said. "It's an emergency."

Clara picked up a pack of cigarettes on the desk and lighted one, sending two long jets of smoke from her ball-like nostrils. She pulled on it again, letting it dangle from her lips, then offered it to me.

I saw the deep wet ring on the end and shook my head. The woman repelled me, and I almost gagged at the thought of smoking after her. She shrugged at my refusal, then put the cigarette back in her mouth and left it hanging there. She never took her eyes off me.

Lorraine sat hunched over her desk picking at her nails until the phone rang. I listened to her garbled recount of what had happened. She kept nodding at the instructions she was evidently receiving from Conway and hung up, thanking him profusely.

She twisted around in her chair and said apologetically, "Frances, Dr. Conway feels that, for the time being, you will be better off in seclusion."

I felt the corners of my mouth twitch in a bitter grin, wondering what she meant by "seclusion."

"Now, it won't be for very long," she said soothingly. "Just until he can get things a little more organized. You'll be very comfortable, and really, you'll be so much better off. You'll have a room like Clara's." To the trustee she gave hesitant instructions. "Take Frances to the room next to yours, will you, Clara?"

Clara, squinting at me through the smoke of her cigarette still dangling from her lips, hauled herself up from her chair and stood waiting for me. When I did not move, the nurse looked at me and questioned, "Is there something else you want, Frances?"

I crossed my arms stubbornly and glowered. "God damn it, woman, I'm naked."

Clara broke out in a hard snicker and the nurse began fluttering again. "Oh, dear. Oh, dear. I'm so sorry. I should have noticed, but things have been so upset." Embarrassed at her vagueness, she said timidly, "Clara, run down to the clothes room and get her a nice little dress of some sort and a pair of slippers. What size do you wear, Frances?"

"What the hell difference does it make?" I grumbled.

"Oh, we do want you to be comfortable. Yes. Yes. You see, there's really no reason for you not to be comfortable."

Clara stood at the door like a bulldog ready to spring loose. "You're a good judge of sizes," Lorraine said to her, unlocking the door. "Pick out something nice, now."

Clara took her time eyeing me up and down before charging through the door. I had never felt so naked.

Lorraine turned, as if to make conversation, but I stopped her with, "Why don't you just shut up?" With that, she huddled over her desk and began rummaging through untidy mounds of paper. I broke the silence by stating, "I have to pee."

Lorraine looked up from her work, startled, then chirped happily, "You can use our rest room here in the office, Frances. Now, why didn't I think to ask you? That's really terrible of me." She almost skipped across the room, and, opening a door to the small toilet, flicked on the light.

The next few moments offered me a luxury I would cherish in the following years—a stool with a seat and a back, and no straps tying me down. But more than anything else, there was the dignity of total privacy. I took great joy in just being able to wash my hands after I had finished.

In a mirror above the washbasin I saw myself for the first time and gasped in terror at the strange creature looking back at me. I hung over the sink, gagging. I turned the cold water on full force and pushed my face into the rushing stream. Then slowly I raised my head, hypnotically drawn back to the mirror. What I saw was not me. It was a thing—a wild, horrible thing. Surely to God, I thought, it can't be me.

I drew closer to the mirror. My face was swollen out of shape. One eye was blackened and pus drained from it. My lips were parched and cracked and the corners of my mouth pulled down into deep ruts. My nose was almost twice its normal size, and a black bruise discolored my chin. My hair was a frizzed maze of mats and tangles.

I pushed my face into the mirror until only my eyes met the reflection. I looked deep, searching for something familiar, something of me, something I could cling to.

The image blurred and I tasted tears, even though I was unaware that I was weeping. I wiped my hands over my face, touching it. Feeling the bones. Hoping somehow to remold it, to wipe away the sudden age. I was the reality of a nightmare.

There was a timid knock on the door.

"Frances, Clara's brought you some clothes. I'll just hand them in to you."

The door opened a crack and she dangled in a pair of moccasins and a dress of faded cotton. It was sleeveless with a round scoop neck and was not only too big for me but much too long. The moccasins were equally oversized and flapped on my feet. Clara obviously judged the rest of the world by her own bulk. But the dress was, at least, clean, and the shoes were nearly new. I dressed quickly, then took one last look at my face in the mirror.

The bruised, frightened woman stared back at me, but I squared my shoulders, opened the door, and said briskly to the nurse, "Okay, toots, where's my suite?"

She took me across the hall to one of the private cells and Clara thumped noisily along. "Is that she-elephant going to shadow me everywhere I go?" I said under my breath. Lorraine, with caution, asked her to check on the patients in the recreation area, and she waddled off, smug in her minor authority.

I surveyed my cell. It was small, about six feet wide and ten feet long, but there was a large window at the end. I walked to it and looked out through the bars. There was an old honey locust tree just outside, nearly full leafed, and I could see other buildings and roads winding through the grounds.

A regulation cot was pushed against one wall, and opposite it, surprisingly enough, was a basin and stool.

"Class," I growled. "Real class."

Lorraine busied herself by fussing over the bed,

straightening the blanket. There was no pillow. She looked up from her task and said shyly, "Frances, I'm sorry about what happened. I just didn't realize."

I leaned in a corner and said grudgingly, "Forget it."

"Dr. Conway said he'd try to get up here tomorrow, but he wants you kept in seclusion until he can see you."

I studied her thoughtfully. She was rather a pathetic little woman. Nervous. Helpless. Afraid. Concerned.

"I'll have Clara bring you some magazines," she went on. "Or a book, if you like. I imagine you enjoy reading."

"Lorraine," I purred, with sudden friendliness. "Do you know what I'd really like?"

She brightened.

"Oh, well." I shrugged and sighed. "I don't suppose. . . ."

"No. No," she interrupted. "You just tell me."

"Well," I said slowly, "I'd like three things."

"Yes?"

"I'd give anything for a cup of coffee and a cigarette."

"Oh, dear," she hesitated. "There's no smoking permit on your chart, and the patients who can only get to smoke twice a day—and then under supervision. But, well, I don't see why one would hurt, do you?"

She patted my arm and concluded, "I'll have Clara get the coffee and, if you promise to be very careful, I'll get you a cigarette."

She started from the cell, then turned. "But you said three things."

I tried to run my fingers through my hair, gesturing helplessly. "Would you have a comb I could borrow?"

She seemed genuinely delighted and went fluttering

through the door, her old self again. Shortly, Clara clomped in with a tin cup of black coffee and Lorraine returned with a cigarette and a large-tooth comb. Clara then offered to get the window pole and open the window, and the nurse nervously complimented her for her thoughtfulness.

I sat cross-legged on the cot and inhaled deeply as she held a match to my cigarette. "Now, be careful," she warned pleasantly. "And don't forget to flush it down the toilet when you're through."

I exhaled slowly and nodded. Clara had opened the window and went lurching through the door carrying the window pole over her shoulder. When she was gone, Lorraine said, "While I'm on duty I can leave the door open, if you like."

"No," I said quickly. "Keep it closed. I'd rather you would."

"All right, Frances." She started to leave, but in the doorway she turned and said, "You've missed lunch, but we'll have supper around six. I'm only on duty in this ward for two hours a day. Clara is in charge when I'm not here and she'll see that you have supper."

Lorraine was beginning to get on my nerves, and sensing this, she pulled the door closed, but peeked back through the wire window and gave me a quick fluttering wave.

The coffee was the usual bitter fluid, but it was, at least, half warm and not so bad with a cigarette. I sipped slowly and enjoyed watching the smoke as it curled and fanned out in front of me. I took my time, and when I finished, I dropped it into the tin cup, ignoring Lorraine's instructions. I watched the short stub slowly disintegrate into the dregs of the black liquid.

I did not want to move from the cot. Lying on my back, I studied the small cell with its gouged walls and filthy floor. The toilet stool was stained and smelled of stale disinfectant. The porcelain basin was yellowed and pockmarked with age. Its one faucet was rusty. There was no soap, or towel, or toilet paper.

Long tits of soot waved from the ceiling, and the corners were thick with dusty, deserted spider webs. The iron cot was crusted with rust, but the overall condition of the cell was far better than isolation had been, and, in general, I was pleased.

I was in what had originally been used as a resident attendant's room. Prior to World War II, it was an established practice for mental institutions to have at least two attendants living on each ward. This was an added bonus to the employee's low pay scale, and the practice not only provided permanent supervision for the patients but offered a home for people unable to earn enough money to house themselves. But, with the coming of the war, well-paying defense work lured away a majority of the employees. Most doctors, competent or not, were either taken into service or else set up their own rewarding private practices. Institutions across the country were stripped, and only crude skeleton crews remained. At the time of my commitment there were 2,700 patients in the asylum, staffed by 300 employees. This is nine times less than the minimum.

It was a critical time. Tax-supported institutions could not provide high enough salaries to entice people away from defense work, and it is an indisputable fact that during this period the asylums were operated by the inmates.

Where I was, wild-eyed patients were made trustees. Homosexuals wormed their way into supervisory positions. Sadists ruled wards. Orderlies raped at will. So did doctors. Many women were given medical care only when abortions were performed. Some of the orderlies pimped and set up prostitution rings within the institution, smuggling men into the outbuildings and supplying them with women. There must be a twisted perversion in having an insane woman, and anything was permitted against them, for it is a common belief that "crazy people" do not know what is happening to them.

Buildings crumbled in filth and decay. Heating plants broke down and went unrepaired. Rats nested in every ward, and it was not uncommon to see them leaping onto food trays, fighting with patients for morsels.

Decent food, clothing and supplies never reached the patients but were either bootlegged by the employees or enjoyed by the executive staff. Women hardly able to function were put to hard labor under the guise of occupational therapy. Old men worked the farm fields day in and day out until they stumbled and fell from exhaustion. Many men, already driven mad, spent ten to twelve hours a day in the slaughterhouse, killing pigs and wading in blood. All day long they clubbed and stabbed and gutted, and then, at night, they would scream in howling misery.

Wards were like neighborhoods, full of intrigue, graft and gossip. Cliques were formed. Enemies were made. Fights were constant. And each ward had a major-domo. In Ward-O it was Clara.

For the most part, the women in this ward were trained in some skill. They worked in the hospital offices, the infirmary, or the library. Some of them worked the switchboards, and others were put on duty as practical nurses, assisting in every conceivable way with other patients. No one in O was required to work as a trustee, nor were they sent to the cookhouse or given cleaning details. O was the top of the social structure—the elite of the madhouse—and Clara had wrestled control of it with her brute force.

Clara was in her mid-thirties, with quivering hunks of flesh attached to her steel frame. Prior to her commitment she had been a chiropractor and had no qualms about disabling any patient who got out of hand. She could snap a back out of joint as easily as breaking a match in two, and did so if she was crossed.

Most of the trustees were picked not for their intelligence or concern but for their brute strength and sadistic inclinations. Clara fitted every requirement. The women on the ward were afraid of her, as was the nurse. And she was secretly despised by everyone.

When Lorraine was on duty or when on the few occasions an official or doctor would come onto the ward, Clara was a docile creature, anxious to please. But when the ward was left to her, when the women returned from their day's work and the door was locked, she became a power-ridden demon who forced the patients to wait on her and pamper her like a potentate. Few incidents ever appeared on the hospital reports from O, Clara saw to that. The staff therefore saw no cause to pull her from her perch. The doctors were more than satisfied with her results, and the women in O knew better than to complain about her treatment.

Sexual favors were freely exchanged in the asylum, for women were desperate for any kind of pseudo-affection, but the ward trembled in awe at Clara's lesbian demands. This appetite was as gargantuan as her lust for food, and secure in her position as trustee, she kissed, fondled and molested anyone who suited her fancy. Few of the women had escaped her.

When Lorraine came to tell me she was leaving for the day, she told me she had checked with Clara and

I would have my supper on a tray in my cell, or, as she called it, room.

Then, with her eyes averted, she cautiously suggested that I try to get along with the trustee, and from the unsaid, I realized that she was telling me that Clara had peculiarities. She was in an obvious state of quandary and concern. She explained that when she was not on duty I would have to be locked in my cell and, as the trustee, Clara would have to have the key. The buildings all were firetraps, and it was a regulation that no patient could be locked up unless someone in charge had a key.

She studied me for a long moment, then made a pointed decision that took far more courage than I had credited her with having. "I'm going to report that I've lost the key to your room. It will take weeks before we can get anyone up here to make a duplicate, if ever."

There would be possible safety from Clara in the open ward, and Lorraine, aware of what was likely to happen, provided me the only feeble protection available—a chance to run if Clara cornered me. I tried to thank her but could not make my words sound genuine. She made things easier by fluttering on her way, telling me to rest well and that she would see me the next day.

Shortly after she left, Clara boomed into the cell and demanded to know why my door was left unlocked. "I'm ward trustee around here," she stormed. "And when a goddamned room is supposed to be locked, I keep the son of a bitchin' key. That's the rule and that's my job. What the hell does that jellyfish think she's doing?"

"She said she couldn't find the key," I said.

Her face was livid. "Then, god damn it, she tells

me . . . not a goddamned crazy broad. I'm the trustee. Who the hell does she think she is?"

"What difference does it make?" I laughed weakly. "None of us can go anyplace, anyway." Somehow I had to avert her attention away from the key, so I said, pouting, "I'm hungry, Clara. What time do we get some food?"

"It won't be for an hour or so," she grumbled. "But you're not going out in the ward to eat, see. Not on your life. You'll eat here on a tray, and as far as the rest of the gals know, this door is locked. Do you get me? Locked. So don't let me see you out in the hall."

I nodded meekly, genuinely afraid of her. "I'm not going anywhere," I said. "I'm tired and hungry. I could eat a cow, I'm so hungry. So if you've got any influence!"

"Don't you worry none about my influence," she snorted. "I run this ward, and what I say goes."

Then she leaned against the wall and slowly ran her eyes across my body. Instinctively I pulled the dress tighter around me.

"You sure as hell are a skinny one." She laughed until the folds of her chin quivered. "That damn dumb jellyfish didn't even know you were naked today. But I sure as shit did."

She moved closer and I felt myself stiffen, then sighed in relief when one of the patients stuck her head in the door and said breathlessly, "Clara, Betty's sick again. She's throwing up all over the place."

"Shit," Clara snorted and slammed the door as though the noise would convince the ward that it was locked. Alone, I began to tremble. There was a petrifying evil about the woman.

I lay back on the cot and pulled the blanket around my shoulders. Too much had happened to me. Numb and sluggish, I closed my eyes but could not suppress the groans that seeped through my lips.

I was disturbed by the difficulty I was having in assembling my thoughts. They seemed blurred and distorted by a distant rolling fog. I lay in this suspended state until Clara opened my door again and brought a tray with a large wooden bowl of boiled pork and potatoes and two cans of coffee.

"This ought to put some meat on your bones." She grinned, holding the tray out in front of her.

I sat upright on the cot and she put it carefully beside me.

"We get about half an hour," she said. "This stuff comes up on a cart in a big kettle and they want it back in the kitchen in half an hour. Never could figure out the damned hurry. Me, I like to take my time, but they got goddamned rules about everything in this place. And I'm trustee here, so I'm the one that sees that nobody breaks them. So, better gobble it down, kiddo. Me, I eat out in the ward with the rest of the gals. Got to keep my eyes on things, you know."

When she was gone, I devoured the tasteless food but could not keep from imagining her humped over a tray, slurping up grub like a vacuum cleaner.

Although I was hungry, I couldn't possibly have eaten everything on the tray. But the skimpy meals of the past days warned me to save what I could. I picked out a large piece of pork and a potato, and wiping the loose dirt off with my hand, I tucked my private larder into a corner of the deep windowsill.

While I was on the toilet, Clara came back for the tray and grinning at seeing me there. She ran her tongue around the rim of her mouth, teasing her heavy lips.

"Any chance of toilet paper?" I asked, ignoring her look.

"Sure, kiddo. You just stay put and I'll bring you some."

She picked up the tray and again slammed the door, mentally locking it, I suppose. A few minutes later she handed me a skimpy roll of paper.

"You know, kiddo," she said and dropped herself down heavily on the cot, "I'm from Seattle, just like you. And do you remember when you came up here a couple of years ago for that big Hollywood premiere?"

I nodded, wishing she would go. Instead, she settled herself more comfortably and went on. "Well, I was just getting started then . . . in my practice, I mean. I'm a chiropractor, you know, and believe you me that's a pretty tough racket for a woman."

She looked at me through her thin-slit eyes for approval, and I nodded in quick sympathy.

"So, anyway, I got me and my lady friend tickets to it. Paid one hell of a price, too, if I remember rightly. And there we were, waiting around to see you onstage, in person, and you never showed up. I was madder than hell about it. You remember that time?"

I nodded again, squirming uncomfortably on the seat.

"Well, anyway," she went on, "I said to my lady friend, to hell with this crap. I was all for leaving, but she wanted to stay and see the picture. So I let her have her way, of course. I remember she was all dressed up, like a kewpie doll . . . and all the big shots were there that night. Remember?"

I nodded and satisfied her of my interest.

"She was all excited about seeing them. And, what the hell, it was a pretty big thing, at that . . . you being a hometown girl, and all. And the papers said you'd be onstage and get the key to the city, I think it was. But you didn't. The only time we got to see you was when you came down the aisle with the mayor, just before the picture started, and everybody stood up and clapped. You remember?"

I shrugged and squirmed on the uncomfortable toilet bowl.

"Sure as shit didn't have any idea that night that you'd end up in this joint with me." This struck her as so humorous she laughed until great tears splashed her fat cheeks.

"The gals here in the ward have sure been talking about you right and left, but I set them straight, believe you me. They won't be bothering you no more. That's for goddamned sure."

She hoisted up her great body and waddled to the door. "I'm trustee of this ward and I got to get it quieted down before lights out. It'll be another hour or so," she added, squinting out the window, studying the sky. "You get so you can tell time by just looking."

I felt a scream rushing up in my throat and I knew that I could not hold it back much longer.

"Yep. I'm trustee and you got to learn these kind of things—like telling time, I mean."

Then she left and banged the door hard behind her.

I wrapped some of the toilet paper around the meat and potato I had kept from supper. As I put it back in the corner of the windowsill, I, too, studied the dying day. The sill was wide enough for me to sit in, and I curled up and leaned my head against the heavy bars that kept the outside world safely at bay. The sky was pale and lonely, and the evening air carried a heavy mist with it.

I had been frightened by the women in the ward screaming and tugging at me, but they were no different from those on the outside who would run down the street in hot pursuit of an autograph, or pull your clothes, or do any of a thousand other embarrassing things to obstruct privacy.

My mind returned to the night Clara had remembered so vividly, and I was annoyed that she had picked an incident and tossed it at me, out of context.

So much had happened to mold that specific night. It was a part of a cycle, a cycle that had started the day I landed in Hollywood.

6

The Hollywood of the thirties cast a wide beam of magic that peered into every corner of the world, and the stars of that era were unique creatures known only to one generation.

Time and economics have wiped out the star system and rendered its species extinct. But for a while I was one of those gossamer ladies who played a small role in the legend known as the Golden Era of the Silver Screen.

There were kings and queens in those days, idols to be adored. All perfect. All untouchable. And there were the idol makers. Men who created the image but destroyed the reality.

I had heard all the wild stories before leaving New York and was jokingly warned that the casting couch was a way of life in California. It was, but I made a firm, irrevocable decision to be accepted for myself and not for my sexual availability. Approaches were made of course, by men and women, but from the beginning it was a hands-off policy and my caustic tongue left no doubt that I meant it. I was a loner, unfriendly and unavailable.

I was also a very small pebble. The giant studios bulged with potential stars, all straining to run the race. All beautiful. All ambitious. All eagerly anticipating the magical transformation from an unknown to a star.

These unknowns were kept in an arena known as Talent Departments, and I reported to such a place on my first day on the Paramount lot. It was a strange experience to find myself in a tense group of young people who had only one thing in common: a six-month contract.

There was an abundant array of beauty-contest winners and muscle-flexing beachboys, none of them trained to act. None sensitized to a performance, and few whose minds extended farther than Ciro's or the Brown Derby. It was an untutored assortment, but from this raw meat the talent coaches waded through and selected, as one would a prize bull or promising filly, a prospect with potential.

We were eyed. Photographed. Told to walk. To sit. To lie down. We were interviewed. Discussed. And, eventually, required to read a few lines.

Then, one by one, the ranks diminished until only a handful remained. Those left were given fundamental exposure to the motion picture techniques of "Lights! Camera! Action!"

No camaraderie existed among this select few, only open competition and unabashed ambition. A do-or-die life-or-death atmosphere left a desperate aura in the air.

But there was one young man in the talent pool who stood out from the rest of the contract players. He had been a vocalist with the Ted Fio Rito dance band and had been signed to a six-month contract with Paramount solely on the basis of his good looks. What drew my attention to him was his frantic determination to learn how to act, and his unsophisticated puppy-dog enthusiasm for everything around him.

His name was William Anderson, but he soon made the preposterous decision to change it to the unlikely Leif Erickson.

I have always considered stage names not only absurd but degrading and never agreed to using any but my own. I went through all the usual deliberations and pressures of "What shall we call her?" and "She sounds like a cookbook," but I was determined to remain Frances Farmer. This was my first battle with the studio. My name was the only thing I'd ever had that was exclusively mine and I would not give it up.

Bill, selecting the Viking explorer, was, in my opinion, not only absurd but disgustingly affected, and I could never bring myself to addressing him as Leif. I called him Bill.

However he impressed me by working hard and studying as though he were on borrowed time, and indeed we were. Most of the options were never picked up and hundreds of young people were left stranded in Hollywood to shift for themselves. Their pride prevented them from returning, and they ended up hanging around casting offices begging for menial jobs in order to exist.

But Bill wanted to please everyone. He yearned to learn, and compared to the other members of the class, he was relatively outstanding. We were given a scene to read in class from Sidney Howard's *The Silver Cord,* and I liked working with him not because he was talented, for he was not, but because he sincerely tried.

About a month after my arrival I was given my first film assignment, a Community Chest "trailer." Not an auspicious acting debut, but it was more than the other players were getting, and it came under the heading of gaining experience.

Evidently someone in the front office was impressed with my work, for shortly after its release I was called to the Publicity Department and told that I was to be "groomed."

I did not pin my hopes on this planned fanfare, but

I went along, mainly because for at least six months I could enjoy a financial security I'd never known.

The one thing I did not like about the movie industry, even as a neophyte, was the gossip. I mentioned my meeting with the publicity staff to no one, but before the day was over, wherever I went, someone commented on my "big break."

From that moment on, I hated everything about Hollywood. The brassy lingo. The lack of sensitivity and individuality. The gristmill philosophy. The yesmen. The crude and influential giants. The Seventh Avenue intrigue. The cruel caste system. The fakery. I hated everything except the money.

In those days my mind's eye imagined Broadway as a pure light, an artistic Valhalla, and Hollywood the disgusting opposite. So I saved as much as I could out of my paycheck in anticipation of the day when I would return to New York and look for stage work.

Although the hundred-dollar-a-week salary overshadowed my disdain, I still grumbled when the tedious publicity campaign began. Press agent brains reasoned that a starlet must be seen in all the right places, so publicity dates were set up for me with some of the studio's leading men. But I balked at any mockup romance. Then somone in the Talent Department suggested that Bill and I looked good together and that possibly I might be more agreeable if he were with me. And I was.

He was a pleasant-enough person, and everyone breathed a sigh of relief when our names began to appear in the columns. Soon we fell into a steady routine, all at the studio's expense, and the maneuver was good for both our careers.

He was my only personal contact in Hollywood, and when we were not involved in a publicity jaunt, we spent our evenings together studying our scripts or analyzing characters.

Through it all I was being ground through an exhausting publicity mill, and overnight, featured articles about me were sprinkled throughout the fan magazines. The hokum I read about myself sent me into a rage. It was demeaning and had no bearing on me as an actress.

Then two months after my arrival, I went into my first movie, *Too Many Parents*. It was a dull, professionally humiliating experience. After working all day on the set, I would go back to my small apartment, lock myself in, and weep half the night. I was convinced that I was selling my soul for the almighty dollar. I hated the fact that I was doing it, but I was too frightened of being broke to walk away.

But I was the only miserable one in the lot. The studio was jubilant about my work and Mamma was delighted with everything. The only thing that made me happy was that I could, as I had promised, send her a little money out of each paycheck.

After *Too Many Parents* was released, the publicity intensified and I was no longer considered just a starlet. I was a "promising" young starlet. I had stepped up the first rung of the ladder.

Many of the publicity shots included pictures of Bill and me together, but though he worked hard, his career was moving at a slow, uneventful pace. Yet he seemed pleased with his progress, but, then, nothing seemed to discourage him.

I was skyrocketing, but I was also going through long morose periods of depression. I was withdrawing more and more. I was remote on the set and openly bored with the constant posing and interviews. I was restless and inattentive in drama classes and finally became so despondent that I fell into the routine of taking long, gloom-filled, solitary walks after work.

Bill sensed my dejection and did his best to cheer me up; but there were times when his puppy-dog attention made me want to scream.

I had satisfied the studio as an actress, but I had them wringing their hands when I refused to give any more interviews or pose for any more pictures. They persisted until I complied.

As a result, I became a spiritual recluse, reluctantly working at a job I did not understand. The kinship I had discovered with the theater had not taken roots in Hollywood, and this void left me emotionally empty.

Working before a camera was uninspiring and consisted mainly of long waits with tedious consideration given to angles and shot dimensions. Scenes were not related or in sequence, and it was difficult to catch a feeling and hold it. A characterization was never given a chance to grow and expand.

In comparison, the theater was alive and orderly. It was also the only thing to which I had ever belonged. My work at the university had bound me to something, but these ties had been severed and I realized that I desperately needed to become part of it again.

Bill was the only compatible factor in an irritating complex, although he was in no way able to lessen the strain building up within me. Then, one evening, when he said it might be a good idea for us to get married, adding that his mother had advised him to propose, it seemed a safe and respectable road to take.

But I neither loved him, nor was in love with him. He was simply an attractive childlike man who seemed to want to understand me. Not a foundation for a marriage, but I agreed. Since I was filming, I could spare only a weekend for the wedding, and we proceeded to make our somewhat slipshod plans accordingly.

As we secretly drove to Yuma, Arizona, I knew that we were forming a union that could only end badly. I told him that we should call it off, for we were not alike in any way. I was too old for him in spirit. Too involved. Too concerned with myself.

If I had persisted and if we had turned back, it would have saved both of us a great deal of pain, but as it was, he calmed my doubts, and four months after my arrival in Hollywood, on February 8, 1936, we were married by a justice of the peace.

I did not go into the union with any dewy-eyed hopes or illusions, and in my mind I was still Frances Farmer, not Mrs. William Anderson, and certainly not Mrs. Leif Erickson.

By marrying secretly, I had risked the monumental wrath of the studio, but fortunately the main powers were pleased with my marriage. Proper announcements were made to the press, and soon we became known as "that beautiful couple, Frances Farmer and her husband, Leif Erickson."

We moved into a small, furnished apartment, and each went about the daily and separate tasks of working. Very little changed between us. We spent evenings learning lines or reading. But my privacy was invaded and most of my solitary walks became uninspiring strolls, for he insisted on going along. Finally we bought sleeping bags and went into the desert on weekends in order for me to get away from anything that reminded me of my work.

I made no other friends, and even though Bill was warm and outgoing, he never seemed to mind the solitary imposition the marriage placed on him. Mamma was happy that I had "acquired a nice husband," and even though everyone liked him, as did I, the wedding band was beginning to strangle me.

A week or so after our marriage, I was given my

first important role in a Class A motion picture. My work in *Too Many Parents* had created a surprising amount of interest with the public, so I was to be cast as Bing Crosby's leading lady in *Rhythm on the Range*.

Crosby, one of Paramount's main stars, was a calm, easygoing man who did much to keep order on the set. Nothing seemed to disturb him. He would show up on time, speak to everyone, and say to the director, "Well, where do I stand and what do I say?" He was successful with this method, but it left me unsure and jittery.

There were two other newcomers in the cast, Martha Raye and Bob Burns. She had a true and delightful sense of humor and was marvelously light and outgoing. Cast opposite her was Burns, "The Arkansas Traveler." And there was I, Frances Farmer, a serious Method actress surrounded by Bing Crosby and his "Ba-ba-ba-boo," Martha Raye and her famous "Ohhhhhhhh, boy," and Bob Burns and his bazooka.

Art, as it were, was simply flushed down the drain, but strangely enough, the only movie I had fun making was *Rhythm*. The role was simple and undemanding, and from a reserved distance I enjoyed the people with whom I was working. But when the day was over, I fell back into my sullen despondency, bored with Hollywood and my husband.

The movie had good reviews and was a hit, so I assumed that I would begin to receive more interesting, challenging offers. Soon after the showing, I received a call from Adolph Zukor, the executive head of Paramount. I was escorted into his private throne room, but rather than assigning me to a new role, he took a fatherly approach and lectured me on my middle-class living habits and general deportment.

According to Mr. Zukor, I was making a name for myself as a rising young actress. (The next step above the rising young starlet.) And he was firm in his desire that I had to start thinking about my image. The first thing I had to do was to pay more attention to my clothes, and then I was to get rid of that "disgraceful old jalopy."

I was satisfied with the way I dressed and told him so. I was more comfortable and much happier in slacks or a tweed skirt, but Mr. Zukor was not to be put off. He screamed for glamor. I let him scream and went about my own business. We never agreed, and I never changed. But, from that point on, it seems that I made a determined enemy out of him, and later I was to ponder the wisdom of my deliberate antagonism.

It became obvious to everyone in Hollywood that I did not intend to follow his edict, but I was a valuable piece of studio property, so the publicity minds decided to use my "eccentric habits" and pegged me as the star who would not go Hollywood.

But I did relent in one instance and bought a trench coat from the wardrobe department that Marlene Dietrich had worn in one of her films. It was my one and only concession.

But in all fairness to Mr. Zukor and his expectations, those were the days of limousines and sables. In contrast, I wore ready-made slacks and drove a six-year-old car. Since I would not change my image, I certainly had no plans to go in debt for a new car. Then, to my pleasure, a Los Angeles automobile agency agreed to give me a new Plymouth convertible, in exchange for some publicity photos. Although it was not posh, this vehicle, I suppose, pacified the standard idea of what a "rising young actress" should drive. At any rate, Mr. Zukor let up, and everyone seemed happier.

I have always been disinterested, perhaps even unaware, of sleek and expensive toys, and I never purchased an automobile, except the original jalopy. I later received an Edsel for my appearance on *This Is Your Life,* and the Plymouth that was given me when I was in Hollywood satisfied my car bug.

After I started *Rhythm on the Range,* Bill and I rented a small furnished bungalow in Laurel Canyon. It was pleasant, but devoid of all the Hollywood accouterments. No pool. No tennis court. No servants' quarters. No billiard room. Just a small house that did not complicate my work by demanding attention. However, after my third salary raise, I had a cleaning woman come in once a week to give the place some feeling of order. It was almost a waste of time, for I would not allow anything to be disturbed, especially my scripts and working notes, which, of course, were strewn everywhere.

But an increasing weekly paycheck had its compensations. I liked being able to buy books instead of checking them out at the public library, and I began building a solid and well-rounded personal library. I also began a devoted effort to build a collection of classical recordings. I bought a typewriter and a phonograph, but nothing to add to the house or its furnishings.

I was living better than I ever had, but I was growing more rebellious toward the industry providing my comfort. Of course there were times when I felt guilty about it, but generally I did nothing to hide my open contempt for Hollywood and the people who lived and worked in it.

It is impossible, however, for anyone not to be slightly affected by public attention, or, if you will, fame. I was becoming well known, and whenever I was asked for an autograph, it embarrassed me to think that my name scratched on a piece of paper could have any possible value. It was a rare occasion when I would respond favorably to a fan.

I was appearing more and more on the covers of fan magazines, and the sheet music from *Rhythm* carried my picture and Crosby's, but it puzzled me that, with so little effort, I could be considered important.

And it frightened me when I realized that, if I wanted it, I could go to the top in Hollywood. No one in the industry liked me, but I was good box office, and that is what counted. I knew I could reach for any goal and attain it. But to do so would mean contradicting everything I believed in.

I decided to wait and see what the next few months would bring me in screen roles, but there was a critical tug-of-war going on inside me. That my attitude and apparent unfriendliness had created a bad image for me did not cause me any inner disturbance. I was not there because I had an overpowering drive to be loved. I was there to work, but in working, I became even more irritable and uncooperative.

My role in *Rhythm* had attracted a great deal of attention. Why, I don't know, for it was an absurd movie. However, Sam Goldwyn asked for me on loan-out from Paramount for the plum dual role in Edna Ferber's *Come and Get It*.

The novel had been a best seller, and the cast was to include Joel McCrea, Edward Arnold and Walter Brennan. Howard Hawks was assigned as the director. It was an exciting, much-acclaimed production and was the turning point I'd been waiting for.

Loan-outs were accepted during this period of motion picture history, but it often resulted in unfair tactics and unjust demands being placed on the performers. In this specific instance, Paramount kept me at my same salary but charged Goldwyn a premium for using me. The studio pocketed the difference. In those days there was no union protection, and stars could be worked day and night, if they were so directed.

This overwork was my greatest aggravation, and later was a prime cause of my smashup.

But I was, for a change, excited about a role. I never devoted greater effort to any motion picture than *Come and Get It.* It was a costume picture set in the Northwest lumber country during the 1890's. At night I took home the stiff corset, the high laced shoes, and the wasp-waist dresses I wore in the film, and spent all my spare time living in them, learning how to walk and move and sit with ease. I practiced breathing exercises and learned to repitch my voice, for I was to play the dual role of mother and daughter.

The mother was a good-hearted, but wayward, saloon singer, and to research it, I went into the red-light districts of Los Angeles, wearing a black wig to disguise myself, and studied the girls who worked the streets. I learned their mannerisms. The way they talked out of the sides of their mouths, with a cigarette dangling from a corner. I acquired their speech inflections. I watched how they drank their liquor and picked up their men. I mimicked their swagger, their cheapness. And I completely immersed myself in the role, studying it from every angle.

Howard Hawks was one of the finest and most sensitive directors in the business, and there was nothing routine or cut-and-dried in his approach. He gave every scene a minute examination, both psychological and visual, and under his direction I was secure and full of anticipation. But midway through the shooting, he had a disagreement with Goldwyn over the story line, and he walked out. William Wyler was assigned to replace him.

I panicked at losing Hawks as the director, but Wyler stepped into his shoes and carried the picture to its completion. I was basically satisfied with my interpretation of the trollop, but the daughter role of a gentle, innocent girl was in no way challenging. My only concern was to bring out the innocence, yet let a shade of the mother shine through, and it worked.

In spite of myself, Hollywood accepted me, and, as a specific honor to me, the picture was scheduled to premiere in Seattle. A unique homage for a newcomer, and it was obvious to everyone, even to me, that I was star material.

A meeting was called at the studio to discuss the plans for the premiere, and tempers flew when I stated that I had no intentions of going to Seattle. But why, they screamed, shouldn't I want to go to my hometown and be feted as a favorite daughter? I screamed back, because I never wanted to see the damn place again. But the publicity had gone out, and there was nothing else for me to do but finally agree to the fanfare.

The mere thought of going home disturbed me deeply. I had been away a year and two months when the premiere was scheduled, and in that time I had made three movies, all favorable to my career, and had married.

I was seriously exhausted by extensive work and emotionally pressured from the realization that Bill and I had made a dreadful mistake. I was not a good or even an attentive wife, but he was never a man who complained, and there were times when the fact that he did not irritated me.

He would play ball in the street with the neighborhood youngsters, and I would seethe inside to think that a grown man, an aspiring actor, would while away his time on such antics when he should be studying. He was genuinely tolerant, but I considered him totally dull. In my mind he had become the youngest pup in a crowded litter, and I could find no place for him to fit. I was miserably unhappy and deeply discontented. Let it be said, however, that no man on earth could have filled my expectations. Bill tried, but the fact that he tried only drove a wedge deeper between us.

The last thing I needed was a visit with Mamma, but when she received the news of the premiere, she went into free-wheeling orbit. She was beside herself by the time the advance publicity crew arrived to "set the stage," constantly underfoot, supervising everything they did. When I was told to get her out of their hair, I shrugged it off. It was their problem, not mine. Secretly I prayed that she would exhaust herself before my arrival.

I was flown in for the premiere, the only one I was ever to attend, and an important occasion for Seattle. The major dignitaries of the city and state, the national press, the usual corps of Hollywood columnists and photographers, the university staff, my high school principal—everyone was there to meet and greet me. The Seattle *Post,* the paper which years ago had led the pack against my trip to Moscow, now featured me as the "fair-haired daughter of Seattle." All was forgotten. All was forgiven.

The studio insisted on furnishing me a wardrobe, which was fine, for I had no intentions of wasting money on clothes I would never wear again. There was an impressive suite for me at the Olympia Hotel, and then began the endless shots of Mamma and me at home. In the kitchen. In the backyard. At the university, where the crowd who had sneered at Hollywood fell all over themselves to be photographed. I posed with the mayor and a Senator, and as an usher at the Paramount Theater. Much was made of the fact that I had once worked there, and now my name was flashing on the marquee.

No one dared mention the scandal I had created a scant year before, and even though I tried to discuss it with Mamma, she would hear nothing of "the past." She was too involved in seeking out another photographer or reporter or latching onto some visiting celebrity. Through it all, Papa stayed in the background, and despite my pleadings, he would not share the limelight. I had a strong feeling that Mamma had deliberately humiliated him. I was her daughter, at that moment, and she was not about to share the rewards with anyone, not even my father.

After the first two days of endless rounds, I was totally disgusted with the whole affair and dug in my heels, threatening to return to Hollywood before the premiere unless the mish-mash stopped. The publicity men were furious with me, and so was Mamma, but I had had enough.

She wanted to stay with me at the hotel, and the evening before the premiere, the old battle between us boiled up again. She was deeply angered that I would not cooperate with the press and argued until my nerves were in shreds. I was on the verge of hysteria as I dressed for the showing.

While a cocktail party was held in my suite with the governor of the state in the living room, I was in the bathroom vomiting. Mamma had wrecked me.

Shortly after the film started, I slipped out of the theater and returned to the hotel to change into a sweater and pair of slacks. I had been primped and begirdled until my eyes were hanging on my cheeks, and I was also hungry. Everyone else had managed to eat, but whenever I tried, there was another picture to take or another place to go. I went to the lunch counter in the hotel drugstore and got a sandwich. I had had enough of Mamma acting like the proverbial stage mother, pushing and haranguing. I simply could not stomach any more.

My disappearance however had created a crisis at the theater, and the call went out to "find her." Finally, a woman from the movie company found me sitting in the drugstore booth reading a magazine and enjoying a sandwich. She told me I had to return to the theater, and I told her to go to hell. Later, *Collier's* magazine did a cover story on me, and this incident was played up to accentuate my far-out behavior.

I finally agreed to go to the reception, but I attended it in my slacks and sweater, amid comments of "Isn't she charming, so natural and unpretentious." I sulked through the procedure and left the following morning, mad at the world, and especially Mamma. She and I had one final blowup after the reception. I had had enough of her temperament to last me for some time to come.

My career accelerated after that particular movie, but from that point on I began reading startling things about myself. A well-known Hollywood gossip columnist did a fair job of describing who I was and what I was doing in Hollywood.

She wrote: "Frances Farmer's manners are none too gracious, and a lot of people cordially dislike her. From the rich double role in 'Come and Get It,' she has stepped out as the prime new sensation of the season. Her director, who has seen them come and go for years, predicts that she will be as great, and probably greater than Garbo. Her dramatic coach says she has everything a great actress needs. Her studio says she'll be reserved for starring roles. And she says she's too busy to talk about 'Stuff like that.' She is as direct as a bullet, sober as a Supreme Court judge, and as industrious as an anthill. Unless all the signs in the crystal ball lie, chances are you are going to hear a lot about Frances Farmer from now on."

Everyone agreed that I could act, but the press tagged me as one of the most difficult actresses in Hollywood.

As an actress, I was reaching a motion picture zenith. But as a woman, I was plunging downhill into deeper and deeper pits of despair.

7

The light in my cell faded into a somber gray.

A faint hum of voices saturated the ward, and the presence of so many women, their restless movements, the rise and fall of their voices, left me uncomfortable.

These, the insane, declared unfit to live in the outside world, had been thrown together in careless disregard for their comfort or well-being, and society expected them to survive this hostile environment. To exist took cunning and dogged determination, and those who strengthened themselves, those who held onto the evasive thread of sanity, learned quickly to dismiss compassion as a frivolous luxury they could not afford. Love died quickly inside the cages, for there was no object worthy of it, and since there was nothing to love, something to hate became the goal. Hate kept one afloat.

I leaned wearily against my cell door. My whole face ached and throbbed. My eye, heavy with pus, was especially painful and seemed to be swelling more. I wet some toilet paper and made a compress for it.

I had been with six doctors and not one had offered to tend my wounds. They had chosen to see only a troublemaking, insulting ex-movie star. How could doctors assume to heal the mind, while ignoring a wounded body? Oh did they too believe the insane could not feel?

Anger and resentment swelled up in me. I gave up trying to ease my eye with the paper compress and instead tried to dig through my hair with the comb Lorraine had left me. I flinched with pain and threw the comb across the cell. I buried my face in my lap and tried to push back the tensions clawing their way to the surface. I had gone into the past, and remembering it and Mamma as she had been and Bill left me distraught.

Keep things under control, I warned myself. Quiet down. I put my head in the stained basin and let the water soak my hair. Gently I combed through the mats and tangles, and by the time I finished I was calmed.

Back at the door, I peeked through the screened window. I had a sidelong view of the ward. Women were walking aimlessly around, some talking to each other, some to themselves. Others had already fallen asleep in spite of the clatter around them. Some sat on the sides of their cots and laughed at nothing.

And then I saw Clara lumbering up the aisle between the cots, dragging along a young girl like a rag doll. As they passed my door, I ducked out of sight. Once they had passed, I sneaked back and peered out, curious to know what was going on.

The girl, about twenty, was obviously terrorized, but not a woman in the ward appeared to notice that something was amiss. I could hear her breathless cries as she was roughly handled by the trustee. I could see them, for they were not far from my door, at the dim end of the hall. Almost at the spot where a few hours earlier the women had swooped down upon me.

Clara had pushed the girl against the wall, her body covering the small frame like an overstuffed envelope. The girl twisted vainly under the suffocating pressure of flesh, but it was useless, for she was hooked help-lessly in Clara's one-arm grip.

I wanted to turn away, but I could not. I wanted to cover my ears and blot out the sound of the girl's frightened whimpering. But I could not. I was trans-fixed as Clara pulled open the girl's blouse with her free hand.

I saw her huge hog head push into a small breast and her bearlike paw clamp onto the other one, knead-ing it like clay. Under the assault, the girl was ce-mented against the wall, and her neck was arched back until the leaders bulged like bright-red ropes. Her eyes were clenched into painful slits, and her lips had pulled back over her teeth in a silent scream.

Then I heard the sounds of deep sucking as Clara hunched her wide shoulders and burrowed her face deeper against the target. Her legs were spread wide apart and planted firmly to the floor, helplessly pin-pointing the girl against the wall. Her bilious slurping defiled the air, and the great paw never stopped the rhythmic grinding against the white, young flesh.

My fingers clawed at my throat, trying to tear out a scream, but nothing came through my clenched teeth, and, in horror, I was swept back to remembering the immigrant girl who had rolled on the deck of the ship. I wanted to help. But I was frozen in my own fear.

And then, as Clara's brutal work went on, I saw the girl twist and struggle until her arms were locked around the flabby neck, and she hungrily pulled the head closer. I watched her fingers rummage through the thin mouse-colored hair, and her body shudder as she responded to the locomotive pushing against her.

Her hands tantalized and begged until the mouth slid across to take and absorb the other breast. Then a great paw reached up and clutched the bare swollen wetness that was left naked, and churned it with the fervor of a gluttonous maggot. Moving. Twisting. Burrowing. Eating flesh with wide stubby fingers. And the girl growled and groaned in pleasure.

Then Clara began to sway from side to side, like a giant tree giving way in a wind, moving the girl with her, first on one foot, then the other, pushing flesh against flesh.

The girl licked the thin, oily hair and began sucking it into her mouth, chewing as though trying to eat it off the monstrous skull. Her hands searched and clutched the bulging back, demanding more, and I watched as her tongue dug deep into Clara's muglike ear, and a river of slobbers ran down through the folds of the fat neck.

And then Clara, still firmly locked to the girl with hand and mouth, separated herself slightly and half unwrapped her arm that had held the girl to her. And as she uncoiled it, she began using the newly freed paw like a giant tuning fork, sliding it up and down the body until the girl began to tremble and gabble incoherently. And, as the paw traveled, it ripped off the skirt and threw it to the floor.

Then slowly, like a sinking mountain, Clara slipped to her knees, her mouth still suctioned to the body as it slid down the quivering and responding nakedness. And the girl, bracing herself against the wall, threw her legs over Clara's shoulders, and the great head shot in between them. She held the girl with her hands cupped under her buttocks, like a grinding saddle, and the girl rode her, almost screaming as Clara bored and moved into her.

The girl's legs shot out, convulsively, then tightened hard around Clara's neck. She flapped the air with her arms, then her hands flew to her breasts, still swollen from Clara's use, and she worked them herself in a wild spasm. And there, with Clara locked into her, she began to shudder until her body shook in completion.

Growing suddenly limp, she made a thwarted effort to undo herself from Clara. She pushed weakly on the woman's shoulders and tried to untangle herself, but the huge head stayed buried, and the rasping wheeze in the girl's throat was drowned by the unsavory sounds that roared on while her secret flesh was consumed by Clara's horrendous appetite.

Then Clara, still in motion, still working her mouth into the girl's body, grunting and chewing, began scooting back on her knees, pulling her mount with her. The girl lost the wall as a brace, but Clara slid her hands up her back and balanced her there, then lowered her slowly until she had her lying on the floor in front of her.

Stretched out on her belly, Clara pushed the girl's legs wide apart by wedging her broad shoulders between them, and clamped down her legs by simply stretching her weighty arms across them. The girl fluttered, like an injured sparrow, but she could not move, and Clara's head pivoted smoothly and undisturbed between her legs.

And then the paws began to climb up the violated body. Forcing. Stopping. Moving. Digging. Rolling tender flesh. Pounding. And the breasts were conquered again and were rolled and pulled.

Still eating into her victim, Clara began using her shoulders as a ramrod and pushed against the girl until her head was hard-pressed against the wall. And then, as Clara shoved harder, she forced the girl's hips into an arc off the floor. Nailing her there, with her legs dangling helplessly in midair, the assault strengthened, and the huge paws began to pump up and down on the breasts, pressing them, savagely. Clara's fingers chewed them like giant teeth, and her head dug deeper and deeper between the legs, clawing with her mouth.

The girl was in agony and clamped her hands to her skull, as though to crush it. But again, as the feverish and incessant grinding churned on, the response repeated itself, and the girl twisted and grunted as Clara snorted and ate. The sounds were wild and distorted, like acid boiling in the depths of a violent pit.

On and on it went, until the girl was in constant convulsions, but Clara never stopped and her mouth never left its place.

She grabbed the girl by the ankles and held her upside down, and then, as one would shove a wheelbarrow, she stabbed her into a corner and stood her on her head. Then she ripped her legs wide apart, holding them in a steel-pinched grip, and slurped at the girl like a greedy hog at a trough.

The girl was silent. There was no longer a response, but Clara continued to maul and deface her body, dangling her from her mouth like a thin skein of yarn.

Hot, scalding water rushed from my stomach, and I hung over the foul toilet and vomited again and again until I was empty and raw. I fell across the cot and knotted my fists until my nails speared painfully into the palms of my hands.

I could not stand the horror. I heard myself begging for my mother to take me home. I promised her everything. I pleaded. I screamed. I wept like a child. But there was no one to answer me. Only the hollow whimpering of my own voice came back.

The two long rings of the alarm bell cut through the ward and, in seconds, the lights went off. Only a few scattered bulbs were left to stand a dim sentry duty.

I heard the sounds of cots giving under the weight of bodies that turned and tossed. Coughs were contagious as women prepared for a sleep that was laggard in coming.

There was no stillness, and in the dim light, the ward moved like stiff dry stalks of corn left bare to a winter wind. It rustled and groaned and whispered and prayed. It cursed and wept and talked of home.

A ward is a living thing, vibrating life in the midst of death. Scratching for heaven in the hot pits of hell. Struggling to live, it lives, tottering on a jagged precipice.

I slipped under my blanket and pulled it closer around my shoulders, for I was suddenly very cold. In the warmth of an early summer, a glacier forced its way into my soul and froze my most intricate self.

I was alone, in a madhouse, and I fell asleep hiding my head under the blanket.

8

The next morning the ward was ripped asunder. A student nurse, assigned to escort the inmates to their work detail, had found the girl tossed in a corner and went screaming through the door.

The girl was naked, and pieces of her hair lay in dusty puffs on the floor. A nipple had been chewed until it dangled from its socket in brown caked blood. Nail slashes streaked her body, and her inner thighs were torn and gnawed until her flesh shivered like raw liver.

She was conscious but had receded into a catatonic state where no pain could ever touch her. Blank. Unfeeling. Never to think again. Never to reason. Void of response and responsibility. Damaged beyond repair. Hearing nothing. Saying nothing. Lost in a living limbo. Pitifully unable to weep, or laugh, or fear.

Who was guilty? No one ventured to accuse. No one gave in to the investigation. The blank, protective wall that comes with insanity was raised, and silently the women turned away and kept a rigid secret.

The girl was carried out and taken to a forgotten cell that lurked in the dimmest recess of the asylum, and when the query had ended, every eye turned to Clara, and judgment was passed by her peers.

Her hold was broken, and the sacrifice had set free

the ward. The aggressor was no more. The great tow-
ering bully dissolved into an errand-running cartoon of
her former self. She scrubbed and cleaned. Fetched
and carried. She was now the court slave, to be
mocked, threatened, ignored and hated.

The code of the ward had brushed aside the right
of outside judgment. The criminal was tried within her
own ranks, and the verdict was never questioned or
appealed. In the unbalanced world of the asylum, the
scales of justice swing confused.

I remained in seclusion for almost two weeks before I had my first meeting with a doctor. But this did
not disturb me, for even though the privacy was inflicted, it offered me a chance to study my situation
objectively.

I still shuddered when I thought that I could well
have been the victim of Clara's rape, but she no longer
concerned me. She had become a timid, frightened
subject.

During the day most of the women left the ward to
work elsewhere in the asylum. Those who, for some
reason, were not on detail sat around in chairs or
walked aimlessly back and forth, killing time, looking
out windows, picking petty quarrels, talking to themselves, or sleeping.

My only communication was a brief visit with Lorraine during her two-hour shift on the ward. Her
schedule varied, but the routine was the same. Now
that Clara had lost her toehold and a new, weaker trustee had been put in charge, the women lined up outside the nurses' cage and peppered her with endless
complaints and demands.

Once, during the two weeks, I was allowed to take a
bath. After it, I was given a clean dress, but I still had

no undergarments and I flapped around in the same old pair of oversized shoes.

Toward the end of every shift, Lorraine would always flutter into my cell and give me a cigarette, but her chatter was bothersome and dull, and I usually ended our conversation by sitting on the toilet, making loud, grunting noises—noises which usually sent her scampering.

But other than the few minutes Lorraine was in my cell and the quick, quiet meals Clara delivered to me, I was alone, and time lay heavy.

I had periods of anger. Remorse. Loneliness. Recall. I took exercises. I sang and acted and talked to myself and thought. Occasionally a curious inmate would peek through my door, but since I was in no mood for visitors, I would scream threats until she ran away in haste.

Then on my second Sunday on the ward, a social worker came to tell me my mother was in the visiting room and that I had special permission to see her. I flatly refused, and no amount of "social" pressure could persuade me to change my mind. Later, the woman returned with a shopping bag containing a pair of flat shoes, two dresses, and an avocado. All offerings from Mamma. Not only did I refuse to accept the package, but I would not allow the social worker into my cell. I drove her away by screaming and cursing.

The next afternoon Dr. Conway sent for me, and a trustee took me across the grounds to his office. It was cramped, dusty and dung-colored. Faded print curtains hung like tired strings at the window. His desk was covered with papers and folders and tacked on the wall was a calendar picturing Jesus agonizing at Gethsemane, compliments of a local funeral parlor. The marbled-tile floor was cracked and gritty under-

foot. I saw the shopping bag in a corner and the avocado sunning in the window.

Clearing a messy space on his desk, he motioned
for me to sit in the straight-back chair opposite him.
He still wore the same loud jacket and tie.

He began unceremoniously, patting his slick hair as
he spoke.

"Your mother called last week and requested permission to visit with you. We usually don't grant this
until we've had a chance to work with the patient, but
she was so concerned and persuasive that I told her
she could see you during visiting hours yesterday."

He dug around the desk until he found a cigarette
and, after lighting it, hunted deeper for an ashtray.

Bastard, I thought, watching the smoke tint the air.
I was tempted to ask him for one, then checked myself, not wanting to give him the satisfaction of turning
me down.

"She left you a package," he went on, nodding at
the shopping bag. "And since the contents were cleared
by Administration, I feel it would be a good idea for
you to accept it."

He closed his eyes, as if to reflect. "Yes, I think
you should be more cooperative, especially when
your mother is so concerned."

I shrugged, still watching the smoke, secretly tasting
it. He twisted around in his chair, reached for the
avocado, and placed it ceremoniously between us on
his desk.

"Your mother tells me this is a favorite of yours."

For an answer, I slumped deeper in my chair and
stuck my legs out in front of me. He reached across
the desk, picked up the avocado and turned it over
and over in his hand. "Interesting," he mused. "Though
I must say I've never been excited about the taste.

Needs to be acquired, I suppose."

Then, putting it down and clearing his throat, he made what I assumed to be professional gestures of getting down to business.

"Let's see, you've been with us a little over two weeks now," he said. "And I've studied your daily reports and I'm sorry to find that you have not shown any marked improvement since your arrival." He hunted through the papers and came up with a folder.

"Ah, yes. Let's see, now. Vulgar. Uncooperative with nurses. Insulting. No interest in personal appearances. Detached. Arrogant. Foul-mouthed. Sullen. Yes . . . just about the same as when you came here, I would say."

He tossed the folder aside and rapped his fingers on the desk, beating out an erratic tattoo.

"I had hoped to have a much better report on you, Frances."

I shrugged.

"Why do you feel you cannot answer my questions?"

"You dumb bastard," I spat. "You haven't asked me any. You've been sitting there listening to your own pontifical crap, and I've had enough."

I started for the door, then turned. "Let me tell you something just in case you're interested. You lock me up in a damn two-by-four for two rotten weeks, and I don't hear a peep out of you. But let dear old mother show up with her concern and persuasion, and the next day you haul my ass in here and say, 'Why don't you treat your mother better?' Bullshit! She can take her shopping bag and her fancy fruit and go straight to hell, and you with her. Now, that's all I've got to say, so get that keeper back in here and lock me up . . . but keep 'Mother' away from me. Do you hear? Keep her away from me."

I yanked on the door, but it was locked.

"Sit down, Frances," he said calmly. Instead, I leaned against the door and glowered at him.

"And another thing," I snapped. "You're so 'hopeful' about my progress, but you couldn't even bother prescribing an aspirin. You saw my face bashed in. You all saw it, and you all knew how it had happened."

"Let's get back to the matter at hand," he said firmly.

"To hell with it. Look, she put me here. Right? So now I'm out of her hair. Right? So why the hell is she still sucking around?"

Again, motioning me back to the chair, he said, "Her complaints against you have been confirmed by your father, and they're both concerned about you."

"She's a hell of an actress, and he's a damn good audience. They make quite a pair those two."

"You feel she's persecuting you in some way?"

"Persecuting?" I laughed. "She's been after my ass from the day I was born."

"Nevertheless, she seems proud of you, proud of your work, of the things you accomplished."

"Oh, Christ. Don't start with the Hollywood routine again. Get this straight, Doc. I'm nuts. Right? I've got bats in my belfry. Right? So, being cracked, I have no logical justification or, for that matter, a rational opinion. But for the record, the next time you talk to her, and, oh, you'll talk to her again and again, because she's got a lot to say. Believe me. But if you can get a word in, ask her about the times Papa tried to put *her* away. See what she says. If you'd stop, look and listen, good Doctor, you'd find out who's nuts in this family."

"Then we have cross-accusations here," he answered slowly.

"Cross, my ass. She's in and I'm out. It's as simple as

that. So when she comes pussyfooting around, I say no. God damn it. No! So what happens? You drag me down here and tell me to be more receptive. Eat your avocado, Francie. Be a good girl, Francie. What the hell kind of doctor are you?"

"Then you feel you are not mentally ill?"

"How in God's world should I know?" I laughed. "I probably am. God knows there's something the matter."

I slumped against the door and dug at my fingernails. "I'm a strange one, I admit, good Doctor. I guess maybe I was carried around in a dirty womb too long. Maybe that's it."

I crossed back to the chair and sat primly on the edge of it. I waited, politely, for a few moments, then, with my voice quivering with the just right amount of dramatic impact, I almost whispered, "I've gone through a lot of hell this past year. But I haven't changed. I'm still who I was. Who I've always been. And all those things your nice nurse reports about me are just that. Me. I'm an unfriendly, secretive, hostile, profane, vulgar image and likeness of God . . . and if I'm crazy, and I well might be, then what does that make God, good Doctor?"

He offered me a cigarette, probably some sort of reward for talking, then took one himself. His hands were steady as he held the match, and I noticed his nails were chewed until they were raw stubs. "That's a rather thought-provoking habit you have there, good Doctor."

He snapped out the match and turned slowly around in his chair, with his back to me.

I began to laugh, insultingly, and grinding out the cigarette on the floor, I said, "You're a fool, you know. But worse than that, you're an amateur and I'm wise to all your Freudian tricks. They're so damn obvious. And you're a ridiculous little man, trying like hell to be somebody and making a perfect ass out of yourself doing it."

I pounded on the desk angrily, scattering papers in all directions. "Why don't you just knock off this shit and quit wasting my time?"

He turned, picked up the phone, dialed two numbers, and said, "Mrs. Anderson is ready to be returned to the ward now."

"Treatment over?" I asked mockingly, then gave him a cocky salute and waited at the door for it to be unlocked. I wanted to get back to my cell. I wanted to be away from everyone. I wanted time with my own thoughts. I had no use for his.

The door opened, and I started through it, but his voice stopped me. "You forgot something," he said, motioning at the shopping bag.

"From me to you," I said airily.

"Frances!" His voice was sharp. "You're to take these things back to the ward with you. Now! And wear those dresses. You could do with some improvement."

I swaggered over and picked up the shopping bag. He pointed to the avocado. "And this, too," he said.

I picked it up, tossed it in the air two or three times, then gave him a broad insulting wink, and left the office, calling back over my shoulder. "Since she's so damn concerned, tell her to send me a toothbrush." I spread my mouth wide and pointed into it. "I've got a million-dollar set of Hollywood ivories in here, good Doctor, and they're turning green."

I dropped the avocado in the bag and swung it, jauntily, as the trustee and I walked back to the ward. Once inside, I headed straight for my cell, anxious for the solitude it offered me, but Lorraine was hot on my heels.

"Did you get to see Dr. Conway?" she asked happily.

"You know damn good and well I saw him."

"Well, I do hope everything went well. It's too bad that he hasn't had a chance to see you before today. Maybe you would already have been down in OT."

"Oh? You think I'm well enough to weave baskets?"

She looked puzzled, hurt by my remark, for my voice was cutting, but she ignored it and dug in her pocket and offered me a cigarette from the pack she pulled out.

"Stick it up your ass!"

"Frances! What in the world is the matter?"

"Look, stupid. Right here and now we're going to get one thing straight. You're a rotten stinking stool pigeon, and I know it. You dare come in here and think you can buy me off with a lousy cigarette. Well, sister, I know what you've been up to. Loud, am I? Vulgar, am I? Arrogant? Sullen? Nasty?"

"I have to make out reports, Frances. It's my job."

"Have I ever mouthed off to you? Have I?"

"Not often."

"Then where the hell are you getting all your hot line information?"

"Everyone in here has a daily report made, and if there has been any trouble, you know someone is bound to tell."

"I haven't been out of this goddamned hole-in-the-wall, and you know it. So what trouble?"

"It's the way you treat the other women, Frances. Yelling those dreadful things at them. You're so unfriendly."

"You're damn right I'm unfriendly."

"If you could just be a little nicer."

"Nicer? Who the hell are you kidding? What am I supposed to do? Go out and kiss asses so everybody will be happy with little Francie. You act like this is some damn sewing circle. It's a nut house, woman. A nut house."

She held out the cigarette to me again, and I grabbed it roughly and ground it in my hands. I snatched the comb off the windowsill and threw it at her.

"You're making it so hard on yourself, Frances." She sighed.

"Yeah. Ain't I, though?"

She left the cell, cosing the door softly behind her.

I was furious, and I beat on the door, yelling, "Let me out of here." I screamed and cursed and rattled the door, knowing only too well that it was unlocked. Once, it flew open, interrupting my tirade, and I hastily yanked it closed. My screams were deliberate and imaginative, but also short-lived, for they were strenuous and soon tired me.

Then I eyed the shopping bag and decided to check it. The avocado looked good, and I was tempted, but I put it on the floor, pressed it with my foot until it split, and dropped it in the toilet. One of the dresses in the shopping bag was the same cotton I'd worn on the day they had brought me to the asylum. Obviously, my clothes had been sent back home, and Mamma's ironic mind had caused her to return the horrid reminder. I flung it on the cot, disgusted.

The other dress was a bright-blue silk she had sent me when I was just starting out in Hollywood. I had hated it then and still felt it was cheap and gaudy. I rolled it up in a ball and threw it in the corner.

Then I stretched out on the cot and, feeling the dress under my head, decided to put both of them to use and make a pillow for myself. I would not consider wearing them, but I rolled them together, fluffing them until I was able to mold a small soft mound. Nesting my head in this new-formed luxury, I fell asleep.

I slept undisturbed until Clara, knocking softly on my cell door, told me that it was suppertime. I finished the meal quickly and put the tray outside my door. I did not want to see anyone else. I spent the rest of the evening, until lights out, stretched out on my cot, staring at the ceiling.

Seeing the doctor had left me angry and disturbed. I could not help asking myself: If Mamma had not tried to visit me, how long would I have waited before he would have seen me? I knew that my refusing to see her had prompted the pseudo-consultation, and I also knew that I had walked into deep water by tossing insults at him that he could not, or would not, forget. He was not a villainous doctor, but neither was he a conscientious physician concerned over his patients' well-being. If he had been so, treatment and attention would have been prescribed for the beating my face and body had taken. The neglected healing was painful and slow, and I was still swollen under the eyes. I had seen myself when I had a bath, in a distorted sheet of tin that was nailed to the wall in the shower room. My face was still sore, and my head had never stopped aching.

After the lights-out, I became restless and worried. Mamma's appearance had disturbed me; I never wanted to see her again. It was all over between us, and the thought of her coming to the asylum, peeping and probing into my affairs, acting as though nothing had happened, set me against her.

I hung to the belief that I was justified in turning my face away from her. I wanted the battle to cease. I wanted the war between us over. And I knew, too well, that any form of communication between us would result in new wounds being inflicted on the same old battlefields.

I knew that I had to find my way out of this nightmare alone, and if I tripped and fell, I had to be the one to pick myself up. I could, therefore, carry no other load. My only obligation was to myself, and nothing could interfere. And Mamma interfered, simply because she could not help herself. It was part of her pattern, as was I.

Dr. Conway had not bloomed with genius when he concluded that the basic conflict was between two women who were, tragically, mother and daughter. But if I heeded his dictum, I would slaughter my own identity. I was the one, not Mamma, who was required to alter, to change, to capitulate, to submit, to admit wrong, to surrender. And if I could not, psychiatrically I would impede my own progress and defeat my own healing, for to all appearances, I was the virulent one. I was the offender. The misfit.

But one does not "go crazy" in a day or two. And one does not end up in an asylum overnight. The road to it is taken a step at a time. And once the mind is locked inside, it takes with it its total heritage and pieces of everyone and everything it has ever known.

Man is built genetically, and there is no deviation, nor is there an escape. Environment may alter but it cannot change the inherited nature. In each, there is a wild, untamed seed that can unexpectedly break through.

I was the result of my parents, and their parents before them, ad infinitum, and my frailties and my defeats, my victories and my conquests were all traceable to that mystic part of my past when I was being formed by those who came before me.

I could, therefore, assume responsibility for my behavior, but I could never assume the blame. I could accept sole responsibility for my actions, but I would never allow the ledger to be balanced only to my debit. I was not some wild plant that accidentally sprung up in some planned garden and spoiled it. I was a person. A daughter. An identity. Living. Breathing. Fearing. Retreating. Failing.

And I had failed so often. Failure had been a faithful companion. From my first memory I knew I had failed to find a foothold in life, and somewhere, somehow, I lost my balance and tumbled into a treacherous wilderness.

It was thus imperative for me to construct a foundation and find a path that could lead me out of it. One that would not sink under me. If I did not, I would be lost forever, I had to begin a quest that would prove to me that I, alone, was not solely responsible, for like Saint Paul, "The things that I would do, I do not, and the things that I do, I would not do."

That night I knew that I had to lay the foundation for my recovery, and it would be difficult to retrace the lonely, unhappy years that I spent as a child. The memory of these years created in me a wild sort of pain that caused me to shudder on remembering.

But I knew that I would have to force the gate to the past even wider, and go beyond my time and even beyond the era of my parents, for my mother and father were also products of a specific heritage and rearing. Here again, I was not a part of it, but it was a part of me.

I scratched deep for the courage to remember, but not without humor, and as the night came on, I curled in the windowsill, which had become my favorite haunt, and with my knees tucked under my chin, I could almost watch the world. I could see the sky and hear the trees creeping into full bloom, and with the window open, I could taste the ever-present mist that came from Puget Sound.

9

To know myself, I would have to search for the promptings that had created me, and for recorded genealogy, it began in the late fall of 1851, when Zacheus Van Ornum, a restless and independent man of twenty-four, left the lake region of his native Wisconsin and began a long and treacherous journey across the Northwest Territory.

The land was primitive and unfamiliar to him, but his curiosity and stubbornness eventually brought him to the frontier settlement of Roseburg, deep in Oregon Territory.

In Wisconsin he had earned his way as a trapper and had sharpened his wits as a trader. He was an intriguing man, blunt and fanatically honest, and his reputation followed him among the white settlers and the Indians as well. He drove a hard, unrelenting bargain, but he was never known to palm off a bad item or to cheat a less experienced trader.

He was one of the few frontiersmen to make an effort to learn the ways of the Indian, and his knowledge became so acute that the government hired him as a lead Indian scout.

But there was terror and surface violence in this fiery-eyed Dutchman. He would not compromise his unorthodox beliefs either in God or man, and if he could not win an argument any other way, he would floor his opponent, sometimes with a fist and quite often with a bullet.

Headstrong beyond reason, giving no quarter and fueled by raw whiskey, he muscled his way through life. Garbed in ragged skins with a great bush of black hair and a wild unkempt beard, he would shout defiance to the heavens and dare God to strike him dead. Then, when nothing drastic happened, he would inflate his chest and shriek his victory over the universe. His favorite word in describing himself was "infidel."

Despite his independence, he was a strong family man and deeply missed his brother Alexis, who had remained in Wisconsin.

Alexis was a direct opposite. He had quietly married and was the father of five. But his brother's letters of the frontier mesmerized the entire family, and they decided to join him in Roseburg.

Alexis, his wife, and all five children moved West in 1860 under the relative security of a commercial wagon train. But at Snake River, the Indians began a month-long attack and all the whites were either massacred or suffered death by starvation.

Only one young boy was taken prisoner. In his grief Zacheus convinced himself that this had to be his brother's son, and for two years he tracked the tribe, leaving a wake of dead Indians in his path.

He finally found a crazed white child in a remote village, and biding his time until most of the men were away on the winter hunt, he single-handedly attacked and rescued the boy. He tied the child to his back and rode with him to Roseburg, but the harm had been done and the lad died without ever remembering his name.

This grief further deranged him, and his twisted disbelief in God became even more bitter and profound. His wild frenzies caused panic wherever he went, and his hatred of the Indian went beyond civilized control.

He became a recluse, never going out except to kill game. But aware that bitterness and loneliness were destroying him, he decided to find a wife.

Women were scarce in the territory, and there were none who would risk the temperament of this wild and puzzling man, so he returned east in search of a bride.

Elizabeth Rowe was a strikingly beautiful woman, fair and fine-boned, and in her own way a pioneer. As a young girl in Lancashire, England, she had yearned for the new land of America, and this yearning had become so intense that she sold herself as a bond servant.

Working and living in unspeakable servitude, she nonetheless kept her hopes pinned to the eventual day when, as a freed woman, she could live out her remaining years in the West.

On the day Zacheus Van Ornum met Elizabeth Rowe, he bought up her bond, married her, and without preliminary courtship, two kindred souls traveled across the continent and returned to Roseburg.

The match was healthy but turbulent, and the frontier soon knew that Zacheus had married a woman who could shout him down and argue him senseless, either vocally or, when necessary, with a skillet to the side of the head.

But she did well by her husband, for she understood his atheistic beliefs and respected his restless spirit. Their union produced thirteen children, one of whom was my mother, Lillian, born in Roseburg in 1874.

As the Van Ornum family swelled in number, my grandfather's zeal for defying accepted traditions attained almost anarchic proportions. He directed his wrath at the majority of the settlers who placidly accepted a literal interpretation of the Bible.

Quiet congregations shuddered whenever the Van Ornums appeared en masse, for they knew that the devil and his disciples had arrived.

Zacheus, along with his brood, would sit on the rough-hewed benches in mock but rapt attention, as the nervous circuit preacher tried desperately to ignore the faces of the notorious infidel and his offspring.

Sooner or later Zacheus would leap to the pulpit, throw the helpless man of God to one side, level a cocked pistol at the congregation, and proceed to deliver a sermon of his own Darwinistic choosing, always ending with a defiance of God and the devil.

When finally exhausted, he would holster his gun, wave for Elizabeth to follow him, and arm in arm they would stomp down the aisle with the children trotting behind.

My grandfather was the subject of many a hellfire and damnation sermon preached throughout the Oregon Territory. He became known as that damn crazy infidel, and this notoriety was indeed well earned.

The Van Ornums lived in a state of high tension, either feuding to the point of bloodshed or extremely close in their affection. And yet, despite this erratic behavior, they shared a deep family loyalty.

My mother would recall her father's exploits with adoration and respect. She was perhaps the closest follower of his free-wheeling philosophy. And like him, once her mind was attached to something, she never relented, never let go.

The Van Ornums did nothing in moderation, and though collared with thirteen children, my grandfather was still restless and decided it was time to move on in search of another land.

Perhaps there were no more pulpits left for him to destroy, or perhaps the territory was becoming too tame. Whatever the case, he and his sons built a covered wagon, loaded it with the family belongings, and they all walked their way down the coast until they reached the Sacramento Valley in California.

They lived in the open until a log cabin could be built, and it was there, on a homestead plot in Chico, California, that my mother was reared.

And it was there that my grandparents, at last, became tired of trying to change the world and instead directed their attention to making their children independent enough to "fearlessly walk the face of the earth."

As could be expected, the Van Ornum method of child correction was not usual. Punishment was meted out only when an offspring could not offer an opinion. Zacheus cared little whether a child's conclusion was right or wrong, as long as he thought something. But to say "I don't know" was an offense punishable by a switch or a hard hand to the backside. He forced them to think and decide for themselves. In such an environment bedlam must have prevailed—to his delight.

No longer able to create havoc in the territory, he thundered down on his family and produced a headstrong, erratic clan who worshiped him.

During this same period eight sons were born to a state supreme court judge in Spring Valley, Minnesota. One of these sons was my father, Ernest Melvin Farmer.

He grew up in the secure comforts of the conservative well-to-do, and each boy did the expected, becoming either a lawyer or a doctor.

Their household was undemonstrative and quiet, even with eight boys, for Grandfather Farmer's word was law, and no one ever considered challenging it. My father's mother, a thin, spindly woman, given to convenient attacks of the vapors, leaned heavily on her husband and sons, and they, in turn, always fearful for her health, stumbled over each other in their rush to provide her with the most insignificant need.

My father dutifully attended the University of Minnesota, studied hard, and pleased his parents. The routine of his life matched his placid personality.

While he was conscientiously finishing law school, Mamma was attending Teachers College in Chico. But shortly after she enrolled, calamity struck the Van Ornum cabin.

Edith, a younger sister, had, unfortunately, strayed down the primrose path and had left California with the local procuress, in order to try her fortune in Alaska. This was too much, even for the freewheeling Van Ornums, and my mother was elected to follow and bring her back.

Mamma mushed through the Yukon all that winter, working her way as a cook, peering into every face and probing into every bedroll in search of her fallen sister.

Like the rest of the Van Ornums, she did nothing quietly, and although Edith by that time had already tasted the forbidden fruit, Mamma convinced herself that some grizzly prospector had taken an unfair advantage of an innocent child and vowed that, when she found him, he would pay dearly for her ruination.

On she trudged from camp to camp, and at some point during that long arctic winter a fur trapper fell in love with her. Thereafter, wherever she went in search of Edith, he followed hot-breathed. So it was an amorous trail that wound its way across the crusted snow.

Mamma had no intention of letting anything or anyone sway her from her appointed task, and when the exhausted trapper finally gave up and left her on the trail, he did so with a gallant and long-remembered gesture. During the long frustrating trek he had whittled a walrus tusk into a Roman cross, inlaid it with a large gold nugget, and inscribed "Virtue is its own reward." I remember she wore it around her neck for years. Dangling on a large heavy chain that reached to her waist, it swung back and forth like an overweight, but virginal, pendulum.

Throughout the winter the trail of the two sisters never crossed, and Edith, possibly weary of the cold, returned to the warmth of the Sacramento Valley, and Mamma, still working her way as a cook, landed in San Francisco.

The excitement of this open city intrigued her and she decided to stay. She rented a house large enough to take in boarders, and it was a success, for her cooking abilities, even then, bordered on near genius.

One of her first roomers was a handsome young Irishman named William Mitchell. Willie, as she called him, worked on the railroad, and my mother fell completely in love with him. They were married after a brief courtship, but unfortunately Willie liked to go on periodic drinking sprees.

Nonetheless it was, for Mamma, a misty-eyed love match and their union produced one child, a daughter named Rita. Shortly after Rita's birth Willie began spending all the money he could find on week-long binges.

Mamma sued for divorce. It was granted without Mitchell's appearing on his behalf. With her feminine ego askew, mother and infant daughter boarded a stagecoach for Idaho to live with—of all people—her sister, Edith, then respectably married.

But the two Van Ornum temperaments blazed, and

shortly after her arrival, Mamma again bundled up her baby daughter and, vowing never again to set foot in Idaho, boarded the first stage West. Eventually she landed in Seattle.

During this time, Ernest Farmer had graduated from law school and taken his father's suggestion that Seattle would offer good opportunities for a young attorney. He was just beginning to establish himself when Mamma arrived in the city.

The fact that she was recently divorced, without funds, in a strange city, and solely responsible for a small child did not hamper her in the least. She managed to acquire a large rental property and again opened a boardinghouse—for bachelors. One of her first roomers was Ernest Farmer.

A short time later, in 1905, when they were both in their early thirties, they were married. One of the strong forces that drew them together was his great attachment for Rita. Whether or not there was a mutual love established between them as husband and wife, I'll never know, for theirs was a long and stormy relationship.

My mother was not beautiful, not even pretty, but she was an impressive woman. She had the strong burning Van Ornum eyes and an almost hawklike face. My father, in contrast, was a very homely man, soft-featured and bland.

They were also emotional opposites. She stormed through life, making it her personal warpath, and he shuffled through it, groping his way like a tired soldier.

After the marriage, she kept the boardinghouse while he worked diligently to build his law practice. Their life together progressed in a relatively normal fashion until after the birth of their first daughter.

My father's devotion to Rita expanded to embrace his firstborn, and he would appear at odd hours during the day just to see the child. This exasperated my mother. She believed in providing all the creature comforts but could not tolerate what she termed "the simpering adulation of addled adults." She had a warm maternal instinct that was completely impersonal, if such can be the case.

My father was extremely proud of his new family, and he persuaded his mother to make a trip West in order to see not only his wife, who was pregnant for the second time, but his firstborn. The little girl was a year and half old when Grandmother Farmer made the trip to Seattle.

My father was concerned because it had been a long and arduous trip for a woman his mother's age, and it was an unseasonably cold January. He was determined to take exceptional care and insisted that she be given the warmest room in the house. Unfortunately this was where Rita and the baby slept. Despite my mother's violent objections, the two children were moved into a small drafty room near the back of the house. Rita suffered a severe throat infection; the baby contracted pneumonia and in a matter of hours was dead.

The shock and sudden loss deranged my mother, and she never stopped blaming my father. She accused him, over the casket, of killing her child. This was a terrible guilt to lay on any man, and his resulting grief was the first of many steps that led to his personal defeat.

The seeds of bitterness were planted early, and nothing was ever the same again for either of them. All that was left was a neurotic need, for the abrasive wounds they had inflicted on each other never healed.

My mother, well into her pregnancy during this tragedy, became seriously ill. She was despondent, vicious, cruel and heartbroken. It reached a point when she was no longer able to sleep and my father feared a nervous breakdown.

But he was never a man attuned to feminine sensitivity, and in desperation he wrote to her sister, Zella, and told her that he had made arrangements to have his wife committed to a sanitarium. He believed she was emotionally unbalanced, and he feared, perhaps justly so, that unless she received treatment, she would lose her mind. He asked her sister to urge her to accept medical help.

Times have changed very little, and in those years a mental breakdown was a great stigma. It still is, but then it was an even darker secret for the family to hide. Perhaps the greatest mistake my father ever made was to confide in Zella, for she immediately shared the contents of his letter with Mamma.

It was a severe and cruel blow. To her way of thinking not only had he killed her child a few months before, but he was now trying to destroy her, and the mere idea that he would betray her in such a way made him her open and eternal enemy. Yet neither of them had any choice at the time except to stay together, and even though she was obviously very ill, my father withdrew his plans to commit her.

He was, however, not anxious for any more children, but he lovingly accepted the son that was born to them.

My mother was no longer able to tend the boarding-house, and shortly after this birth she agreed to give it up. The family moved to 312 Harvard Avenue, and during the next four years, even though the marriage was faltering, my father's law practice began to thrive.

He was gaining a small reputation as a promising attorney, but money was still a problem. His frugal attitude drove Mamma to distraction, especially when he insisted that she skimp on the food budget.

He was deeply disturbed and disgusted when she became pregnant again, if for no other reason than he could not see his way clear to assume another responsibility. The son was four years old when a daughter was born to them, and although he had great affection for his family, he insisted that enough was enough. As he often put it, he had not married an incubator.

My mother was justified in her resentment. According to her he acted as though she had raped him and deliberately saddled him with another child. He blamed her lack of sexual discipline and held her responsible.

Sixteen months later I was born, and there was never any question but that I came unwanted and certainly unplanned.

He now had three children and a stepdaughter, all of whom he loved, but he also had a nervous highstrung wife, much given to eccentricities. If money had been scarce before, it was now reaching a crisis, and in order to support the family he was away from home most of the time, taking any case, no matter how trifling, and lingering around the city jail in the hopes of finding an extra client.

While he was attempting to survive in this manner, my mother withdrew more and more. It is not difficult to understand their separate frustrations. He was a man from a tightly knit family, brought up in a well-organized house. Mamma, on the other hand, was from a freethinking, independent clan who never concerned themselves with routine or material order. She was a creative woman with no outlet, married to a man whom she could no longer accept or understand, and she was surrounded by four children who brought little interest into her life.

It was during this time, probably in the hopes of lessening her discontent, that she began an aggressive, almost abnormal study of dietetics. Her natural flair for cooking presumably prompted this drive, but it soon became more than an interesting, healthful outlet—it became a fetish. In short order she ignored everything except her studies.

By the time I was three the family relationship had reached a point of desperation. Mamma would lock herself away in the spare room and spend hours delving deeper into her work. Ignoring my father's complaints, she decided to analyze the commercial bakery products sold in the city. To everyone's dismay, her tests produced some alarming findings on the synthetic ingredients used in bread. This spurred her to personally see to it that every bakery in the city was closed down.

Ordering new stationery with the letterhead "The Mothers Want To Know Why Club—Lillian Farmer, President," she began to write scorching letters to the newspapers attacking the bakeries for using dark and evil food substitutes in their breads and pastries. She always ended her letters by claiming a club membership of "a million strong and growing every day."

My father tried to explain that this was dishonest, but she dismissed forewarning and continued her campaign.

Her wealth of knowledge in the field of dietetics, all self-taught, was impressive, and when the papers began printing her articles, a city-wide controversy arose. Shortly thereafter she scraped up enough money to start printing her own pamphlets and distributing them personally in front of every store that carried the tarnished products. The newspapers recognized good copy, for she was indeed a flamboyant individual with a colorful vocabulary. She became a Carry Nation with a potholder.

In a very short time everyone in Seattle knew Mrs. Farmer, and my father was horrified. But even though her tactics were a bit too theatrical, she succeeded in forcing the local board of health to pass strict baking requirements.

Her first taste of publicity fascinated her. She relished the attention, although, in reality, she was looked upon as somewhat of a crackpot.

Heady with success, she notified the press that she would next tackle the local board of education. She was disturbed by the menus being served in the public schools. She stormed a board meeting, armed with statistics. The press backed her up again and very soon the school board met her demands. This resulted in the schoolchildren of Seattle eating balanced meals.

My father, horrified and humiliated to have his wife a local joke, demanded that she curtail her activities. She responded by announcing to the press that she was devoting her life to writing books on nutrition. Although this caused no great flurry, it further angered my father.

Once again he made the fatal mistake of writing to her sister, Zella. He begged her to try to reason with his wife and asserted again that he was having her committed. And again the sisters exchanged the news. But this time it was too much for Mamma to bear. She left my father and took us to Los Angeles to stay for a while with Aunt Zella. From there we moved to a small house on Cole Avenue, near Hollywood Boulevard and Vine Street. Papa sent token payments of support but would not agree to a divorce. What money he did send was never enough to make ends meet, so while Mamma worked, Rita looked after us. She became my mother-substitute and I loved her dearly. When she married a few years later, I hid myself and wept because I had lost the only warm, stable person in my unsettled life.

That year the United States entered the First World War and Mamma threw herself into the home-front effort with all the fire of her Van Ornum blood. She attended bond rallies, rolled bandages, worked in factories, and probably provided the only good laugh the people of California had during the whole war.

In our backyard she had not only planted a vegetable garden to ease the war shortage, but raised chickens as well, and although her imagination was always unique, she then launched her most bizarre undertaking.

She wanted a vivid way to express her patriotism and temporarily laid aside her dietetic studies to devote herself to breeding a red, white and blue chicken. She crossed a Rhode Island Red, a White Leghorn and a Blue Andalusian. Eventually a bewildering mutation with red, white and blue feathers growing at random pecked its way into Mamma's world. While her barnyard miracle was growing, Mamma sewed herself an Uncle Sam suit, "made of genuine satin," top hat, vest and all, to complement the fowl.

When bird and garb were ready, she called the newspapers proposing that her "Bird Americana" replace the eagle as our national emblem. The newsmen had a field day, and pictures of Mamma in her stars and stripes holding her cackling curiosity were plastered over the front page of every Los Angeles paper. They were the hit of bond rallies and parades.

The crowds loved them both, but the constant excitement was a strain on the bird and it died, possibly of vertigo. (It was not eaten.)

When the chicken died, she lost her news value but her wildly creative mind began to churn again. This time she reached for an even higher zenith and decided to develop a totally new breed by crossing a turkey and a chicken, which, of course, she called a turkhen. Once again she had her teeth into a cause, and the activities of the household focused on its outcome.

Her aim was to produce a bird the size of a turkey with the meat of a chicken. Why? God knows! But this experiment in barnyard genetics was something less than a stunning success. All she came up with was a ridiculously confused chicken with an exceedingly long, naked neck. It had great difficulty in keeping its balance and staggered around the yard as if soused to the gills.

Undaunted at this slight imperfection, she once more announced her findings to the press. She fashioned some sort of collar for the fowl, hooked a log chain to it, and proudly posed for the photographers, leading the staggering turkhen around like a prize poodle. Nothing revolutionary ever came of her new breed, but Mamma had made news again and she loved it. The turkhen soon died without reproducing itself. (It was not eaten.)

During the flu epidemic she turned to a more serious cause and worked long hours as a practical nurse. This, like her cooking, came as a natural ability, and one of the few things I ever enjoyed as a child was having my mother tend me whenever I was ill.

She would change, it seemed, and become very gentle. She brewed wonderful-tasting broths, and I can still remember her hand pressed against my forehead and her voice whispering, "You'll feel better soon, little sister."

Most other times any show of affection would seem to embarrass her, and often, in order to have her attention, I would pretend to fall asleep at the supper table just to be carried to my room and tucked into bed. I felt a rare sense of safety in her arms.

Money was an acute and desperate problem to us now. Papa had promised again and again to send a set amount each month, but it seemed more often than not that no money came and Mamma worried and fumed.

One day at the Cole Avenue house Mamma had been more high-strung than usual, and the pressure kept mounting until the air was charged with her temper outbursts. Whatever I did, I can't remember, but without warning she threw a large pair of scissors at me with such force that they stuck quivering in the wall next to my head. I remember screaming and running into the yard crying, but in a few minutes she called me back and acted as if nothing unusual had happened. But I was afraid of her after that. Even though I was accustomed to her outbursts of temper, this was the first time it had been expressed in a physical attack. For weeks I thought she wanted to kill me, and I used various excuses to keep out of her way. I realize now it was simply an accidental flare-up brought on by too many pressures. But it left an indelible mark.

A short time after this incident she began to threaten suicide, if we misbehaved. I can remember lying in bed night after night, wondering if she would really do it, then crying because I did not want her to die. She was everything I had and I couldn't lose her.

When I was about nine, we moved from Hollywood

to a cabin in the family homestead at Chico, in the Sacramento Valley, where we could live rent-free.

I made no friends partly because of my somberness, but mainly because I felt we were different, and of course we were. Most of the other children had fathers and we, by comparison, were ragamuffins. I realized, from adult glances, that people felt sorry for that "poor little Farmer girl," and I hated their concern. Even then I could not stand sympathy. I preferred, and still do, cold calculation to compassion.

We managed to live in Chico until I was nearly eleven, but the strain of trying to raise a family without any support was telling on my mother. The household was neglected and chaotic, discipline was inconsistent and haphazard. As a result I was growing into a headstrong, resentful, rebellious child. I learned to cope with Mamma's inconsistent disposition by staying clear when a storm brewed and relishing her attention when she sought me out.

Life was a powderkeg, Mamma its fuse, and one night everything exploded. Without any warning she informed us that we children were leaving for Seattle the next morning to live with our father. I was stunned that she would consider giving us away to a stranger, and I told her so. I screamed and threatened to run away. The next morning, as we drove off with Aunt Zella, I did not look back at my mother. I hated her for her disloyalty. I later learned that she had notified Papa that she was going to force him to provide for his children. She was through. She informed him to make his plans accordingly, and he agreed to meet us in Albany, Oregon, the halfway point.

He was waiting at a hotel, and I suppose he approached this reunion with understandable forebodings. I had made up my mind during the drive from Chico that I would not like him. How could I? He was the cause of all my problems, and if he had done right by us, I could still be with Mamma. These were my feelings and I did nothing to hide them from him.

He bought some magazines at the newsstand, and as he herded us onto the train, I heard him ask Aunt Zella, "What in the name of God do they eat?" It was then that I became acutely aware that I was now in the hands of a total stranger, and, at that point, my childhood ended.

I sat across from a man who had no idea how to console me. He was awkward in his attempts at humor and conversation and I slouched deep in my seat and glowered at him.

I had no way of knowing that the breaking up of his family and our long separation had had any effects on him. I later realized that his law practice had deteriorated and that he was down and out. He had lost all drive and ambition to pursue a career and merely plodded along, picking up trivial cases whenever he could. He was already a defeated man and my cold hostility must have stung him deeply.

Even though he had known for several weeks that Mamma intended to send us to him, he had not looked for a place for us. We spent a night or two with a family in the suburbs until he found a two-bedroom apartment in the center of town near his office and apologized to us for its smallness and sparse furnishings, not knowing that it was far better than anything in which we had previously lived.

We had been there three days when I started breaking out in blisters, and within hours the three of us children were covered with them. Papa, rather frantically, called in a doctor who told him we had chicken pox.

The doctor quarantined the apartment, and I was

not too upset when I found out that Papa could not stay with us. He explained that he had to work but promised that he would come by every evening and check on us.

But after he left, misery set in. I was sick. I was frightened. I was alone and I missed my mother. I wanted my mother. Chicken pox is not a fatal disease, but to an eleven-year-old left alone, it can be a wretched experience.

Papa kept his word and each evening would prop a ladder against the window and hand through groceries. He would caution against scratching the blisters and urged us to take care of ourselves. Then he disappeared until the next night.

But after the quarantine was lifted, a marvelous thing began to happen. Little by little Papa and I were becoming friends. He was wise enough not to force his way, and even though I was still resentful, he was becoming comfortable to be around. He was very different from Mamma. He seldom raised his voice and he smiled at me a lot. In spite of myself I was beginning to like him, for I felt he was beginning to like me. I wanted to be friendlier, but I was afraid that a sudden misfortune or the unpredictable actions of adults would take from me that which I most desired—their attention.

As it developed, my apprehension was justified. One evening Papa told us, with some relief in his voice, that Mamma was moving back to Seattle. The Chico cabin had burned down. Before Mamma agreed to return, she demanded that he buy a house and guarantee one hundred dollars a month for support. She was agreeable to allowing him weekend visiting rights, but was adamant that she would never share the same roof with him. She made no secret of the fact that she intended to file for divorce, but Papa was a hopeful man and thought that eventually they would patch up their broken marriage.

I was not sure how I would feel when I saw her again. Inwardly, I was responding to Papa, for he was becoming an affectionate and conscientious parent. He worried and fussed over me like a mother hen, and I liked his attention. But I no longer felt that I needed Mamma or, for that matter, wanted her. I still resented her "giving me away," although it had been working to my advantage, and now that she was coming back, all I sensed was that she was spoiling the only good thing I'd ever had. I dreaded the commotion that she generated.

Mamma had lost all her writings in the fire, and after the newness of the house wore off, she once more occupied herself with her new book. For a few months things were quiet, but then Papa began falling behind with his support payments, and the sparks flew. Regardless, he would still show up on Friday evenings and Mamma would block the door with her body.

"You're nothing but a cheap shyster," she would shout as he pushed her aside. The haranguing would last most of the weekend until he grudgingly handed over a few dollars. I like to think he never deliberately withheld funds from us. He simply wasn't earning enough money, and I'm sure he would rather his children consider him a tightwad than to know he was a failure. On the other hand, I can understand the frustration he put Mamma through, for she was literally worn out from years of haggling with him over money.

Life continued tumultuous and noisy, and to escape it I began to spend more and more time with my books. I read everything I could find at the public library, for I had decided to become a writer. The fascinating experience of learning began to fill my life, and my surroundings became obsolete.

At fourteen I was a very intense high school freshman, reading well beyond the normal level for my age. I lived in a world of words and books, and my family held little interest for me. I no longer bothered to pretend they did, and I was beginning to see Mamma as an eccentric, high-strung woman who was brilliant and well informed but who, unfortunately, missed the mark at being a mother—or, rather, my mother. She often embarrassed me with her wild and overwrought gestures and attitudes, and the house was usually in such bedlam that I seldom invited any one to it.

During my first year in high school I made no friends, except for Lottie Stevens. I worked hard and helped put out the school paper. I also joined the debating team and was relatively successful. When I lost a debate, it was always because the judges felt I was too intense about my subject matter and all too dramatic in my presentation. I stressed my points with the vigor of a hack actress, for I was, in many details, much like my mother.

Through most of my high school years I was not interested in boys, and I accepted dates only when I needed someone to take me to a special event. They soon learned not to paw, and any adolescent attempt at lovemaking resulted in a tongue-lashing that sent them scampering from the front porch. I was not curious about them and they did not repel me in any way. I simply had no interest in sexual experimentation.

During this time I grew deeply concerned with what I felt was the spirit of man and I began to question many things. One was God. I had never been unduly impressed with religion, but I was growing curious about it and felt that if I intended to become an honest writer I would need to know more about this strongest of human attachments.

Occasionally, Mamma had sent us to the Congregational Church, but it seemed farfetched to hear the minister sermonize about God as though he had a personal acquaintance with Him.

I did not like the idea that somewhere there was a something that could make me well or happy or rich or poor, as suited its fancy. I read the Bible, but it seemed more like a contradictory fairy tale. Prayer seemed nothing more than a potluck experiment, and certainly nothing that I would care to rely on.

I began reading Nietzsche's philosophical tracts in which he also expressed the same doubts, only he said it in German: *"Gott ist Tot."* God is dead. This I could understand. I was not to assume that there was no God, but I could find no evidence in my life that He existed or that He had ever shown any particular interest in me. I was not an atheist, but I was surely an agnostic, and by the time I was sixteen I was well indoctrinated into this theory.

I talked over my opinions with Mamma whenever possible, but her spare time was scarce. She was almost always buried in her own writings, yet there were moments when we would sit on the porch and I would ask her pertinent questions about life and God. Either her responses were vague or she reverted to her advice that I should think for myself.

"Don't follow the Judas goat. Think things out for yourself."

When I was seventeen, I bought a much-coveted $2.95 hat which quickly disappeared in the clutter of the house. I accused everyone of taking it. I was furious. I hunted and hunted, but it was nowhere to be found, and in desperation and without really thinking, I made a dramatic declaration at the supper table: "I am going up to my room and ask God in prayer to find it for me."

I stayed on my knees for quite some time waiting for something to happen. Nothing did. But when I went back downstairs, I suddenly realized that I had not searched behind the couch. And there it was.

I ran to my mother waving the hat triumphantly and declared, "You see, I asked God to find it for me and He showed me where it was."

An odd look came over her face and she did something very unlike her. She kissed me on the forehead and said, "I'm glad you found it, little sister."

The next day in creative writing class, our teacher, Miss Belle McKenzie, gave us two weeks to write an essay based on a personal experience. It was to have great impact on our final grades. The hat incident had left me halfway believing in prayer. Yet when I learned that a classmate had just lost both parents in an accident, I was appalled that God helped me find a hat but permitted a young girl to lose her family.

I told Mamma I was going to attack God in an essay entitled "God Dies." Busy with her own writing, she looked up from her work briefly and mumbled, "If that is what you think, little sister."

A few days after we had turned in our essays, Miss McKenzie told the class that she had slected three which she thought suitable for submission to the *National Scholastic,* a well-respected educational publication conducting a national essay contest for high school students. She did not tell us whose work had been chosen, and I dismissed the whole thing from my mind.

A few weeks later she announced that Frances Farmer had been selected as the national winner. I was to receive the first prize of one hundred dollars. I was so excited that after I had been personally con-

gratulated by the principal, I was allowed to go home
for the rest of the day.

I could not wait to tell Mamma, and she responded
with full-blown maternal pride. She was ecstatic. I
called Papa and he made a special trip out to see me.
That night at supper I was the guest of honor. Later
given center stage, I read the essay out loud. It ended
thus!

. . . God became a super father that couldn't
spank me. But if I wanted a thing badly enough,
He arranged it.

That satisfied me until I began to figure out
that if God loved all His children equally, why did
He bother about my hat and let other people lose
their fathers and mothers for always? I began to
see that He didn't have much to do about people's dying or hats or anything. They happened
whether He wanted them to or not, and He stayed
in Heaven and pretended not to notice. I wondered a little why God was such a useless thing.
It seemed a waste of time to have Him. After
that, He became less and less, until He was . . .
nothingness.

I felt rather proud to think that I had found
the truth by myself, without help from anyone. It
puzzled me that other people had not found out
too. God was gone.

I had never seen such pride in my mother. She
could not have been happier, and when the check arrived, I insisted that we use it for household expenses,
and that pleased her even more. I was the best in the
land. I was the apple of my mother's eye. I was queen
of the house, and I played it to the hilt.

Then all hell broke loose. When the essay was published in *National Scholastic,* it brought with it an avalanche of local press headlines.

SEATTLE GIRL DENIES GOD, WINS PRIZE

Mamma wasted no time in calling the editors of every paper in town and demanding a retraction.

The national press picked up the story, and within a week I began to receive letters from all over the country. Some were from students who applauded my protest, but a great majority came from disturbed citizens who threatened me. At my own school most of the students shunned me. Most of Seattle's Christian community was outraged. I became the perfect example of "pagan youth." One editorial read, "What is becoming of our country when a young girl gets one hundred dollars reward for celebrating the death of God? Atheism," it said, "was rampant in the public school."

I had unwittingly released a monster, and Mamma threw a saddle on its back and rode it for all its worth. She was completely on my side, but the last thing I wanted was a militant, dramatic defender. I desperately hoped that the whole thing would die down, but it kept building, with Mamma adding fuel to the fire.

A city-wide church meeting was announced and the subject was to be my essay and its evil effects. A prominent minister was to deliver the sermon, and he announced to the papers that he was going to destroy the creeping atheism among our nation's youth. He had been "called" to speak out.

That night Mamma notified the press and headed for the church service with both barrels loaded. I begged her not to go, to let the whole thing die, but she would hear no argument. "You have every right to say what you think, and those idiots are not going to browbeat you for it." Neither Papa nor I would go with her.

The minister was a fireball. "If the youth of Seattle are going to Hell, Frances Farmer is leading them there." He pictured me as a tool of Satan, and Mamma somehow managed to bide her time until he was nearing his peak. In front of clicking cameras and a wide-mouthed congregation, she let fly with her own ringing denunciation. Since she was never at a loss for words, she would have made Grandfather Van Ornum proud. The meeting was dissolved as she marched back down the aisle with chin high and victory tucked under her belt.

She was elated by the news coverage. But I nearly died of embarrassment. I went to Papa's office in tears, and he consoled me, for he had experienced the same chagrin many years before.

But if I made the papers during my junior year in high school, Mamma took the headlines from me when I was a senior, and her escapade amused Seattle and struck a kindred note with every frustrated wife in the city.

It had a shocking effect on the family, and I was even more humiliated by her antics than by my own literary volcano. Perhaps it was the exhilaration of her battles with the local ministry that gave her the necessary vigor to focus her attention on her own marital problems, for soon she began an allout campaign to sue Papa for a divorce. However, he stood firm and pulled every string he could to thwart her efforts and, for a time, succeeded in leading her in an endless legal circle.

It was obvious that Papa really wanted his family, but he would never follow through with responsibilities, and Mamma was left to face the financial and emotional outcome. The house payments were always late. The grocery bills piled up. There were no provisions for medical or dental bills.

Finally Mamma heard of a woman lawyer who was a stalwart defender of women's rights, and Mamma, at last, found herself a helpmate. She was a tall, skinny creature, with bushy black hair that always had a pencil stabbed through it, over her ear. There was no question about it, Papa had, at last, met his legal match and the divorce went through without a hitch.

The court awarded Mamma a hundred dollars a month in support, and Papa was given unlimited visiting rights, so nothing was radically changed, except, at long last, Mamma had her freedom.

Papa resented the divorce deeply and became even more stubborn about meeting his court-ordered support payments. But he still showed up like clockwork every Friday evening. She would spend the whole weekend screaming at him while he puttered around the house, ignoring her, whistling to himself.

Finally, he was two months behind in his payments, and she was down to rock bottom. When he was ready to leave on this particular Sunday night, she warned him, "Mark this down, Ernest Farmer, someday I'm going to shoot that penny-pinching head right off your shoulders."

He put on his hat and coat, kissed me on the cheek, and grinned. "Now, Lil, that's not a nice thing to say in front of Frances."

He winked at me, and I giggled, but he left with Mamma standing in the middle of the floor, stomping her feet and beating her fists together.

The next morning, dressed in her best finery, Mamma bought a small revolver at the local hardware store and had it loaded with blanks, explaining to the owner that she only wanted it for protection around the house and assuring him, as only she could, that, for the life of her, she would never hurt anyone.

With the revolver in her purse, she boarded the streetcar and headed for Papa's one-room office in the main business district. She flung open the door, flame in her eyes, and without saying a word, pulled out her gun, took aim, and fired repeatedly at Papa.

He dived under his desk, screaming for mercy. People came from all directions, and they found Mamma standing in the middle of the room, waving her gun in the air, shouting wildly, "Take me away. I'm guilty. I did it."

Papa was still under the desk when the police arrived. Once Mamma was safely impounded in the patrol wagon, Papa called a colleague and told him to go down and check on Mamma. At that point of the escapade, no one realized that the gun had been loaded with blanks, and Papa was deeply anguished that his Lil would try to kill him.

Mamma was brought to jail in hysterics, screaming her confession and denouncing Papa. The police reporters seized the story, and, once again, the Farmer skeleton began to rattle across the front pages of the Seattle papers.

A firm interrogation had her pretty well calmed down, and she ended up telling a coherent but somewhat unbelievable account of what happened.

The police checked to see how Papa was faring and confirmed that he was unhurt. Then the hardware store verified her claim that she had purchased blanks. However, she was held under bond until her first court appearance. All ended well, though, for, of course, Papa would not press charges, and the case was dismissed.

Mamma returned home exhausted but triumphant. By now her personal scrapbook was beginning to bulge, and she carefully clipped and pasted the records of her latest adventure.

I thought I would surely die of shame and humiliation, for I saw no humor in the story. However, Mamma's antics delighted most of my senior class, and she became somewhat of a comic book heroine.

For the remainder of my senior year, little or nothing adverse happened. I continued to mope around the house, as Mamma put it, and read long into the night. I seemed to thrive in my solitary life and concentrated on writing volumes of short stories.

Words became pure melodies to me, and I worked with them like precious tools. I wrote about everything I encountered, except my family, for they were too real and painful and private to put down on paper.

If I were to look back over my childhood, to examine my roots, I would say that I existed in a deep gloom, and with each passing year that gloom intensified.

I loved my mother deeply, but, at her insistence, it was always from afar. And those years of such intimate separation ate through the frail ties that held us as mother and daughter.

Many times as a child, and even as a young adult, I would slip into her room and touch her hairbrush or nuzzle my face into a dress hung in her closet, simply to be near her. But these unrewarding substitutes took a toll.

I was never harmed by physical want, for poverty should never serve as an excuse for discontent or as a reason for failure. But I was deprived in more subtle ways. Ways that my mother, to her death, never realized or understood.

So much of her was evidenced in my behavior. The fire. The determination. The will. The curiosity. The impromptu acts of violence.

Perhaps too much of her lived within me, for more often than not, it seemed that when I felt her retaliation, it was as though she were purging herself through me and my weakness. She could be cleansed if she brought my defects into the open for ridicule or punishment.

And much of my father flowed through me, as well. His slowness. His irrational dreams. His failure to triumph over himself. His obvious love that was slain by the sting of my mother's aggressive venom. His ability to harbor secrets. His silence. His chronic need for solitude.

On this incompatible foundation rested my rehabilitation and on this erratic family tree I hung suspended and adjudged insane.

During the past two weeks, despite the bedlam, I had been able to recall, in scattered order, the conditions and events that had deeply affected me, and somehow I had been able not only to digest them but to reach unbiased and satisfactory conclusions about them.

I had not absolved my foes of guilt, nor had I been able to forgive or lay aside the foaming hatred that boiled within my spirit. I was still resentful and angry, but I had come to the realization that I had to learn to cap the volcano and keep it under control.

I wanted out. I wanted to be free.

The price I had to pay was self-control, and in my mind an embryonic resolution began to form.

The only escape open to me was to react and respond as Dr. Conway and Mamma expected. I knew that altering my attitude would go far toward securing me my freedom, and since Mamma would have to accept and sign for my parole, I would have to handle her with greater diplomacy. I could not let anything she might say or do upset me.

The hostility had to cease, for I was waging a war that I could not possibly win.

10

I put my new resolutions into immediate effect. I no longer screamed or cursed or threatened. I was quiet and pleasant to Lorraine and to any of the patients who happened by my cell. I appeared to be responding, and it took a great deal of self-control not to ask Lorraine if my daily reports noted the change.

Three days after my consultation with Dr. Conway, two orderlies fastened a belt, with built-in handcuffs, around my waist and manacled my wrists. Leg irons with about a foot of chain circled my ankles.

I offered no resistance.

Taking short, hopping steps I was led through a large door, and as I heard it clang noisily behind me, I knew that I had pressured my way into a nightmare. My new leaf had been too late in turning.

I looked down the long line of beds filled with naked women twisting, jerking, groaning, screaming, while others ran up and down the aisle repeatedly ignoring anything that got in their way. Some gibbered to themselves in animated conversation. Those tied in chairs shook their heads as if trying to clear their minds of cobwebs. Others drifted aimlessly through the ward, carrying mops or rags.

The ward bristled with attendants. This was the area of shock. Electric shock. Insulin shock. Hydrotherapy. Experimental medication. Women who had not been able to adjust were brought here for treatment. And I was petrified.

A cart being wheeled down the aisle carried a black girl, lifeless except for great beads of sweat that hung on her face like a heavy dew. Her tongue twisted out of her mouth, and her throat muscles jerked as though she had gagged on something. Two attendants flopped her on a cot, and as the sheet was pulled off, she lay in a twisted, naked heap, unaware that urine was pouring from her body.

The orderly unlocked my restraints, and the nurse told a dull-eyed trustee to take me to my cot, halfway down the room.

"Prep her for hydro," she called after us.

The trustee pointed to an unmade cot, telling me to remember which one was mine, then steered me through the ward into a small room fitted with three bathtubs.

Women were in two of them, their heads sticking out from the canvas sheets stretched tightly over the tubs. Their bathing caps made their heads look like skulls.

One woman was screaming, her voice hoarse. Her eyes popped and blazed, seeing nothing as she thrashed under the canvas. She kept screaming for someone named Arnold, then would sink into babbling.

The other woman was motionless. Absolutely still. Her head draped to one side, and her eyes were half open. I wondered if she might be dead.

Then I heard the water rushing into the tubs, and I instinctively drew back.

"You ain't goin' nowhere," the trustee said. "So just settle down and take your clothes off. Don't make it hard on yourself, babe, cause I'll knock the hell out of you if you try anything. Now strip."

She gave me a shove, for good measure, that slapped

me against the wall. "Strip," she ordered. "Shoes and all."

I quietly obeyed. I was determined to keep my resolution, regardless of what might happen.

She tossed me a bathing cap and two large wads of cotton. "Stuff this in your ears and make sure you plug 'em up tight. Then put on the cap."

My own violence was my strength, and without a show of rage, I felt vulnerable, frightened. At the same time I was fascinated with my ability to obey with such meekness.

Before I could organize myself, the trustee had taken down three canvas straps from a hook on the wall and had looped one around my chest, pinning my arms against my sides until my breath was cut short. The second was buckled around my thighs, and the third around my ankles.

She left the room as I tottered to keep my balance. I tried to hop after her but tumbled headlong. My chin cracked against the floor and I felt a sharp pain as my teeth sliced my lower lip. I lay there screamig, flopping, trying to maneuver myself into a sitting position, but, tied as I was, I was unable to do little more than rock back and forth on my stomach.

The trustee returned with a student nurse and another attendant, who pulled me to my feet and stood behind me while the nurse checked my bindings, easing the one around my chest. I was still screaming and gabbling, spitting blood from my mouth, but the wound was ignored. They picked me up, one by the ankles, the other by the shoulders and dropped me into the empty tub, bruising my spine.

They pulled the heavy canvas sheet up to my neck, and while one tightened the neck drawstring, the other took a long dirty rope and looped it under the lip of the tub, gathering the canvas into the lasso. She tugged and pulled while the other one stretched the sheet across the tub. The rope was wound around and around until it made a tight band that kept the canvas secure.

The first crash of icy water hit my ankles and slipped rapidly up my legs. I began to shake from the shock of it, screaming and thrashing my body under the sheet, but the more I struggled, the more I realized that I was helplessly restricted in a frozen hell.

I began to gnaw on my lip, flinching from the pain of my teeth digging into the wound but praying that it would take my mind off the freezing water that burned my body like acid.

The three of them stayed there until they were satisfied that the water pressure was adjusted to the drain and would not overflow the tub, then the student went to the woman who lay in semiconsciousness. She pulled open one eye, studied it briefly, then the three of them left. I was still screaming when the door slammed the rest of the world away.

Hydro was a violent and crushing method of shock treatment, even though it was intended to relax the patient. What it really did was assault the body and horrify the mind until both withered with exhaustion.

I lay there in the glacier grip until my mind had gone blank. I felt it slipping from me, but I tried to keep it active by thinking of addresses, phone numbers, nursery rhymes. I counted forward and backward. I became confused. I recited the alphabet, but everything was jumbled. I struggled, and screamed, and froze. Then, like the incoherent woman calling for Arnold, I slid out of awareness and tumbled into a gibbering, scrambled maze.

I do not remember the other two women being taken from the tubs. And when they finally came for me, I was past audible speech or functional movement. I remember being lifted onto a cart, and then the straps fell off. The cap was pulled from my head, and my ears were unplugged. Somewhere, I heard a voice, but it was like a resounding echo.

"My God," it said. "She's nearly chewed off her lip. She'll have to be gagged next time."

A dry blanket was wrapped around me and I felt the seasick motion of the cart as I was wheeled back into the ward area. It was night, but the veneer of sleep was thin and the patients tossed and rustled like dry leaves.

"We'd better take her to the station and try to fix up her mouth," another voice said. "Damn, but somebody will sure catch hell for this. She's in a mess."

"What's wrong with me?" I tried to say, but the words came out thick and unfamiliar.

"Don't try to talk, honey. You're going to be all right."

The movement of the cart rattling along was making me sick to my stomach, but then it stopped and turned, then stopped again.

"What's her name?"

"Wait till I look it up, for heaven's sake."

I could hear with sharp awareness, but when I tried to open my eyes, I could not move my lids.

"It's Anderson. Frances Anderson."

"Who's her doctor?"

"Conway. Wouldn't you know?"

"Well, he'll play hell blaming us for this one. See what time she went to hydro."

"Jesus!"

"What's wrong?"

"She went in at three thirty."

"Good God, that's ten hours."

"What are we going to do about her mouth?"

"What can we do until Conway checks her? Wipe it off, I guess."

"If she's been in water ten hours, we'd better rub her down first."

Hands, from far off, hardly seemed to touch me, but then inch by inch they moved closer until my flesh became sensitized. I heard a deep groan roll from my throat and I tried to speak.

"Don't move your mouth, honey, if you can help it. We're going to put a compress on it until the doctor gets here."

I felt a warm, moist cloth being laid across my lips, but its soft pressure bore down like a slab of lead, and I tried to lift my hands to take it away, but they were frozen in place. I wanted to see the voices and forced my eyes open, but only a dull blur colored my vision. I groaned again, low, like a hunted animal, and slowly moved my head from side to side. The cart once more squeaked and rattled its way back into the ward, then stopped.

"Lift her easy. She's almost out and she'll sleep straight through."

I was laid on a cot and a blanket was pulled under my chin. A foreign hand soothed the hair out of my face and rested briefly on my forehead, then went away.

I was quiet and warm, and everything vanished as I entered a lifeless sleep.

11

For the next twenty-four days I was depersonalized in hydro. The physical pain, the spiritual injury, the mental torture mashed one day into another, until all thoughts hinged on either being in or out of the tub. Nothing else existed.

I have only vague recollections of Dr. Conway showing up, but after he left someone put a thick sick-tasting salve on my lips twice a day and a roll of gauze was stuffed into my mouth during each treatment. I remember very little about eating or walking or hearing or seeing, but I have nightmare recall of two personally humiliating experiences during those three weeks.

Soon after the treatments started, I began to menstruate, and a trustee brought two small paper sacks and put them by my cot. In one was a pile of worn sheeting that had been torn into narrow strips. These were to be folded and used. When the rag was soiled, I was told to put it in the other sack, and at the end of my period, I was responsible for washing them out for reuse. There were no pins or belts of any kind allowed in the asylum, so the rags were simply held in place by keeping the legs pressed together. Later I learned that many of the women fashioned slings by tying a rag around their waist and one between their legs.

Hydro was prescribed for a three-hour duration, but seldom did the treatments terminate on time, and the endless hours in the cold water attacked my bowels and bladder. Lying in the water, with my nerves and system violated, knowing that my blood and waste were mingling with it, offended and grieved my spirit beyond description. My femininity was mauled, my power to reason or struggle vanished. I simply existed in chilling confusion.

I was unnaturally calm at the end of three weeks, for I had been systematically deenergized. All personality was washed away and all that was left was a water-clogged robot. Each day I was led to the tub and undressed when I was told to. I stood like marble while the straps were tightened around my body, and I waited patiently while the cotton was stuffed in my ears and the cap pulled down over my head. I did not struggle when the gag was crushed into my mouth, and when I was put in the tub, I hardly flinched as the fluid hell claimed me.

I had been tamed.

After three weeks, when I was no longer physically or mentally able to function, I was left to a recuperative period. I was not required to do any ward work, but allowed to remain in bed and vegetate. It seemed a miracle, but inch by inch my strength returned, but my mind was slow and cloudy. It was difficult to think. It was almost impossible to remember.

During the later part of my treatment, I was mouth-fed by other patients. Women who had undergone shock and could hardly function themselves were given ward work. They cleaned toilets, fed other patients, or mopped up filth and vomit. They chattered constantly, without making sense, but I suppose they were confused at being able to think again. It mattered little whether their thoughts were in order or, for that matter, rational. The pertinent fact was the excitement and challenge of the mind returning.

Within a week, I became one of them. I carried food to other patients and fed them, personally disinterested in their limp conditions and untouched by their misery. They, like I, would survive it. I mopped floors. Changed foul sheets. Scrubbed toilets. Washed rags. Emptied bedpans, and tried to start myself thinking again.

I worked until I felt that most of my life had been spent in this ward. I could remember little else. I had been separated from the rest of the world and was immune to its problems. I was dull-minded, slow moving and uninvolved. I had been turned into a full-fledged inmate.

And then, one Sunday, Mamma came.

I was given a clean dress and sat quietly in a chair while an attendant combed my hair. I had no desire to see her, but somewhere, during the flood, I had lost the vigor to become upset or fretful.

I lined up with those few in the building who had visitors and waited to cross into the "recreation area," a big hall in the Administration building. I smiled wryly on seeing the number of orderlies on standby duty in case a patient got out of hand.

I saw her sitting across the room, and I felt my heart grow pinched as I walked toward her. She stood up, unsmiling, and waited for me to come to her. She made no other move, but remained firm-footed until we were face-to-face.

"Let's sit down, Mamma," I said, pulling up a chair.

"Well. Well," she said. "You've put on a little weight."

"I don't think so. I don't see how, anyway."

"You certainly do look heavier to me."

"Could be the place agrees with me."

"Now, don't you start acting smart."

"I didn't mean for it to sound wrong. I guess I was just trying to make a joke, and it came out wrong. I'm sorry."

"That's all right, Frances. I just hope we don't get off on the wrong foot, like you usually do. So tell me how you are."

"I'm really very tired."

"Do you have to work here?"

"You could call it that."

"What do you do?"

"I wait."

"That doesn't make sense. Have you made any friends?"

"I've been too busy."

"Well, really, Frances, that's what I asked you. Do you do any work? You're not making sense."

"I'm sorry, Mamma. I'm doing the best I can."

"Now are you going to sit there and tell me that after all these weeks you haven't got anything more to say than 'I'm sorry, Mamma'? Honestly! Tell me what it's like in here. What you've been doing. Tell me about some of your new friends. Talk."

"It's hard for me, Mamma. I suppose I'd rather not have to think about it. Maybe that's it."

"That's no way to get well. You've got to bring all this out in the open."

"Mamma, please, I don't feel like it."

"Have you been sick?"

"They tell me this place is a hospital, so, yes, I suppose I've been sick."

"Do you eat all right?"

"I guess so. You said I'd gained weight."

"Really, Frances! I was only making conversation. Why must you always insist on taking everything literally?"

"Do you have a cigarette?"

"Are you allowed to smoke?"

"Everyone else is."

"I didn't think to ask your doctor. Do you smoke in your room?"

"I don't have a room."

"Well, wherever. Do you smoke there?"

"No."

"Then why do you insist on taking advantage of a situation? You can get me in a lot of trouble if you're not allowed to and I give you one."

"If I ask the orderly and he says it's OK, do you have a cigarette for me?"

"I'll ask him."

"Let me do it, Mamma. Please."

"Now you sit right where you are. You've got no business moving around all these. . . ."

"Crazy people."

"I didn't say that. But, well, after all you never can tell when one is likely to get. . . ."

"Violent?"

"Well. . . ."

"I live with these people, Mamma. All day long I live with them. And at night I sleep with them. And you know something? You're right to be afraid. They're a spooky bunch."

We sat in silence until I said again, "Are you going to ask him, or may I?"

"I'll motion for him." And after a long involved conversation of listening to her explain that I was Frances Farmer—"You know, the actress?"— the orderly shrugged and mumbled, "Why not, lady? It's OK with me."

She dug in her purse and came up with a crumpled pack, took one out of it, and handed it to me, then held a match, forcing me to bend forward in my chair to reach it.

"You have a nice doctor, Frances. He's never too busy to talk. I keep close tabs on you, you know."

I had no answer, but I managed a smile and nodded in agreement.

"He tells me you're just doing fine. You're responding, he says."

I smiled and nodded again.

"Why haven't you written me?"

"We're not allowed to have pencils."

"In heaven's name, why?"

"They're pointed instruments, Mamma, or didn't you realize that?"

"What in the world does that have to do with it? Of course they're pointed."

"Well, you just think about it."

"You're making it up. Why don't you just say you don't want to write me and be done with it? Don't expect me to swallow some stupid excuse."

"It's true, Mamma. But I promise that as soon as they think I'm well enough to trust with a pencil, I'll write you."

"Well, young lady, I'm going to check with Dr. Conway about this. It's ridiculous, and I think it's just some more of your weird imagination."

"Maybe it is, Mamma, so you check with him."

"Don't take that condescending attitude with me. In heaven's name, do you think you can ever straighten yourself out, or am I going to spend the rest of my days making bus trips out here?"

"I don't know how to answer that."

"Well, you think about it, young lady. You just think about it. You've got to help yourself and get rid of that awful attitude. That's your problem, you know. That, and those so-called friends of yours. Where are the big shots now? Skipped, that's where. They drained you dry, then skipped. So you straighten yourself up. If you have any trouble, you've brought it all on yourself."

"I probably did, Mamma."

"I don't want anybody blaming me for this mess."

"Nobody's blaming you, Mamma. It's all my fault."

The silence that followed was awkward and heavy. I wished she would leave, but she had settled herself down in the chair and stared moodily at me.

"Do you have another cigarette?"

"You smoke too much."

"Come on, Mamma. Please."

Her eyes narrowed as she shook her head in refusal, and we sat there, looking through each other until I broke the silence.

"Listen, Mamma. You don't have to make trips out here. It's too hard on you. It's a long bus ride. And really, I don't mind. Maybe on holidays, or something special, but don't feel that you have to come just because it's visiting day."

"It's my duty."

"Mamma!"

"And anyway, I've met a lot of nice ladies on the bus today. You know I always could make friends. We had a good visit on the ride, and most of them would like to meet you."

"Meet me?"

"Why do you act so surprised? They know who you are, and they said they'd like to meet you. What's wrong with that?"

"I'd rather not."

"Well, I told them you would, but you'd probably embarrass me and make some smart remark."

"I won't do that, Mamma."

"It'd be the first time. Why do you fight everything I ask you to do?"

"I'll do what makes you happy."

"That's better. A group of us plan to go back on the first bus. I don't like being out after dark, you know. They said it would be announced over the loudspeaker when we have to leave, so when you meet the ladies, I want you to try and be real nice to them."

"I will, Mamma."

There was little to say after that, and so we sat together in stiff silence until her bus was called. I noticed eight or ten other middle-aged women getting up from their chairs, making ready, and Mamma waved and called to them from across the room, causing all heads to turn in our direction. "Girls. Over here. My daughter, Frances Farmer, wants to meet you. Over here, girls."

It was a humiliating moment. Puffed up like a mother hen, Mamma bounced off the names of my pictures and leading men.

Mamma had come and gone. She had left her mark on me, but we had not touched.

Mamma visited me twice during the next two months, and each time was much the same. My reactions were curbed and under control. I could hear her, but I had learned not to listen.

During the third month, I was moved to another ward. I had graduated from shock, and as a reward, I was housed with the aged and infirm, the theory being that an inmate fresh from shock was incapable of any responsibility except the most menial. Those of us who were put on practical duty were expected to take care of the aged bedridden.

The old were pitiful in their wrinkled agony. Toothless and blind women, rotting away, were given only the most primitive care. We were to feed them once a day, on no particular schedule. We would wait until the soup cart was brought to the ward, for their one meal was always a weak, colorless broth, and those acting as pseudo-trustees filled buckets from the soup kettles and went from bed to bed, feeding with the same spoon, from the same bucket.

Sheets were changed only when the patients had so befouled themselves that they literally swam in the filth and waste. No soap was provided for us to launder them out, so sanitation was impossible. The odor. The filth. The misery. The despair. All vied for prominence.

Patients were never washed or talked to. They lay on their thin, filthy cots and waited for death. No one ever visited them. No one ever inquired about them. Forgotten relics doomed to lie in a grave marked only by the state.

And they died, I remember, mostly in the wee hours of the night. They would slip away in the blackness, and we would find them in the morning, already cold. Their bodies stiff, and their sightless eyes open, milky and dead.

And in such a way I passed through the summer of 1945. By fall I had been promoted once more and was put to work in the clothes room, sorting apparel as it was received, and distributing it as requisitions came through.

It was a large and complicated operation and required, what seemed to me, an endless routine of badly planned procedures due to a confused method of disbursement.

Of the twenty-seven hundred patients in the asylum, only a few supplied their own clothing. Some of the apparel came through outside donations, but for the most part, things were made by the patients in occupational therapy. As a result, few luxury items, undergarments, shoes or hose, were available. During the cold months, women wore men's socks when they could get them. There were never enough shoes to go around, and it was almost impossible to class them according to sizes, for most had been worn until the size letters were indiscernible.

To further complicate the operation, we not only handled donation packs as they came through, but disbursed the laundry on a daily basis.

About twelve of us, all women, managed the department, and it was hard, physical labor. But I did not mind, for by the time my work was finished, I was ready for sleep as soon as I was returned to my ward.

When I was assigned to the clothes room, I was also moved to better quarters. I was still under full security and could not have outside or ground privileges, but moved from the ward to work in a group. We worked a ten-hour shift with a half hour off for our midday meal. But there was one advantage to working in the clothes room: We were the best-dressed women in the asylum.

I had been without underwear for so long that I concentrated on the donation bags until I managed to accumulate three decent pairs of pants and a worn but wearable brassiere. I kept this booty hidden in the sleeve of a threadbare sweater, for such prize possessions would be stolen without a second thought.

As the weeks passed, and I obviously appeared capable of the work assigned, I was given ground privileges. And this was worth the backbreaking labor in the clothes room. We had one day off a week, on a staggered schedule. I spent my day off away from the ward, walking, walking, walking. Always alone. I had not made friends with any of the patients, nor would I discuss my problems or listen to theirs. I relished the solitude of my private walks.

I did not think back during this period, nor did I risk contemplating the future. I suppose I simply existed in a suspended state, giving off the essence of a calm but moody woman. I was still regarded as unfriendly, but I was no longer reported as being hostile. Outwardly I was in full control, for I had kept my resolution and never once resumed the role of the antagonist. But I had not amputated the anger. It still lived. I had only let it grow thin and undernourished, and it worked to my advantage.

I did not see Dr. Conway during this period, but I knew from my promotions that my daily reports were being read. I was behaving in a manner that seemed to suit him, and he was doling out the rewards.

The weeks struggled into months, and I had gone through three seasons when winter came. During the summer the wards had been airless heat boxes, filled with insects and sweat. But winter was the most frustrating time of all. The thin cotton wrappers, our standard uniforms, offered no protection in the drafty damp buildings, and only a small amount of heavy clothing was available. In one respect I was fortunate to work in the clothes room, where I would put on two or three dresses against the bone-chilling air, and a torn pair of overshoes helped when the winter rain and snows came. Later I claimed a coat with a scaly fur collar that had come through donations, and, all in all, I made out rather well.

During the winter I had the grounds almost to myself, and I would walk the snow on my day off, feeling its wetness slip through the overshoes, soaking my feet. But it was a natural discomfort, and since the world I lived in was so unnatural, it was a welcomed normality. I loved the fresh, cold air. I was brought to life by it. But inside, the cold became an enemy that sent us to bed shivering. We slept in our clothes and shoes, hoping to evade the overpowering gloom of the icy dampness.

Just before Christmas, after seven months as an inmate, I was told to appear before Staff to discuss my parole.

Although I desperately wanted to be free, I was frightened by the news. My confined life offered a kind of twisted security. Rules were made, and if they were broken, the offender was punished. There was safety in routine. The thought of being thrown back into a world where money and ambition created a pressure pot terrified me. As I dressed for Staff, I was tense and nervous. I wondered whether I could remember how to act "normal," or if I had been caged too long.

I met before the same group of doctors but with no confrontation on my part. When they brought up the question of my career, I felt myself shrinking back behind my wall. I tried to explain that I planned to take up some other kind of work, and then the sparring began. They were not satisfied until I admitted that my attitude toward so rewarding a career was a flaw in my makeup and not a reflection against my profession. Since they evidently considered making movies a sign of mental soundness, who was I to challenge such wisdom? Only a crazy woman would turn away from wealth, fame, glamor. And they let me know that I could not hope for recovery by avoiding such a prominent factor in my life. I wondered if I had been a waitress or a shoe clerk or a cleaning girl, would they have placed so much importance or whether or not I resumed my work?

As the interview progressed, I was manipulated into thanking them for the "care" they had given me and acknowledging positive results from my confinement. I did exactly what they wanted me to, for I knew that my future rested in their power. They could let me out or send me back, and I could not risk offending them.

I wanted out. I wanted to leave the cage. I wanted to control my own spirit and develop my own destiny. I wanted to eat and sleep and dream in freedom, so throughout the interview I remained calm and composed.

When they brought up the basic hospital charges of four dollars and twenty-seven cents a week, I explained that I did not have any money, but that when I went back to work, I would begin making payments to the state. As an afterthought I mentioned the work I had been doing in the clothes room, but I was told that patients were not paid for occupational therapy. Work was considered an important part of the treatment. It was ironic that I had spent months laboring at a breakneck pace, lugging heavy sacks of clothing six days a week, ten hours a day, only to learn that none of it was worth my board and keep. I had to bite back the words boiling inside me, but again, I kept calm and outwardly, at least, accepted their reasoning.

Then I faced a long session of questions as to where my money had gone. Had I squandered it? Had I made bad investments? What had happened to it? I had no logical answer. I did not know where the money had gone. I had had a manager who handled my affairs, but I did not know until I had been placed under Mamma's guardianship after my smashup in Hollywood that I was broke. An appeal was made to the courts claiming I was a pauper, and I had no means of counteracting the claim.

I explained to the staff that brooding over financial losses would probably hinder my recovery. This logic seemed to please the group, and the interview was closed.

I returned to the backbreaking work that was curing me and waited for word about my parole. At first, every time a door opened I thought it might be a message from Staff. I lived on hope and I waited.

Christmas came and I did not take part in any of the pitiful festivities. It was nothing more than another day, and by mid-January every woman in my ward had appeared before Staff. There was nothing for us to do but wait.

Then, in the late spring, when the endless hours had whittled down any expectation, my parole was granted, placing me in my mother's custody. Only two others in the ward made it. Most of the other women were notified that their guardians could not accept custodial responsibility and that they were to remain until "next time," or until further arrangements could be made. These women were bound by law to remain as inmates until a responsible party would assume custody, and the realization that they were helpless to help themselves drove a stake through their hearts. In a matter of hours after the news reached the ward, I watched these women give up the struggle, and one by one, they were removed. Others took their places, proud that they were getting better. Encouraged that they were being given responsible jobs to do. Hopeful that they would soon be getting out. They saw three who had made it.

When my release date came, I received a package from home. I had written Mamma and asked her to send me some clothes, and she had managed a nice cotton dress and a pair of straw sandals. As I dressed, I was told that she was waiting for me in the Administration building.

I wanted to walk out of the asylum alone. I had been carried in alone, and I wanted the right to shed the stench of it by myself, but Mamma was there, waiting.

It took only a few impersonal minutes for my papers to be processed, but even so, Mamma insisted on talking too much and offering suggestions as to how to expedite the papers more efficiently. Finally it was over.

As we walked to the gatehouse to wait for the bus, I turned off her constant babbling. I was rising from a grave, I was free. And for a moment I forgot that I was still bound to her by law.

I was paroled as "improved" and learned that it had been in full agreement with the Staff. I was told, by the release clerk, that during the next year, if no adverse attacks occurred, I would meet before the Staff for another interview, and if I passed, I would then be able to apply to the court for a motion to restore my competency.

A year, I told myself, is not such a long time. It would pass, and I could wait. The parole, of course, imposed certain restrictions, but on the bus ride back to Seattle, I did not dwell on these problems.

I sat by the window and watched houses pass. And children. And trucks. I saw stores. And cabs. And phone booths. Things I had not seen for nearly a year. And I saw them through clear, unbarred glass.

I became aware, after a while, that Mamma had stopped talking, and I looked at her sitting in the seat beside me, asleep. The bus pitched and turned, jostling her head on her chest. She was an old, timeworn woman. Deep lines of age cut her face, and her hands were cracked and spotted from the years.

This woman, who had carried me in her body, was someone I never really knew. Everything about her was unfamiliar, and yet we had fought, almost to our death, perhaps only for the sake of fighting. I could not say. Perhaps the battle between us might now end, for surely, I thought, there could be nothing left to fight about. Mamma and I had waged a long and bloody war, and the causes of the battles had been lost in the attacks.

She was old. Her life, at most, was nearly over, and I wondered if her last years would be mellow. We would have a slim existence for a while, but in time I knew that I would be able to give her some of the basic comforts. I wanted to work at something, but according to my parole, I could not. Lawmakers have a certain wisdom and consideration, for who would employ a crazy woman just out of the asylum? But when "recovered" was stamped on my record, I could seek work. Until then we had to live on Mamma's mysterious avenue of supply.

She moved in her sleep. Her eyes twitched behind the locked lids. Her fingers creaked, and as I looked at her, I was able to release any anger harboring within me.

Carefully, feeling almost like I might be putting my hand in a trap, I eased my arm around her shoulder and let her head rest against me. I steadied it as the bus turned and moved its way toward home.

Her breathing was deep and contented as I held her tucked against me, and, so no one could hear and invade this one uncomplicated moment, I whispered to myself, I love you, Mamma.

12

The armistice between us was shattered on my first morning home. Before I had finished breakfast, a flock of reporters began arriving at the house. Mamma, on her never-ending quest for the limelight, had notified the local papers and wire services of my release. She had even extended them a personal invitation to come to the house to interview me.

I was furious at this, but I knew that if I let a glimmer of hostility show, the reporters would sense it and a series of distorted stories would reappear. My only recourse was to smile and pose while fielding a barrage of humiliating questions that ranged from rude queries into my personal life to solicitations of what it was really like to be an inmate in a state institution.

I was shocked to find that Mamma had saved all the fan mail that had accumulated during my internment, and when she blithely suggested they might like a "heartwarming" picture of me reading it, I gritted my teeth but patiently obliged by curling up on the sofa, and pretending, for the sake of the cameramen, to be absorbed in the stacks of yellowing letters that were heaped around me.

When they had drained all the schmaltz from that pose, one of the photographers suggested getting a picture of me with my dog. In spite of the disgust I felt over the experience, I have kept this news picture for my records. The caption reads: "Miss Farmer receives an enthusiastic reception from her pet dog, Sheba, who went into ecstasies as soon as her mistress returned from the State Hospital."

The picture shows Sheba standing on her hind legs reaching up to lick my face. This is the same animal Mamma testified I had tortured.

To pacify everyone, I admitted to "glowing health and mental competency" and, for the most part, gave printable quotes. Through it all, Mamma was running inside and out with a steaming coffee pot, her way of insisting that everyone make himself at home, and doing whatever she could to lure them into just one more picture. And the neighbors, who a little over a year ago had watched me being hauled from the house in a straitjacket, now lined the sidewalks lapping up the razzle-dazzle of flashbulbs and reporters.

Finally, I feigned exhaustion, and everyone left. Their leaving was none too soon. I was so incensed with Mamma that I had the maddening urge to take my fists and hammer her to a pulp. All else paled in comparison to the scorching wrath that was close to exploding in me.

She seemed completely unaware that she might have deeply offended me, but instead busied herself with straightening up the fan mail. I stood behind her, clenching and unclenching my fist, to keep from hitting her in the back, and only when she turned, suddenly sensing my presence, did she recognize my fury and, true to her fashion, began an artful maneuver to demean it with her own accusations.

"Don't you stand there and give me your dirty looks," she roared. "I'm trying to make something out of your life again, and don't think you're going to mess it up."

I knocked the bundle of letters out of her arms and shoved her onto the couch.

"Listen to me, Mamma," I screamed. "You keep your goddamned nose out of my business or someday you're going to push me an inch too far and, so help me, I'll kill you."

In response, she threw up her hands, waving them like banners of war and let out a bloodcurling howl as she bounded out of the front door, shouting for help. I grabbed her before she was off the front porch and yanked her back into the house. I slapped my hand over her mouth and muffled her shrieks. I had learned the ins and outs of fighting in the asylum, and she was no match for me. In spite of her kicking and struggling, I hurled her back on the sofa with one final warning.

"Don't you ever again mention my name to any reporter, or dare give out another story about me. If you do, Mamma, you'll regret it. And if you know what's good for you, you'll keep your mouth shut around me, too, for I haven't a thing to talk to you about. With your 'help,' I've damn near wrecked my life and I hate the very thought of you."

I threw her roughly aside but she crouched on the rim of the sofa, open-mouthed. To give final imprint to my warning, I took my finger and jabbed her soundly in the chest.

"You sweat it out for a change, old lady," I growled. "And keep out of my way. And another thing, don't start that look-what-I've-done-for-you crap, either, because I've paid tenfold for this goddamned house and everything in it. All you've ever done for me is nothing. Nothing! So just keep the hell out of my way, or else!"

I had frightened her and I relished it. For the first time in my life, I saw fear in her, and for several days after that she scampered around the house like a timid field mouse. I did not regret the severance nor did I feel guilty about it. I had no desire, however remote, to seek even a superficial reconciliation with her.

I was through! Finished! As far as I was concerned, the war was over. I had lost it, and I knew what the eventual outcome would be, but even that did not disturb me. I knew she would bide her time until she could recommit me, but I was not afraid. In fact, I waited, with a curiosity of sorts, to see what overt act would finally provoke her to the point of sending me back.

Why she had petitioned and arranged my release was a puzzle, unless she genuinely believed that I would pick up my career in Hollywood. In her mind, I suppose, she still envisioned me as a star, but, in reality, I was something Hollywood wanted to forget. Although I still rated exploitation in the papers, I had been swept under the rug and was best left there. I was bad news, and there wasn't a legitimate studio willing to take the risk. I was notorious. From the time of my arrest in Santa Monica, I had become open and fair game.

The vivid truth of this struck home one day when I found a bulging scrapbook in a desk drawer. Mamma had carefully kept the clippings in chronological order, and through them I viewed my rise and fall as reported by the press.

Everything was there in lurid detail. I saw pictures of myself fighting with policemen. I read the one-sided accounts of a screaming match between me and a judge that ended with him shouting down a jail sentence. I read reports that I had broken the jaw of a hairdresser in a fight at the studio. I saw stories in movie magazines, given by some of my "closest friends," to the effect: Poor Frances had always acted peculiar.

I saw pictures of me on the cover of *Life* magazine.

I learned, through a news clipping, that my husband, Erickson, had divorced me and remarried the same day. I read where I was declared insane.

Some of the reports blamed my smashup on liquor. To some, I was a hopeless alcoholic. And then, I read where I was an addict. It was reported that in court I had said, "They sneak benzedrine in my orange juice to keep me alive." From that, it was assumed that I had been driven insane by dope.

Then I read where I supposedly had said that all that was the matter with me was a broken heart, and the sob sisters picked it up and assumed that I was so disturbed over my bust-up with my husband that I had been driven mad. God!

I read on and on of all my ills, temper and idiosyncracies. I was "Hollywood's Cinderella girl gone back to the ashes on a liquor-slicked highway."

It was easy to see that the party was over, and all that was left of the glitter and gold was shoddy speculation and a label that I would never be able to shed.

Day after day, I spent hours pouring over the scrapbook, studying the clippings and reading each article time and time again. I clung, abnormally, to the book and read about a woman, me, whom I had never really known.

I could not deny the pictures, crass though they were, but neither could I accept the final conclusion that they were of me. They were of a stranger, and I brooded over this. I would sit in front of the mirror studying my face, then compare it to the features of the woman in the photographs. In my mind's eye there was no relationship or similarity. The majority of the incidents were vague. Most of Hollywood was a blur, but as I read about myself, I had to consider the reports as something near the truth. Yet none of it seemed real. It was all too bizarre and unlikely.

I read that I personally boycotted Japan as early as 1939 by refusing to wear silk clothes, and there was a big news splash about my attempts to get all the leading actresses to join in my boycott.

I read of my efforts for the Loyalists in the Spanish Revolution, and the reporting of this was none too kind. Then I read where I had gathered a quarter of a million signatures to petition the government to subsidize the theater with federal grants, and there was a picture of me personally delivering the petition to the Secretary of State.

I mulled over the success I had on Broadway starring in *Golden Boy,* and it was from this specific point in my career that I noticed the news copy about me changing. If the reporting was accurate, it seems that from Broadway on I was rude, critical and demeaning toward the motion picture industry. I appeared to belittle everything about it.

A picture taken of me on the set of *Flowing Gold,* a mediocre film made after my return from the stage, showed me drenched with mud, and the story was that Hollywood had, at last, gotten even with me when the director insisted on fourteen retakes of a scene that called for me to fall facedown in a mud puddle. It was now the industry's turn to throw it, and the trade seemed delighted in the get-even method that was used.

Things began to go bad for me when I dropped Hollywood to work with the Group Theater on Broadway. To do so, I demanded a release from my contract at Paramount, and I went off salary. In spite of all the consequences I reached the peak of professional fulfillment while working with the Group.

Unfortunately, I was slow to realize that it was not so much my talent they wanted but only my name, and they had used it to get *Golden Boy* on the boards. Nevertheless, it was meaningful to me, and I willingly worked for minimum salary during the run of the play. Money was no object as long as I could be involved with people I then considered the elite of the theater.

It was during the initial days of *Golden Boy* that I became intimately involved with Clifford Odets, the playwright for the Group, and items began to appear in the gossip columns linking us. Erickson, who was not working in Hollywood, came East and got a modest part in another Broadway production and, for a few weeks, stifled the rumors. But our marriage had collapsed long before I left Hollywood, and in New York, it became such an intolerable arrangement that we finally made a public separation. The reports were that my temperament and ambition had caused the split . . . and perhaps it had. Whatever, I knew that I had to close that episode in my life—and I did.

Odets and I made vague attempts to avoid attracting public attention, for at the time he was married to a European actress who had two Academy Awards tucked safely under her belt, but who also knew of the financial woes of both the Group and her husband. She calmly remained aloof to the difficulties and machinations that spewed in all directions.

Golden Boy was an acclaimed hit, though somewhat controversial in its leftist leanings, and I went on the road with the company when it closed on Broadway. During this time, plans were made for me to take the show to London at the end of the American run. I notified my agent in Hollywood and asked for an extended release on my contract. I made definite arrangements to tour abroad. Members of the Group were not given to prudence in their expenditures. They were broke, but a search for money produced total backing for the London engagement, providing a specific actress would play the lead.

Without bothering to tell me of the change in plans, even though I was with them every day, they notified the press that someone else would take the show to England in my place. I was left with quite a bit of artistic egg sticking on my face. I had been unceremoniously dumped.

Later, when times were bad again, members of the Group showed up on my doorstep broke and jobless. They came time and again, asking for personal loans. These amounted to nothing more than handouts, for they were never repaid. One of the leading directors of the Group not only borrowed three thousand dollars from me to get himself "established," as he called it, but also lived at my home until he was able to find a job. Later, my father tried to collect from him, but this director, who is now a Broadway legend of sorts, denied the debt.

Even Sophie Rosenstein, who had initially taught me that Hollywood was a wormy apple and a jug factory, sought me out and asked me to use my influence to get her a position in the drama department at one of the studios. I did this without questioning the fact that she had compromised, and the things she had taught me in college were never mentioned between us.

In spite of everything and regardless of the personal frustrations, I was, for a while, a working part of the theatrical legend. I lived and worked with heroes, but I can now look back on the Group Theater dispassionately and recognize the flaws and tawdry maneuverings that went on within the cult. It was eventually destroyed by these flaws. In principle, it vehemently denied the capitalistic system yet sought it as a bed partner. It scoffed at money, but stooped to anything in order to acquire it. When the chips were down, art was not the high and mighty God. Plain cash talked.

Unrealistic though it might appear, the shock of having my faith in the theatrical ideology shaken was the first and heaviest blow leading to my smashup. And perhaps such a total commitment would appear naive and even foolish to a layman. Nevertheless my hopes and my Valhalla had always been with the Group, and when I was finally shocked into realizing that I had been nothing more to them than a rung on a ladder, I lost faith in almost everything else. My artistic id was clobbered to shreds, and the emotional trauma that climaxed the relationship with Odets finished the job.

His ardent and bold attachment, his promise of marriage ended with a wire to my hotel which read, "My wife returns from Europe today, and I feel it best for us never to see each other again." That was the last I ever heard from him.

He was a man who had sought me out and who had convinced me that my place was on Broadway. He had mocked and belittled my marriage and had done everything a man could do to convince a woman that he was in love with her.

The profession knew what had gone on between us and everyone had been waiting in the wings, so to speak, for the last laugh. It came when he jilted me. It seemed that I was the last to know that his "love" had been nothing more than a well-planned effort to keep me involved in the productions. I was good box office, and I was needed in that respect. I can admit only that I was still naive enough to be hoodwinked.

Odets was a strange, almost ugly man, but he was everything I could ever imagine, at that time, admirable in a man. He was a fiery, fascinating intellect with strange sexual drives, and I reacted like a smitten schoolgirl. I believed in him passionately, and I was radical in my defense of his work. I drowned myself in his doctrines and political theories, and had he not severed the affair, I probably would have followed him to his far-left politics.

As it was, when Congress started investigating Communist infiltration in the arts, I was safely tucked away in an asylum. I wonder what I would have said if I had been called to testify before the committee. Knowing my penchant for truth, I would no doubt have provided the rope to hang many of the industry's luminaries.

The card carriers lied through their teeth, but no one was fooled, and careers that had bloomed quickly fell to oblivion . . . as well they should.

Odets maneuvered me as he would a character in one of his plays. He toyed with my attitudes and reactions. He was a psychological button-pusher, able to crush me with a word or sweep me into ecstasy with a gesture.

One moment he would marvel at my brilliance and minutes later he would curse me for my stupidity. Sometimes, locked with me in his apartment, he would plead like a schoolboy for love and favors, and then, suddenly and with insulting accusations, he would assault me as though I were a streetwalker.

From the time he first singled me out and asked me to appear in *Golden Boy,* I was mesmerized. The serpent beguiled me and I did eat. He would insult me in front of everyone, belittling my performance, and he was satisfied only when he had reduced me to tears and sent me sobbing to my dressing room.

There were times after such incidents when he

would not speak to me for two or three days. At other times, he would force his way into my dressing room and make a great point of not only locking the door behind him, but further securing the room by propping a chair under the doorknob, and then he would tear off his clothes and scream his love and need for me with all the fire and passion of a Rococo Thespian. He would threaten to take his life and mine, unless I loved him. The fact that I was genuinely attached to this man compelled me to try to gratify his physical appetite. His sexual behavior was a complicated maze of weird manipulations. He would deftly maneuver me to a point of fulfillment, then withdraw and mock what he termed my base and disgusting desires. After searing my feminine spirit in this bed of humiliation and degrading me in every possible manner, he would begin again with the shyness of an innocent lad and explore me with tender fascination.

This was no ordinary man. He was a creature who pried open the psyche with the intention of sticking it with pins. I cannot say that I loved him; a more apt description would be a passionate hatred coupled with a physical fascination. Whatever it was, it did much to destroy me.

Whereas I had once lived secure within myself, after Odets I became a bundle of raw hesitant nerves, confused and almost without purpose. And it was during my affair with him that I became dependent on liquor. Whenever we had been together for any period of time, he would invariably destroy what beauty had been shared between us, and in the hours that followed, I unfortunately began to rely on drinks to see me through.

While I was struggling with this, Shepard Traube, the man who had been instrumental in securing my screen tests, brought a seventy-five-thousand-dollar breach of contract lawsuit against me. The suit stated that I had failed to pay him 10 percent of my salary over the years for his representation. I claimed his representation had been solely on that one contract, and the subsequent trial and the trauma of a court battle (which incidentally came out in my favor) added fuel to an already-roaring emotional fire. I sensed that I was being pushed to a disastrous brink.

When *Golden Boy* closed, I went into rehearsal of a play called *Thunder Rock,* but I was no longer able to cope with the building pressures and I found myself trying to keep my stability by drinking even more.

To study a scrapbook that pinpoints your life in detail is an eerie experience, and I found myself absorbed in reliving the rapid-fire events that eventually defeated me. As I read, I came to the uncomplicated conclusion that what finally whipped me was simply overwork.

To recapitulate, in 1936 I began my Hollywood stand by making a quick movie called *Too Many Parents* and married Erickson. During March and April, I made *Border Flight.* In May, I was filming *Rhythm on the Range.* From these I immediately went into the heavy production of *Come and Get It.* Then I was signed to do *Ebb Tide* with Ray Milland, working on that set during the day, and at night shooting scenes for *Toast of New York* with Cary Grant. Before *Toast* was finished, I was working on *Exclusive* with Fred MacMurray.

In August, 1937, I went East, where I did summer stock in Westport, Connecticut, and starred in *Little Women* and *The Petrified Forest.*

In September of that year, I went into rehearsal

with *Golden Boy.* The play ran through May, and after the Traube lawsuit was settled, I left immediately for Hollywood and was cast with, of all people, Erickson. We made a dreary movie called *Escape from Yesterday,* but I muddled through.

A news clipping from the New York *Times* brought back memories. I read:

> Paramount is pleased with the tranquility surrounding Frances Farmer's brief resumption of her screen career. Following her substantial Broadway stage engagement of "Golden Boy," the studio rather expected fireworks when it came to casting her. However, when she was assigned a role in the modest film "Escape from Yesterday," there was no objection from the star, who attained note for, among other things, giving voice to caustic opinions about Hollywood in her New York interviews.

There were none of the expected fireworks simply because I was too exhausted to bother and too disturbed to care.

I finished this film and returned to New York, where I rented an apartment in Gramercy Park. I remember I spent long hours in solitude trying to establish some balance in my life.

In September of that year, 1938, the Group sent one of its most persuasive ambassadors to lure me into the road tour of *Golden Boy,* and I accepted. We opened in Chicago to good reviews and ended the run in Washington, D.C., in December.

While in Washington I made a point of meeting the Spanish Ambassador to the United States, Dr. Don Fernando de Los Rios, and at the embassy I kicked off a national drive by donating large amounts of food to the children of Spain.

In January, 1939, back in New York and under Elia Kazan's direction, I went into rehearsal of *Quiet City,* a play by Irwin Shaw. In April the play was closed after a short, unsuccessful run. In May I appeared on the *Kate Smith Dramatic Hour,* a radio program, opposite Luther Adler in *Men in White.* I also went into summer stock that month in Mapleton, New Jersey, and worked in the East through August.

In mid-September, I began rehearsal of Robert Ardrey's *Thunder Rock.* It opened in New York on November 14th and ran for twenty-three performances.

Franchot Tone was cast opposite me and played an unforgettable role in my dilemma. Every day I was finding myself more and more keyed up and drinking heavily. I was having desperate bouts with myself and my id, and all through rehearsal and the short run of the play, Tone would invariably make his way close to me and whisper dreadful things, repeating comments from Odets and calling me a lush and a whore. I loathed this offensive man, and his crude talking did much to grate further my already-raw nerves.

I was so disturbed after the play closed that I refused to see anyone and stayed locked in my apartment. This went on for several days, and then the Theatre Guild offered me *The Fifth Column,* a production in which most of the Group Theater was involved. I went into rehearsal an emotional wreck. I was also near physical collapse. We were hardly into rehearsal when I called a halt to everything, and left the show. Catherine Locke replaced me, and due to my walkout I was fined fifteen hundred dollars. This was also the end of the Group Theater. It had fallen apart and degenerated into a jealous, temperamental pack. Only remnants remained of the original hotbed of genius.

In February, 1940, I returned to Hollywood, and in March I was on radio in a play called *Woman in the Wilderness,* an appropriate title for my personal quandary. On the sixth of March I began work on *South of Pago Pago* opposite Jon Hall, and in July started shooting *Flowing Gold,* with an ex-Group member named John Garfield. When *Gold* was finished, I went back East for another season of stock.

By the end of the summer run I was in serious condition, but the only thing I knew to do about it was to barricade myself against everyone and in privacy try to understand what was happening to me. If I had had a friend at that time or anyone who cared about me, perhaps things might have taken a different direction. As it was, word was out that I was a hopeless drunk.

Nevertheless I stayed through the winter and left New York in March, spending two months driving alone across the country. I stayed in out-of-the-way places, hoping that I would not be recognized, and I registered with my married name, Mrs. William Anderson. I had little success traveling incognito until I bought a black wig and a pair of dime-store glasses. With this rather simple disguise I managed to finish the trip in nervous privacy.

Arriving in Hollywood at the end of April, I decided to throw caution to the wind. I had always lived modestly, but if I was a star, I would like to live like one before everything crashed around me. I rented Dolores Del Rio's former home in Santa Monica and surrounded myself with the trappings of the "idle rich." A butler whom I didn't know what to do with, and a staff of servants who completely baffled me. Alone, spending hours on end brooding about my life and its dark aspects, I rattled around the house for a few weeks and then invited Mamma down. She arrived and adjusted to the luxury with the flair of a dowager queen. She had visited me in New York, on several occasions, but did not respond to Broadway as she did to Hollywood. It pleased me, at that time, to spoil her, and we would eat together in the great dining room and chuckle over what a far cry it was from the tiny kitchen in Seattle.

I especially enjoyed my private suite. The bedroom had a glass roof and I was able to lie in bed during the day and watch the clouds. At night I could look deep and long into the stars.

At the end of April, 1941, I began a film called *World Premiere,* in which I costarred with John Barrymore. He was so dissipated at the time that he moved and spoke by rote. He would reel up to me and try to say something, then his pale watery eyes would go blank and he would stumble off to his dressing room muttering to himself. He was already a dead man. His career had become a mockery and there was nothing left of him as an actor, but even so, it was still a deep pleasure for me to have worked with someone who had given so much to the American theater.

In May I began a film with Susan Hayward called *Among the Living*—which I was not. I was, rather, an emotional zombie, but on the day this film was finished in July, I began shooting *The Bad Lands of Dakota* with Robert Stack.

When the picture was finally completed, I knew I had to have a rest, and since Mamma was still in Hollywood with me, she suggested that we take a vacation in Mexico. Being physically drained, I saw everything through a haze. Mamma, a devoted tourist, wore me out. The vacation in Mexico did nothing except emphasize my exhaustion and deepen my sense of melancholy.

When we finally returned to Hollywood, I convinced her that she should wind up her vacation and head for Seattle. She was reluctant to leave, but I finally put her on the train for home.

Desperately needing privacy, I spent the months of August and September, 1942, completely alone. I knew within myself that I was beginning to slip away, and I lived with the eternal fear that there was nothing that I could do about it. I was afraid to see a doctor, and I was afraid not to. I was in no condition to make any kind of a decision, and so again I did the worst thing I could possibly do: I locked myself away from any hope of help and remained alone. In every sense of the word there was no one whom I could trust. This was not the fancies of an ill woman, but was a reality, for Hollywood has never been known for its brotherhood.

Drinking did not enter the picture at this time. For that matter, it was only when I was in New York that I felt the desperate need to escape and used this means to transport myself.

I turned down all film offers during this phase, and I filled my time by beginning to write my memoirs. At first, the ego that prompted this undertaking amused me, but, as the manuscript grew, I realized that perhaps through this self-examination I might be able to purge myself. Ruthlessly I delved into the darkest crevices of my mind and came to rather startling conclusions. I was unloving and unloved. I was completely detached and void of all involvements. Absolutely nothing or no one mattered to me. I was miserably unhappy, and as I wrote, I would have long hysterical crying bouts.

I stayed completely to myself during this period until one night I gave in to the repeated urging of an actor with whom I had worked, and I agreed to go to a party being held at the home of Deanna Durbin. Having decided to make a quick appearance and be off, I insisted on driving myself.

It had been several months since I had gone out socially, and as I dressed, I remember taking two or three drinks to prod my lagging enthusiasm.

As I left the house that night of October 19, 1942, I nearly changed my mind. I sat in my car, debating and arguing with myself, and, had it not been for the recollection of having once spent an extremely pleasant afternoon with Miss Durbin and her husband, I would probably have gone back into the house and followed my usual habit of going to bed early.

At this time, the coast of California was under dimout restrictions. But I admit to having my mind on other things and I forgot about being in a dim-out zone. For that matter, I was so personally disturbed about my private war, that I remember driving along and growing more and more apprehensive about the social commitment ahead of me.

The thought of being with people was so distressing and even terrifying that I suddenly burst into tears. I pulled the car to the side of the road and buried my head against the steering wheel, oblivious to everything except my most intimate misery. Unfortunately, I neglected to turn off my lights.

I cannot recall how much time passed before a motorcycle policeman pulled alongside and approached the car as though he expected to find, at least, Tokyo Rose behind the wheel. He bellowed out one accusation and insult after another. Infuriated and startled by his manner, I jumped out of the car, still crying, and yelled at him to shut his mouth. I demanded that he give me a ticket for whatever I had done and leave me alone.

To complicate matters, I had left my driver's license in another purse. I made an attempt to identify myself, but instead of recognizing me, he accused me of trying to make a fool of him. By this time I was almost hysterical, and after he insisted on smelling my breath, he accused me of being drunk.

With this we reached a verbal knockdown drag-out, with me yelling at him to keep his goddamned mouth shut. One word brought on another and it ended with him calling a squad car that took me, not peaceably, to the Santa Monica jail, where I was charged with driving without a license and failing to have observed a dim-out zone.

How ironic that what should have been a minor reprimand actually started a landslide. In night court, I was sentenced to one hundred and eighty days and put on probation. Ironic, too, that even though this was a first offense and no other traffic charges had ever been logged against me, the maximum sentence was invoked. I was appalled and shocked, not only by the sentence, but by the flurry of publicity involved in the recording of the incident.

Since my license was suspended and since my car had been impounded by the court at the time of my arrest, I made arrangements for a garage to deliver it to my home. I remember taking a taxi from the court, and when I arrived home, I did the only thing I could think of to protect myself: I refused to see reporters or studio representatives or anyone else who tried to pry into the incident.

Then, alone and feeling terribly sorry for myself, I began to suffer the perils of "if only." Perhaps if only I had followed my inner urging and remained at home that night, none of the calamities that followed would have occurred. Or, perhaps, if only I could have sought the professional care I obviously needed, or, if only I had taken time to rest, I might have been able to handle the complications of my life and career. Or, if only I had found someone who could have loved me and whom I could have loved in return, things might have been different.

As it was, Mamma was having fits in Seattle, insisting on returning to what she called "the scene of the crime." Nothing I could do would dissuade her, until I promised to come to Seattle as soon as possible. I would have agreed to anything to have kept her out of Hollywood at that time, for I knew that, if she showed up, she would get to the press and start spouting her own theories on the incident. She was primed for battle with her cannon loaded. Unfortunately, the fodder turned out to be me.

The month after my arrest I spent in isolation. I cut my household staff to a minimum, with only the housekeeper-cook living in. During the day, I never left my bedroom suite, but at night I roamed the grounds with the darkness safely surrounding me.

I knew I was losing control, and when I examined my life minutely, I was left with the desolation of having nothing of real value. Life was a monotonous, unrewarding prison, and a persistent melancholy cloud hung over me.

I had reached a point where I believed all incidents and relationships, whether impersonal or intimate, seemed to pivot on the fact that I was a movie star. There was no sympathetic concern over a woman who was obviously cracking under emotional pressure. I was a property, something that could draw a certain gross at the box office, and nothing more. The fact that I was troubled or losing touch with reality was passed over. Once, during the filming of *Ebb Tide,* I had collapsed on the set and the studio rushed me to the hospital for a checkup and rest. This should have been a warning sign especially to me, but it went unheeded.

It was as if seeing a locomotive barreling down a track and remaining frozen. I knew my personal defeat lay directly ahead, but I could not stop it. Or could I? Perhaps I was overreacting to a minor incident. The initial press reports of the incident were understated. Yet every word of the account was a looming insult to me personally, for when it was all said and done, I was the one who ended up with an undeserved, humiliating jail record.

I read on in Mamma's scrapbook, where, immediately after the sentencing, I accepted a role in a movie to be shot on location in Mexico. I have vague recollections that my agent urged me to accept this job rationalizing that it was a way for me to get out of Hollywood for a while and let the situation cool off. It made sense, so I, without even asking to see a script, signed with a shoestring production company and was flown to Mexico City in a chartered plane.

As soon as I reached Mexico, I requested a script but everyone stalled, pleading last-minute rewrites. I waited around for two weeks and finally walked out on the part. But before exiting, I left my own unique imprint on the producer by verbally ripping him apart.

I returned to my home in Santa Monica, sullen and annoyed, and to my horror found it occupied by a strange family. When they would not let me in, I thought some bizarre prank was being played on me. In no humor for jokes I called my agent, screaming.

He finally got through to me that he had sublet the house, thinking it was best not to run up extra bills while I was out of the country. This surpassed his authority and I thought at the time that something was indeed beginning to rot in Denmark.

To my further amazement, he went on to say that my "things" had been moved to the Knickerbocker Hotel, where a room had been taken in my name.

"My things," as he called them, could not have possibly been contained in a single hotel accommodation, and had I been able to reason things out at that time, there might have been some way for me to protect my property.

I went to the Knickerbocker, and when I inquired at the desk, I was given the key to my room. In it, I found a few clothes and nothing more. Every personal possession was gone, and I flew apart.

There is nothing quite so exasperating as a run-around executed by experts, and I heard more feeble excuses about my vanished property than I could possibly remember. I hit a blank wall wherever I turned.

I finally gave up trying to find my personal effects, but I kept hounding everyone I knew, asking for the manuscript I had been writing. This was the only thing that really mattered to me. I had not written it as an exposé, but evidently someone had read it during my absence, sensed the danger in it, and must have ultimately destroyed it. While I was in Mexico someone had thoroughly and deliberately cleaned me out, but to this day I have never been able to prove who or why. However there is every indication that the spoils were divided, for only three years ago I received an anonymous package at my home. It contained an expensive cut-glass decanter that had been a part of my property while I lived in California. When I opened the package, I wondered what strange twinge of conscience had prompted the return of an item looted three decades past.

I had reported my loss to the police, but when I could not give an itemized inventory of the missing goods, they claimed they could not help me . . . and this is probably true. I must have made little sense to them, accusing unknown culprits of stealing property that I could neither list nor remember in detail.

All this happened just before Christmas of 1942, and I remember spending the holidays in solitude. And then, early in January, I began working on a King Brothers film, ironically called *There Is No Escape*.

By this time a good part of me was slipping away. I heard myself talking in a voice that was not mine. I was aware that I was behaving in a peculiar manner. I wanted to run, I wanted to get away from everyone.

I was suffering severe head pains almost constantly, and it frightened me to find that I had also developed a nervous twitch in one eye. My head hurt so that I could hardly bear to have my hair combed, and sitting for makeup was a nerve-wracking chore.

There were times when I knew that I was incoherent, and yet the studio was determined to get one more scene out of me regardless of the personal consequences. A great deal of money was riding on a product, me, and every effort was made to secure the expected profits.

I knew I would not be able to finish the picture, and after trying to get through one particularly difficult day, I had to call a halt. I remember going back to the hotel, somehow getting to my room, and actually feeling myself collapse.

I knew then it was all over. I had drained the pond

dry. I remember undressing and not bothering to put on nightclothes. I took a sleeping pill and waited, facedown, for it to take effect, then in the wee hours of the morning I was shot out of my sleep when the police began hammering on my door demanding that I "open up." To be startled from an induced sleep is bewildering, but it is even more so when the law is confronting you with a warrant for your arrest. It was a frightening experience for me. I was confused and touched paranoia in that I thought, at first, that another weird prank was being played on me.

Of course I would not open my door, and of course they would not leave. Finally, they forced admission into my room with a passkey, and two of them came toward me with handcuffs and a drawn gun. I knew then that it was no prank.

I cannot recall all the assorted violence and confusion that followed. I was naked and putting up one hell of a fight. I remember locking myself in the bathroom, and when they finally broke down the door, they found me hiding behind the shower curtain.

I still had no idea as to why I was being arrested, nor was I informed. This being the case, and considering my disposition, it follows that I did not agree to go peaceably, to say the least. Standing in the tub with the shower curtain wrapped around me, I was handed the warrant by a police matron.

I began to fight, and it took the two policemen and the matron to dress me. Later, reports were handed to the press that I had danced nude in front of the officers, but in truth I was only trying to find something to wrap around me when they broke into my room.

After I was dressed haphazardly, I was bodily hauled through the hotel lobby, kicking and screaming. Anchored between the two policemen, I was put in the squad car. When I began a fight with the matron who rode in the back seat with me, they stopped the car and a wrestling match ensued until I was in handcuffs.

I was terrified. Everything was becoming confused.

It all came back to me, as I read the clippings in Mamma's scrapbook and saw the horrible pictures she had so carefully trimmed and pasted for posterity. This was the first time I had ever seen the full-blown newspaper accounts of the incident, and it jarred me.

From the hotel, I was driven directly to the Santa Monica jail and put in a cell. I was still uninformed as to the cause of my arrest. The disgusting thing to me is that the law set out to serve a warrant on me but first called the press and obviously invited them along to record the proceedings. There were photographers and reporters at the hotel, and after I was put in a cell, they were allowed to shoot pictures of me through the bars. One of them requested that the cell door be opened so that he could get better shots, and the police obliged.

The next morning, when I was taken into the courtroom, I learned then that I had been arrested for violating probation. When I tried, at first calmly, to reason with the judge, asking for more explicit explanations, I was told that unless I kept silent I would be held in contempt of court. I was still without legal representation at that time, and I was not permitted either to call a lawyer or postpone the hearing until I could retain one.

With that, it swung into a three-ring circus, fit for the citizens of Rome. The judge was offended by me and I was appalled by him. The reporters and photographers were having a field day, and while I was loudly trying to explain that I was unaware that I was expected to report weekly to a probation officer whose name I did not know, the judge attempted to hammer me into silence with his gavel.

When I finally realized that I was actually going to be sentenced to serve the 180 days in jail, I exploded. The judge, redfaced with anger, shouted orders to the police to take me to the Los Angeles County Jail, but I cut him short. I grabbed an inkwell off the bench and threw it at him, with perfect aim. I then did everything I could to destroy the courtroom. It finally took five policemen and a straitjacket to subdue me.

Pictures of the infamous incident were splattered across every front page with blow-by-blow accounts. I trembled as I reread them in the scrapbook and wondered why Mamma had wanted to save such horrible reminders. Why should a mother seek to nurture a recorded decline of her child?

I knew I was considered offbeat and uncooperative as an actress, but every report of this incident, except one, seemed to relish in my fall. I was the brat, the smart-aleck who finally got her comeuppance, and the pictures printed were shocking. I had to force myself to accept that they were really of me.

I went back to the scrapbook time and time again, hunting for evidence of better days, but always I returned to the scene of the crash, mesmerized by the printed account of the destruction.

My downhill slide was in full gear, and when I was in the Los Angeles jail, I was booked for the work detail, which of course I had no intention of doing. I still had not seen a lawyer, but I never stopped screaming and fighting for my civil rights. But if anyone heard, no one answered.

Then Mamma appeared on the scene, hotfooting it down from Seattle, and called her own press conference. It was through her interviews given during that period that reports of possible mental derangement appeared. It was Mamma who planted the first seed.

True, I was acting like a raving lunatic, and I was deep in the throes of a nervous collapse, but Mamma started the ball rolling by insisting on a sanity hearing. She said point-blank that I was crazy.

The next article in her scrapbook confirmed the court order declaring me a mental incompetent. I also read where the county, upon investigating my case, had found that I was "without funds." I was broke, but rather than have me committed to an institution, the Screen Actors Guild requested that I be sent to a private sanitarium.

In the meantime, Mamma had succeeded in being appointed my legal guardian, and in one legal swoop I lost all my civil liberties.

These actions were perpetrated without my ever having had a lawyer of my choice, and I was to wage a long, hard battle before I could again regain the security of citizenship.

There was only one columnist who came out in my defense, and today I still keep a copy of this report as one of my most valued possessions. John Rosenfield wrote:

WHAT HAPPENED TO FRANCES FARMER SHOULDN'T HAVE HAPPENED AT ALL

Just when the movie industry is winning the public's attitude and admiration, Hollywood breaks out in a rash of petty scandals. It is not a tribute to a part of the press that some of these episodes have been played well beyond their merits of news.

It was the lesser part of sagacity that the industry permitted some of these affairs to get out of hand. The Frances Farmer incident should never have happened. This unusually gifted actress was no threat against law and order or the public safety. Something that began as merely a traffic reprimand grew into a case of personal violence, a serious charge and a jail sentence.

And all because a sensitive high-strung girl was on the verge of a nervous breakdown.

Fortunately, the law came to its senses in time to spare Miss Farmer the ignominy of prison.

Miss Farmer, who is no prodigy of emotional stability or sound business management, needed a lawyer one unhappy night last winter. A helping hand might have extradited her immediately from nothing more than a traffic violation. The terrible truth is that she stood alone, and lost.

I would belabor a point if I continued to stress that what should never have happened did. Now, when I look back over the Hollywood melee, it seems almost as though it never happened to me at all, and yet the horrible truth is that it did.

When I was sent to the private sanitarium, selected and paid for by the Screen Actors Guild, I was encased in a clean, well-appointed hellhole, and the psychologist who headed it was nothing more than a glorified witch doctor.

According to the records that I have acquired in order to authenticate this book, I was put under immediate treatment and subjected to a series of ninety insulin shock treatments over a ninety-day span.

Insulin, now considered an obsolete and ineffective treatment for the mentally ill, was a horrible and brutal physical attack which not only stunned the brain cells, but shocked the body as well and left the patient racked with nausea and pain.

It is difficult to recall the time I spent at the sanitarium or, for that matter, the events that followed during the next weeks. But as I went through Mamma's scrapbook, I read reports where I had been released after six months, so obviously I must have made my way back to Seattle tucked safely under Mamma's court-appointed wing.

Through the scrapbook I was able to trace a path that was dim in my memory, and since it still remains vague in my mind, I cannot relate it as a part of my memoirs. Whatever happened during these periods of blackouts is not a part of my life, as I know it.

Insulin shock succeeded in doing one principal thing to me: It deadened my mind to a point where recall was almost impossible. Electric shock has similar effects, even though the medical claim is that a patient will eventually be able to remember what has been deliberately shocked out of the mind.

I cannot challenge this concrete theory, well documented by those involved in psychiatric research, except to ask if any doctor who theorizes has ever survived three months of daily shock therapy.

I have. Day after day, until I had hardly any faculties left with which to function, and regardless of what is claimed by those devoted to research, there are blank spots left in my mind that have never been filled. There are months of my life that are gone and they never seem to surface, even in fragments.

In some respects, the treatment for the mentally ill has been partially humanized with the advent of tranquilizers, but the effect is still the same on the patient. People are left with great gaps in their recall. So whether it is done with a pill, a shot, or an electrode, the results are still permanent damage.

I faded from the limelight after my release from the sanitarium, with only occasional bits of news as to my whereabouts. It was reported that I was committed briefly to a state hospital and released, only to be committed again. Mamma had not had time to clip the pictured reports of my last release. But being in a house, even under the strained conditions that existed between us, had a gradual healing effect.

I began to listen for all the everyday sounds that are so taken for granted. The evening paper hitting the front door. The relief of looking through a window without bars. The neighborhood sounds of cars starting in the early morning and of children leaving for school. The security of sleeping in a room and closing the door for privacy. The pleasure of a morning cup of coffee or of sitting on a porch at twilight and listening to the quiet sounds of evening. These, and so many more, gradually came back to me and became a part of my life again. Inch by inch, despite the handicaps, I was learning how to function in an everyday world, but I was also adhering to Mamma's law that I could not leave the house.

Since her press conference we had stayed as clear of each other as possible, and even when Papa would show up on Friday nights for his regular weekend at home, we exchanged very few words.

He was a man I had always wanted to love, but the gulf between us was too wide for either of us to bridge it. I never inwardly expected or even dared hope that he would switch his loyalties and abandon Mamma in my behalf; he obeyed her even though they still lived apart.

The good manners and gentle weaknesses that had

somewhat endeared him to me over the years left me
frustrated and cold. Now he seemed almost like a whin-
ing dog. Obviously my strength and determination to
survive flowed from Mamma's bloodline. Papa never
had any strong convictions, and his routine of arriving on Friday evening and puttering around the house
for the weekend irritated me until I finally reached a
state where I did not even want to look at him.

Mamma still bullied him and he still irritated her
with his feeble retaliatory jibes. He also made ag-
gravating efforts at insignificant conversations with me.
He wanted to talk but refused to answer any questions
I had or discuss with me anything relating to my commitments. I wanted to know why he had stood by and
allowed Mamma to suck the very life out of me. When
I would confront him with it, he would shake his head
and walk away. But he always turned back just long
enough to ask that I try not to cause any more trouble.

This went on for three weekends, and during the
intervening days Mamma and I had almost nothing to
do with each other. We ate separately, each fixing her
own meals, and whenever she would come into a room,
I would leave it. Only the barest communication went
on between us.

One morning, after an extremely trying weekend
with Papa, I noticed that not only had she straightened
the living room (which was rare), but she was also
wearing her best dress. Thank God, I thought, perhaps she is going out to visit with someone for a few
hours or go downtown shopping. When the doorbell
rang, Mamma rushed to answer it. The actress Zasu
Pitts came in. From the hallway, wrapped in a skimpy
housecoat, I stared at her in shock.

Mamma fluttered in excitement over the visit, outdoing even Zasu and her famous nerves. The only course left open to me was to hide in my room and refuse to come out. Nothing could have forced me to sit and talk to this woman whom I'd never met before.

But my disappearance did not hamper Mamma in the least. She kept up a faint "Yoo-hoo, Frances, dear. Come down now" routine and succeeded in keeping the poor woman there for nearly an hour. When Miss Pitts was finally able to escape her hospitality, Mamma came charging up to my room, clutching her autograph book and spitting fire.

I had insulted her in front of her favorite actress, and in so doing, I had humiliated her beyond repair. It seems that she had phoned Miss Pitts at the theater, introduced herself as my mother, given her what I am sure was a soul-searing story about poor Frances wilting away, and gone on to persuade her that a visit from someone from Hollywood would be wonderful therapy for me. I can hear her crooning that if she would just come to the house and let me know that I was still remembered, I would be cured.

I have no way of knowing what the woman must have thought, for that one brief glimpse was our only meeting, but I am sure with Mamma's sales techniques she was coerced into making the trip. I meant absolutely nothing to her, nor she to me, and quite frankly, the last person on earth I ever thought about seeing in the midst of my dilemma was Zasu Pitts.

I let Mamma rave until she had almost run down. Then, without saying a word, I got up, walked over to her, drew back my hand, and slapped her full across the mouth. I grabbed her by the shoulders and shoved her out of the room.

"Don't come near me or I'll kill you."

When I first arrived home, I had taken a table knife

from the kitchen and by wedging it between the door-jamb had used it as a makeshift lock for my room. She must have seen it on the dresser, for she dropped her autograph book and ran out of the house, yelling for help.

I knew there was a possible chance that I might hurt her, but this frightening self-knowledge came not from an insane mind but was born out of desperation. I feared being pushed too far.

I closed my door, wedged in the knife, and went back to bed to wait for the inevitable. When she returned to the house, hours later, Papa was with her. He knocked on my door and asked if I would come out and talk to him. I opened the door and followed him down the stairs.

When we reached the kitchen, where Mamma was waiting, the first thing he said to me was, "Now, Francie, you haven't been acting like my sweet little girl."

And so I hit him. I doubled up my fist and drove it as hard as I could into his face, knocking him off balance. As he fell, Mamma began beating on my back and pulling my hair. I swung my arm around and struck her on the side of her head, throwing her on the floor. I stood in the middle of the shabby kitchen with the two people who happened to be my parents lying at my feet. I studied them for a moment, then said, very quietly, "This is the overt act you've been waiting for. So make your call. You've got good reason now, so for your own good, send me back. If you don't, you'll keep pushing me until something really dreadful happens to us."

Papa crawled over to Mamma and wrapped his arms around her, his face ashen, and for the first time in my life I saw an exchange of affection between them. She leaned her head on his shoulder and trembled.

"Neither of you have any idea who I am, do you?" I said calmly. "You've tried to make me into something that I can never be, and to vindicate yourself and your mistakes, you've pushed me into a corner. I can't escape from you, you know. If I left here, I would be a fugitive, and no matter where I would hide, you'd track me down and bring me back because you've convinced yourselves that I'm insane.

"Mamma, you've done everything that you can to destroy me. You've lied to the doctors and to the press, but most of all, to yourself.

"And, Papa, you're a man of the law and yet you took part in railroading me into an asylum. You made it possible for Mamma to have her way. You helped it happen.

"We are a sorry lot. A sick depraved cartoon. Just look at us. To all appearances you're two old people who have just been beaten up by a crazy daughter, but the three of us know better. But that doesn't matter. What does is that now you have just cause to send me back. So set your legal wheels in motion, Papa, and get it done, all according to law.

"And you, Mamma, rehearse your testimony for the doctors. Make it good this time. Make it good enough to stick. Tell them you're afraid that I'll kill you. And who knows, maybe I will. There's only one thing I want you to remember, and mark it well, the two of you. Don't ever try to see me again. Don't show up on visiting days pretending that everything is all right because I won't see you. I don't want to hear from you or even remember that I have a mother or father. I'll go quietly this time, but don't try to follow me, because

I pray to God that I never have to see either of you ever again."

I left them sitting on the floor staring after me and wearily returned to my room.

When the state car came for me the next morning, I walked between the two attendants without a struggle. I climbed into the back of the security truck and never looked back at the house.

It was only when the door was locked and we began to move that I cried.

13

Violent . . . having qualities in such a degree as to produce a very marked or powerful effect, especially in the way of injury.

Ward . . . a division in a lunatic asylum containing a certain number of beds.

Oxford Universal Dictionary

There can be no chronological narrative, no orderly sequence of events for the following five years of my life. Nor can I specifically remember incidents except in shocking jabs of recall that still jolt my consciousness and affect my behavior.

Five years. Five long bleak years of my life that passed. There were no calendars or days of celebration when work was laid aside. There were no Christmases, for there was no Christ. There were no Easters, for there were no resurrections. Days were hammered out hour by hour.

So I cannot say it all began in such and such a manner. I only faintly remember the first shock of being physically shoved into the cage. But I must attempt to relate the horrors as I recall them, in the hope that some force for mankind might be moved to relieve forever the unfortunate creatures who are still imprisoned in the back wards of decaying institutions.

I write with the passionate plea that lawmakers pause in their deliberations to remember the more than one-half-million souls currently committed to state or county mental institutions, and the other half-million confined to homes for the mentally retarded. I ask for extreme efforts and charitable assistance for the millions who exist as outpatients, neither sane nor insane.

Never console yourself into believing that the terror has passed, for it looms as large and evil today as it did in the despicable era of Bedlam.

Is this a humane and civilized society when the legislature of one of the most progressive states in Midwest America refused to appropriate the necessary funds to permit those housed in mental institutions or homes for the retarded to bathe twice a month instead of the authorized once a month? The argument against was that the state budget could not cope with the additional increase in the cost of soap and water. This means that children, the aged, the bedridden, and the crippled are not given the simple human consideration of a bath every two weeks but are left to endure their own stench for a month at a time. Twelve baths a year. Yet this same legislature appropriated an adequate fund to replace and to refurbish the picnic tables at roadside parks.

In every state there have been recurring scandals of flagrant misappropriation of funds in mental hospitals or homes for the retarded. A tour of some of the more decent wards accessible to the public would shock the average citizen into action. But since the conditions still exist, it appears that few are interested.

A meal taken in the children's ward would turn a strong stomach, and even a brief glance at the filth and decayed garbage would offend the pious conscience of the most fervent antilitter campaigner. Rats, roaches, spoiled vegetables, malfunctioning plumbing, irresponsible, poorly paid and often neurotic personnel still abound, and the beatings still occur . . . the abuses still continue.

To see children housed in wards with little supervision or devoted care given to their scarred psyches is shocking. To look at them staring from behind bars, their innocent eyes asking "Why am I here?" "Why doesn't someone come?" "Where is the world I want to see?" primes a sense of helpless frustration.

To see the old wandering through lost memories, slumped on rough wooden benches, bare-gummed, vacant-eyed, dirt caking their hands, trembling in fear and grief should cause passionate despair; and yet they are forgotten.

To find patients who have been confined thirty, even forty, years because no one wants them at home, no one wants to be bothered, is a moral crime.

Go to any state or county, and look into the ancient buildings or behind the modern façades. Search through the long dim corridors and peek into the grieved souls of the patients . . . and then say to yourself, if you can, "Things are getting better." Indeed, in comparison to our times, they regress, and the terror of insanity still screams into unresponsive ears. And so, as I recall the five years that I spent locked in the violent ward of a state asylum, I do so with the knowledge that the same force of evil still lives in so-called hospitals.

My story is not unique.

Patients with a history of readmission (and this was my third) were not processed in the customary manner. They were sent to the back wards which housed the hopelessly insane. It was, and still is, customary that if a tenure of confinement exceeded one year, the patient was considered incurable and no longer given any form of treatment or therapy.

Readmission is a mental death sentence and thus as a recidivist I was not granted a reevaluation of my sanity before Staff. I was taken direct to the ancient barracks where the chronically ill were housed. Set in a compound were crumbling, single-storied stone structures with wooden floors and boarded-up windows. Roofs that did little to keep out the rain or heat covered the overall neglect, and vents in the roofs provided the only air.

I was assigned to Ward T, a long, narrow building, probably eighteen feet wide and at least a half block long. The main ward ran most of the length and was just wide enough to permit two rows of floor mattresses and a narrow aisle between.

Next to the main security door was a vestibule of sorts. This was the nurse and orderly station and ran the full width of the building. A narrow cage of steel fencing separated the vestibule and the patients' area. The vacant cage served several uses. It was where medication, when available, was administered, and it was the only admitting station for the habitually returned patient.

A narrow gate was the only access from the vestibule, and a padded door served as the entrance into the ward.

In this cage I was told to strip, and my shoes and clothes were taken from me. The orderly then peeled back my fingernails and toenails to the quick and some of them bled. Then my arms and legs were tied to my body with belts and the hair was clipped off my head. This, I learned, was done about three times a year to every patient.

Upon completing his job, the orderly went back to

the vestibule and motioned for me to stand against the fence near him. Poking his fingers through, he unbuckled the belts. I watched, fascinated, as he began turning a large iron wheel mounted on the wall, and I followed the moving chains that worked a pulleylike contraption overhead, and stood there as the padded gate creaked open a scant foot.

The grinding metal stopped, and I felt a pole jab me in the back, pushing me through it. "Move on in." He jabbed me again, and I edged sideways into the screaming, milling mob of naked women.

There was an old woman of perhaps seventy who was completely mad. She could not walk but crawled along the floor, dragging her shrunken legs behind her ... gabbling like a choked animal.

A hairless, purple-veined skull wobbled on a spindly neck spiked onto her rawboned shoulders. The shriveled flesh of her breast was all that was left to identify her as Woman.

Blinded by cataracts, she would focus her curdled eyes at a blank world and flick her white-caked tongue from between her lips, stabbing it in and out of the toothless cavern as would a lizard.

She spent her years crawling from corner to corner, dodging kicks, abused and mentally decayed, beyond hope of repair, but still shivering in the cold and panting from the heat. Still feeling.

A girl in her mid-twenties screamed incessantly. She ran back and forth with her hands clasped over her ears, her eyes ablaze with fright, shrieking until her voice gave out. Then came inaudible sounds, still heard by her in her mind. Days later, when the vocal cords had somewhat healed, the screams would start again and continue until once more they died away to silence. In time, due to this constant damage, blood replaced spittle and oozed pink from the corners of her mouth.

A mongoloid of about age fifteen, with horrible, ugly eyes, stared at the only world she would ever know. Balloon-headed, with naked yellow skin and gaggling tongue, a freakish imbecile, she was the object of extreme cruelty; but she gave no sign that she was affected by the brutality. Pinched, slapped, stamped on by other patients, the object of unmentionable obscenities, her sexual mouth pulled and stretched by insane perversions, she, nevertheless, continued to move and live. Instinct guided her, as it did the rest of us, to fight at the fence for food, and like all the others, she lapped the waste from the floor.

A middle-aged woman tripped haughtily in her nakedness and paraded back and forth, spreading her legs apart with her wrinkled fingers, hawking lewd and foul favors to receptive inhabitants.

A young girl, vaguely familiar to me, huddled against the wall, her legs pulled under her, and only one breast was nippled. The other had been chewed off. And then I remembered. Her eyes were still dead, and the only sustained activity was the constant chattering of her teeth.

Women who thought they were men masturbated invisible penises with swaggering pride.

Women who dreamed that they had given birth to the Messiah watched constantly for His return.

Women, freaks in their baldness, talked of their breathtaking beauty and sexual prowess.

Women with menstrual blood streaming down their legs giggled and pranced, ignoring the reality of madness.

Women with only thin threads of life anchoring

them to this world lay on bare floors and suffered from inconceivable maladies.

Women quietly struggling to retain their sanity removed themselves into safer areas and huddled together in this Neanderthal world, to watch other "ribs of Adam" drink of their own urine and savor their own dung as it fell, steaming, from their bodies.

Winters were cold and hard. The damp air of the north drove icy spikes into the always-naked flesh. Frost lay everywhere, and in the frozen tomb, unwashed during these frigid months, the stench of filthy bodies and decayed breath overpowered any remaining sensitivity.

The summers were hotboxes of hell. Insects swarmed the air and were caught and eaten. The temperature soared, bringing with it even more rancid odors of bitter sweat.

Food was thrown into the pen once a day. Sometimes it would come early in the morning. Sometimes it would come far into the night. It was shoveled through the gate and pounced upon by the strongest. It was fought over and grabbed, even though, ironically, there was always enough to feed the horde.

Those who still felt a cut above the wild carried the remains cupped in their hands and fed those who could not otherwise have survived. Epidemics of vomit followed every feeding, and doglike, it was lapped up by the human scavengers.

There were secret rooms in the violent ward, with solid doors. These rooms were prisons within a prison, reserved for the killers and executioners.

Women with a violent lust to maul and mutilate were locked away in these dark closets, feared by all.

And women obeying a personal edict from God,

who were bent on executing all evil-doers according to His will, were chained in these formidable holes. From behind the heavy doors, their Godforsaken screams would come awesome and wild.

These were days of battles without victories. Sleep was never assured. Strange, ugly hands would creep across unsuspecting bodies, and dry, foul-smelling lips would clamp themselves onto sister lips.

Sometimes, in the tumultuous darkness, the soft birdlike touch of another human being would flutter briefly on another hand, and, for a moment, the clamor would subside as creature met creature in breathless and innocent contact.

There were beatings. Hard bars of soap were knotted into towels and slammed against skulls. But there was mercy in the pain, for at least for a while blackness blocked out the anguish.

There were rapes. Strange men smuggled their way into the cage to assault. Spewed from a derelict gutter and joined by comrades in crime, they devoured women whose maladies served only to incite the attacks. Rape, in its most vicious form, scarred and claimed every inmate.

There were chains. Restraints that lashed with steel links the ankles and wrists. And naked women who were not fit to roam loose, even in such a confined society, were tied in sacks or straitjackets, or hooded like untamed falcons.

There was water. Shot through a powerful hose that came in unexpected force through the steel fence, it quieted the ever-recurring riots that furiously sprung into life. Its force subdued the ward, pinning both the guilty and the innocent against the walls, rolling the frail down onto the floor like marbles, stinging the flesh with a thousand needles, but quieting the calamities nevertheless.

There was flesh. Flesh that was gnawed away by human teeth. Fingers chewed until blood poured from the stubs were stared at in mad fascination and then eaten again.

Once, in the dead of winter when food was scarce and almost always frozen, a cat crawled into the cage. Somehow it had slipped through, perhaps hunting warmth or a place to curl.

It was taken alive. It clawed and screamed as its eyes were pulled loose and eaten. It was ripped and torn, gutted beyond recognition. It died slowly and in agony.

Rats were eaten, when they could be caught, as a matter of course, but the slaughter of the cat brought quick retaliation.

In my record was the testimony from my mother that I was a torturer of animals, and to satisfy the "civilized," someone had to be accused of perpetrating this inhumane act. I was appointed as the guilty and put into one of those dreaded secret rooms.

In the wild, unbelievable melee, I had tried to take it away and save it. But I was caught with the mutilated animal clutched in my arms, half-eaten, bleeding strings of flesh hanging on its body, and I was automatically convicted.

I was put away in a small dark closet without heat or light. I could tell when day would come by a faint whiteness shining through the small opening at the bottom of the door.

Sometimes, but not often, a scrap of food was shoved through this slit, and there were occasional saucers of water . . . but the door was never opened.

I could stand upright in this secret room and take four steps before I hit a wall. I could stretch both my arms and touch the sides with my fingertips. I broke the monotony by sleeping with my head sometimes at one end and sometimes at the other.

I made my toilet in one corner, keeping it in a small animal-like mound. When I was awake, I would stretch out on my bare stomach and press my ear to the crack in the door and listen to the world outside. It was, even in its most deformed sense, my only contact with reality.

I had no thoughts of any depth during those days of exile. I was without the energy needed to spark a rebellion. And so I waited, like a patient creature, until the door finally swung open and I was allowed to crawl back into my familiar environment, grateful that my enforced hibernation was past.

Death came often in the violent ward. It was brazen and lewd in its demands. It rattled and struggled for attention, but those who could still hold to their senses turned away. And those whose minds were already dead stared at it or giggled in its face.

Death came in the winter and left in its wake blue stiff bodies that no longer shivered. It came in the summer, smelling and bloated, with swarms of flies to testify to its coming.

Death came to the young. It visited those born damaged, and it relieved the old of their tiresome burden.

Death was carried away in a long gray sack with a drawstring at the neck. It was hauled out like a stiff shaft of wheat.

And death also came to those who continued to breathe. Living skeletons, threadbare leftovers died a relentless and deathless death. Living parts of their spirits were buried as each moment sluggishly passed. Segments of their souls, the most intricate part, subsided, never to be reborn.

In time, death killed all hope. It did not attack it mercifully but taunted the life out of it, slowly and with deliberate intent. And then, with hope dead, there was nothing left.

God did not come to the violent ward, nor did He send His emissaries, for this was the physical millennium wherein the devil reigned his thousand years. The demons and malicious spirits of lunacy ruled in the inferno, and God was not to be found.

He was called for and begged for, but He never came. He was ever expected and still believed in, but He never confirmed His existence.

"Whither can I flee from thy spirit? If I descend into hell, thou art there." In the maggot-ridden food? In the twisted thoughts of the deformed? In the dead minds of the undead? In the cold chains that pinched the image and likeness?

No. The ward behind the wire fence was no fit place for a God to visit . . . and He never came.

And so, in this Godless crypt of the damned, I somehow managed to survive.

I entered it on the twenty-second day of May, 1945, and left it on the twenty-fifth day of March, 1950.

14

On the cold, damp morning of March 22, 1950, while I was still lost in the back wards, I was told to appear before the medical staff that afternoon for a parole hearing.

Over the years there had been no drastic changes in my behavior pattern to trigger the prospect of a release, and I was cautious and fearful that some deceitful trick was about to be played.

In the five years I had wallowed in a nightmare, I had all but resigned myself to ending my days in this black dilemma. I no longer hoped for miracles. During all the years in the violent ward I had little if any contact with the outside world. I had not seen a newspaper, watched a movie, listened to a radio, talked on a telephone, or read a letter.

The months had come and gone, and I had finally adjusted to the reality that I was all but forgotten. To be informed suddenly that I was eligible for a parole hearing made me wary and suspicious.

I was taken from the ward to the admissions building. There, under supervision, I was allowed to bathe and wash my hair. I wanted to shave under my arms and my legs for the five-year growth was long and matted, but this was refused. Our heads had not been clipped for the spring months, and as I ran a comb through the short hair, I wondered what I looked like. I was then given a clean dress to wear and a pair of oxfords, without shoelaces. When I was dressed, I was taken to a small office outside the main conference room and told I was to wait there until my name was called.

In personal defense and in order to establish the unlikely turn of events that followed, I will quote *verbatim* from my hospital records in the hope that it will confirm that people are, in many instances, incarcerated far longer than need be simply because no one makes a move to have them released. Once committed, almost forgotten, is the drastic burden an inmate must learn to carry.

On July 18, 1948, the records show that I was transferred from Ward T to Ward L, and the report reads:

> Patient is mildly cooperative and helps on the ward. She has periods of being high and requires restraint and confinement. This restraint included three belts. She has not been able to see her parents at any time.

The next entry is on September 15, 1949:

> Patient is cooperative but never volunteers conversation with others. She sits in a corner with a blanket covering her head, but she has learned to answer pleasantly.

The following is dated December 5, 1949:

Patient is receiving routine restraint and treatment.

Nearly four months later, on March 22, 1950, the entry reads:

Patient presented to staff. Nurse reports that on ward she is helpful to the feeble patients. Physically the patient is not robust.

Staff unanimously recommends that parole be granted.

The last entry is March 25, 1950, and it reads:

PAROLED.

In the nearly two years prior to my release there were four brief entries recording my condition, and judging from them it seems that I had learned to keep my mouth shut. In so many words, I was a quiet, skinny woman who sat around with a blanket over her head, but who was, nonetheless, good to old people. Nothing more.

Nevertheless, and without quite understanding why, I *was free!* But unknown to me, one major change had come about. I was needed at home. Mamma had suffered a slight stroke and Papa's health was failing rapidly. So the thinking members of my family had reached the decision that the logical one for them to get to take care of the situation was sister Frances.

Papa, prodded on by the idea, had written the hospital requesting that I be released into their joint custody, explaining that I was desperately needed to assist them in their old age . . . and within a week I was paroled.

It was that simple!

Much later, I found a letter in his files written to him by the attending physician assigned to my ward and dated March 22, 1950. It read as follows (verbatim):

DEAR MR. FARMER:

The Superintendent directs me to acknowledge receipt of your letter of recent date regarding your daughter Mrs. Frances Anderson, a patient in this hospital.

We are glad to report that Mrs. Anderson appeared before our medical staff today and was found to be sufficiently recovered to warrant a parole. Parole to you and her mother was granted, and she will be delivered into your custody when you or Mrs. Farmer can call at the hospital and sign responsibility for her.

Papa arrived on the twenty-fifth to take me home. For five years I had survived every conceivable torture and had been considered too dangerous to be allowed at large. Now, suddenly, not only was I sufficiently cured to warrant a parole, but also I was considered capable of accepting the responsibility of caring for the two people who had been singularly responsible for my commitment.

I was insane one day and competent the next, and now, whenever I reread my hospital records or study the court charges brought against me by my parents, I find that I can forgive their actions, but I cannot forget.

What is so painful to me is the knowledge that at any time during my commitment my parents could have obtained my release simply by requesting it. But even more terrible is the grief that comes from knowing that I was left there with little or no concern for what was being done to me until they became unable to care for themselves. How twisted it was that the insane member of the family was the one who was brought back into their world to tend to their needs.

This action contradicts their previous motives. They had put me away because I was crazy, and yet I was brought out and expected to handle the responsibilities of two aging people, who were, in all respects, my most dreaded enemies.

No one welcomes the inconveniences and traumas of caring for the old and sick, and yet the other members of my family had no qualms about leaving these two in their last days to a woman who was, in every sense of the word, a second-class citizen.

People who have been declared incompetent have no civil rights. They cannot make a contract or write a will, or marry, or vote, or sign a check, or drive a car. They cannot buy or sell property or enter into any business transactions. They cannot be insured, or be licensed for a trade, or be issued a passport, or bring legal suit. They are a stigma to society, to their families and to themselves.

So the question that badgers me to this day is that if my family really believed that I was insane and had kept me all those years in an asylum, why would they risk bringing me out, ever? To be released from a mental institution after so long a confinement is practically unheard of. Yet the facts, in my situation, are indisputable. A simple letter from my father asking for it freed me.

The question then arises: What was I doing there in the first place? It is distasteful for any one to believe that the innocent suffer. Society insists that only the guilty are punished. But is that always the case?

The law reads that any "interested person" may initiate a petition to the courts for incompetency, and it is a fine legal distinction to judge whether an individual is eccentric or insane. None is safe from this danger despite constitutional protection. A neighbor, an employer, a husband, or an angered stranger can petition the courts against any individual, and, by law, a competency hearing results.

In court actions the law affords most accused persons the right to bail. This is done to allow the marshaling of a defense. But the mentally ill are often detained literally incommunicado, with no right to bail and with no opportunity to prepare a personal defense. Once the finger of suspicion is pointed at an individual, the stigma remains. Any unusual act or reckless behavior triggers a consequent doubt as to that person's sanity.

The Eighth Amendment also prohibits "cruel and inhuman punishments." The treatment of the mentally ill—that is, the use of lobotomy, shock treatments, and indefinite incarceration—certainly qualifies as cruel and unusual. Even if it were conceded that after a person is convicted and hospitalized, drastic curtailments of his civil rights would be in order, it would seem that, as a matter of course, as soon as he is released from the institution, these rights should be restored. Unfortunately this is not the case. The patient, declared ill, is paroled like a criminal.

Another controversial question is the fact that most mental patients are obliged to perform a variety of menial and demeaning tasks while they are in the hospital. This work is supposedly done in lieu of payment for services which may only include custody, or in lieu of therapy, even if none is given. For example, washing dishes for eight to ten hours a day may be considered therapy for a serious mental disorder, but such forced labor falls within the meaning of the term "involuntary servitude" as used in the Thirteenth

Amendment. This prohibits all forms of slavery under whatever guise.

Another point worthy of reiteration is that the person accused of being mentally ill is rarely given access to the psychiatrist who may or may not testify in his behalf, while the individual making the accusation usually has relatively unlimited access to such experts to recount the weird behavior of the accused. When the person so accused is hospitalized, it may be that he has been denied the "equal protection of the laws" guaranteed in the Fourteenth Amendment.

In my particular case both my parents had offered damaging testimony against me and had acquired guardianship, and I was thus helpless to defend myself or to testify in my behalf.

So when I met Papa in the main office of the hospital and waited while he signed the stacks of forms that finalized my parole, I did so with some bitterness.

I had little to say to him on the bus ride home, and when he tried to drape his arm around my shoulder and hug me to him, I moved to another seat. I could not bear his touch, and I was unmoved by his shocking feebleness. I had aged too, and even though I was grateful for anything that had been instrumental in bringing about my release, I could not find it in myself to offer him any more than a cold acknowledgment.

My interview before the staff had been drastically brief. They had asked if I knew what kind of a day it was and I said, "Yes, it is rather cold." Then they asked if I felt that I had been helped, and I answered yes. They asked me if I would like to go home, and I said yes. They asked me to count backward from one hundred to fifty, and I did. Then they asked me to count forward from one to fifty, and I did. There was nothing more to it than that, except that when I was released, I was not told that I was expected to act as nurse and housekeeper to my parents, and I had no idea that the price I would be required to pay for my freedom would come so high.

When we arrived home, I was horrified at the shambles. It was almost as bad as the asylum filth. Mamma was as cantankerous as ever and immediately began ordering me around, in her most grandiose manner. She was relentless in her demands.

She and Papa still argued constantly, and he was always underfoot, for he had finally convinced her that he should move back to the house and economize. They lived under the same roof, but they were inevitably at each other's throats.

In reality what had happened was that I had exchanged one violent ward for another, but I was even more of a prisoner at home with Mamma's swaggering attitude of chief jailer than I had been when I was held behind the impersonal bars of the asylum.

If I would leave the room without asking her, she would hobble after me screeching that I had better not try to pull the wool over her eyes or she would "send me back." And Papa would come tottering after her to join in on the threat. They were both absurdly childish, but their natures grew even more spiteful and vindictive as each day passed.

Papa would wet on the floor several times a day, and Mamma would scream until I mopped it up. At night, when I could finally get away from them and go to my room, I would collapse on the side of my bed with my face buried in my trembling hands.

Day in and day out I heard over and over that if I refused to "mind them," they would send me back. I lived with the gnawing fear that they would do it at the slightest provocation, and as a result I became something I had never been before: a whimpering whipping post.

When I displeased them, which was constantly, I would beg and plead for another chance. If a meal was not exactly right, and the majority of the time they made a great to-do about hating my cooking, they would fall into menacing discussions, acting as though I were not there, about when they were going to call the police to come and get me.

I would panic at these threats and actually subjugated myself to them by falling to my knees to plead for mercy and another chance. Mamma would throw back her head and laugh at me, and Papa would cluck his tongue and shame me for not having any pride.

I was resigned to this threat hanging over me for as long as they lived. Neither of them ever told that notice of my competency was issued in 1951, and I discovered it only by chance, years later, among the legal papers in Papa's file.

On May 15, 1951, he had written to the superintendent of the hospital the following letter (verbatim):

DEAR SIR:

On March 22, 1950, my daughter, Mrs. Frances Anderson, appeared before your medical staff and was granted a parole to go to me and her mother. She has been with us ever since and has at no time indicated by word or action that she is not normal and sane. She has waited faithfully upon her mother who has not been at all well during this period and has done all the house work, and to me and her mother she is absolutely sane.

I intend to apply to the probate court for a decree of competency, but if you wish to have her examined by your medical staff prior to this, kindly name the time and place for such an examination.

No examination was required, and in 1953 I discovered that on March 25, 1951, by order of the superior court, I was discharged from the jurisdiction of the state hospital as "fully recovered and so ordered, adjudged and decreed and restored to competency and civil rights."

A major question must be answered regarding this devious deception perpetrated by my parents. Why would they deliberately and with planned intent keep the knowledge of my restoration from me? What twisted delight did they experience from badgering me with hourly threats? To keep me in line? Perhaps. Or was it their final effort to cling to something secure, regardless of the costs, and so long as they could keep me harnessed to them, they were not alone? They knew that as long as I remained in ignorance I would do nothing to defend myself, and they could have found no stronger weapon to bind me to them than the threat of recommitment.

Papa was taken suddenly ill and I had done everything that I could for him at home. He and Mamma had both fought against having a doctor, but when I finally overruled them and called one, he sent Papa to the hospital, where he was operated on for an abdominal obstruction.

I had to leave Mamma alone at the house while I waited for him to be returned from intensive care, and when I finally saw him, I knew that in a matter of time he would be dead. Yet the old are capable of conjuring strength from some invisible source, and he made it through the operation, although he never recovered his prior vigor.

The doctor, sizing up the situation, knew that it would be impossible for me to take care of him at home, especially with Mamma still insisting on running the show, so arrangements were made for him to be admitted to an "old peoples' home." There was no money to pay for this care, so the Elks Lodge, of which he had been a lifetime member, managed to handle the admittance on a charity basis. When I saw him he seemed contented. He had struck up friendships with what he called "old codgers," and I can only assume he received competent care.

With Papa gone, I was then faced with the problem of Mamma, and she was becoming more and more difficult to manage. The stroke had left her vague, and, if possible, even more ill-tempered, and once Papa was gone, she insisted that we were out of money. There were many days when she would dole out a quarter for me to run the house on, and, in short order, I reached a point of sheer desperation.

Since I believed I was still on parole and knew, by law, that I could not seek employment, I decided to take a cautious step and write to the superintendent of the institution to ask that I be presented to the staff in order to petition that I receive a discharge.

I received a prompt reply that puzzled me, for it stated that the court, on the request of my father, had already decreed my recovered status and that my civil rights had been restored to me.

I was appalled and angered that this had been done without my knowledge, and yet the whole bizarre commitment had been handled in what seemed to me if not an unlawful, then an unorthodox manner. So I took it upon myself, for my own personal satisfaction and proof, to seek an attorney and find out where I stood legally. I explained that, regardless of any previous court order, I wanted to appear personally

before the judge and petition in my own behalf not
only for restoration, but also for a discharge of my
mother's order of guardianship. He told me it was not
customary for a second hearing, but I insisted, for it
was the only way I could be sure. I trusted no one,
least of all my family.

Arrangements were made for me to appear before
the hospital staff on July 1, 1953. Almost three years
after my parole date, I returned to the place that
had been my private hell. It took more courage than I
thought I could muster to walk back onto the grounds
and wait in that same colorless admitting room, along
with other patients, until my name was called.

The hospital had taken a testimony from my brother
regarding my position, and I again quote, verbatim,
from the records. This entry is dated July 1, 1953:

> The brother was interviewed and says his sister
> was under the impression that she was on parole
> status only, and in his opinion the parents have
> held the institution as a threat over her. He says
> she has done a good job taking care of her par-
> ents since she left here.

The following is an accompanying entry also dated
July 1, 1953:

> Patient was presented to staff for discharge at
> her own request. Patient says she wishes a dis-
> charge in order to seek employment and support
> herself. Says she was not aware that she had any
> freedom unless she had a discharge stating that
> she had recovered. Says both her parents are quite
> ill. Mother is 79; Father is 82. Says she has been
> staying home taking care of them. Says she would
> accept any type of employment that would bring

in a steady income. Does not have any plans to go ahead with her acting. Patient says that in her opinion she had a nervous breakdown but feels she now has overcome the previous emotional problems that were troubling her. Patient says that she has lived the past three years under the impression that on the slightest provocation she would be returned to the hospital. Had the feeling that the door has always been open to her return. Patient says she has tried to do a good job looking after her father and mother. She has kept house and made repairs on it and has raised a garden for food.

On the third day of July, accompanied by an attorney, I went before the Superior Court of the State of Washington on "The Matter Of The Insanity Of Mrs. Frances Anderson."

By Judge Lloyd Sharett the following was decreed (verbatim): "The above entitled cause having come on to be heard before the undersigned judge of the above entitled court on petition of Mrs. Frances Anderson for restoration of natural competency, and said Mrs. F. Anderson being present in person, the court being fully advised in the premises does now make and enter the following order: Now, therefore it is ordered, adjudged and decreed that the above Mrs. Anderson should be and hereby is restored her mental competency. Done in open court this third day of July, 1953."

I had only one more step to take finally to sever all legal ties to Mamma, so on July 27, after again petitioning the court, I secured an order discharging Lillian V. Farmer as my guardian.

And so at last, after ten years and nine months, after an era that began in October, 1942, and ended in July, 1953, I was legally freed and unfettered.

But those years had wounded me. I was barely human and no longer capable of compassion. I concentrated so intensely on basic survival that outer conditions had little or no effect on me. I felt nothing. I was an empty and frozen vessel, and determined calculations motivated my every move.

The final macabre power play by my parents left me without any tangible emotion for them—neither love nor hate. I looked at them with a detached, bitter eye. I would take care of Mamma as long as I could manage it, but I was determined to maneuver circumstances in such a way as to solidify and guarantee my freedom.

The first thing I did was to hunt for a job, and after searching the newspapers, I applied to the Olympic Hotel in response to an ad for a valet girl. I was hired to pick up and deliver cleaning and laundry to the guests and was paid seventy-five cents an hour. The job was treadmill, which drained me of a great deal of energy, working seven days a week, ten hours a day. I would eat a hot breakfast in the morning before leaving for work and wait until I returned that night to eat supper. The way things were, I could not afford to take out lunch money from the small salary I received.

But while I was economizing, Mamma had taken to having two quarts of pure cream delivered to the house every day. She had become obsessed with eating shredded wheat with cream, and I was distressed when so much of my salary was going for such an uncalled-for luxury. I begged and tried to reason with her, but she could not be swayed.

I had been at work three months before I could begin to accept myself and my life with a little less tension. Papa was firmly ensconced in the old folks' home and Mamma seemed content to rattle around the house all day listening to her soap operas and munching her shreaded wheat. She still threatened to send me back, and even though I had disarmed her, in the back of my mind there lurked the constant demon that she had done it before and perhaps, somehow, she might be able to do it again.

I would come home at night, dead tired, and listen to her rambling on and on about how she had sacrificed her life for me and how she would get even with me for it. Finally, I knew that I would have to take further precaution to protect myself. Even though the law had dismissed her hold over me, I wanted more absolute assurance. I made the unemotional decision to marry.

Without any deep concern as to who the man would be, I started looking around for a prospect. I began making friendly overtures to the girls I worked with, suggesting that I might join them one evening after work. One of them told me she knew a man, a bachelor, who would like to meet me, and after playing coy for a while, I demurely agreed to the blind date.

I was never emotionally or physically attached to him, and I knew that he was not the kind of person who could engage my loyalty. After our first date, when he kept saying, "I'm going to marry you, Frances Farmer," I knew that I would not be using him unjustly. I might have felt qualms, though I doubt it, if he had said, "I'm going to marry YOU," and left it at that. But he always declared to the point of thumping his chest like an overhormoned ape, "I'm going to marry you, Frances Farmer," so obviously he had some sort of hangup about marrying an actress, even one who had been declared bonkers . . . and I graciously complied.

I can think back on this interlude, and it was that, without a tinge of guilt or bad conscience. I never professed to be in love, but I do have this to my feeble credit: As long as I remained with him, I did what I could to be a satisfactory wife.

He was not a particularly attractive man, although he was relatively kind and quite understanding toward my parents. So much so that both of them developed a sincere attachment for him.

As for me, I used this marriage as a lever to shift the bulk of responsibilities off my shoulders. Papa was settled and cared for, but Mamma was another matter. So after we were married, we moved into the house with her until, as he put it, we could lay aside enough money to buy a new one. He did set about refurbishing the living room with some medium-priced furniture, which he bought on credit, co-signed by me, and it was a general help to have a man around, if only to do some of the heavy work. A month after our marriage I had to quit work because Mamma was requiring more care and becoming very feeble and absent-minded. It was no longer safe to leave her alone.

With a husband in tow, I managed to influence Rita, my half-sister, to share in the care of Mamma by having her go to her home for a visit.

The day she left, we drove out to the home and picked up Papa so that he could go to the airport with us to see her off. Somehow I think they both knew that this would be their final good-bye. When the plane was called and it was time for Mamma to leave, he held onto her hand like a small child and wept. But she was too excited about the trip to respond to his grief and tottered off to the plane, turning back only once to wave at us.

Papa cried all the way to the home, and when we left him in the lobby, it was the last time I was to see either of them again.

Something about my cold handling of my parents triggered my husband's righteous indignation, and by the time we returned to the old house he was furious with me. I thought it most abnormal, but he had cried on leaving them both, and I had stood as unmoved as a stone.

That evening he began drinking and did not go to work the next day. He became progressively abusive when I refused to argue in defense of my behavior, but nothing he could accuse me of upset me.

With Mamma and Papa gone, I had accomplished the major phase of my overall plan, and I had lived in the grim world of reality too long to bother with pretending I felt something that I did not.

He was appalled at this indifference and worked himself into such a drunken frenzy that, by the weekend, he had literally wrecked the house and everything in it.

The new furniture was totally destroyed. He jerked pictures off the wall, threw chairs out of the windows, turned over the old cookstove in the kitchen, yanked mattresses off the beds, tore up clothes, and broke every dish in the house.

I sat on the porch impervious to the violence, and this incensed him all the more. What he failed to realize was that physical destruction was old news to me. He forgot that I had lived through years surrounded by violence, and even though his spasm was complete and the havoc he wreaked was total, it nevertheless left me unmoved and unconcerned. I could not even bother to venture a reprimand.

After he passed out on the floor with an empty fifth in his arms, I went back into the house, rolled him over on his stomach, and stripped his wallet of sixty dollars. I left him an equal amount.

About ten o'clock at night I put on my coat and looked back one last time. Everything was wrecked, as if an isolated tornado had swooped down and twisted the old house on its foundation.

For a long moment I stood there absorbing the scene, then I quietly closed the door and walked to the corner to wait for a bus. I felt neither elation nor regret. A chapter had ended.

When I reached the city, I walked to the bus station and asked at the ticket window how far fifty dollars would take me. The teller wanted to know which way I was going, and I said whichever way the next bus was headed. He studied the schedule, added up forty-eight dollars and seventy-two cents, and gave me a one-way ticket to Eureka, California.

15

During the next three and a half years I subsisted in a neuter exile, but for the first time in my life I was unencumbered. I was responsible only to myself.

My emotional field lay fallow, and I used this sabbatical of self-inflicted isolation in Eureka as a time to repair the shreaded remnants of my life.

I found a job working as a typist for a commercial photographer and rented a bedroom in one of the ancient boarding-houses that lined the side streets of this small coastal town.

During this strange hiatus, I made no personal commitments. I went to work, walked home for lunch, and at the end of the day walked back to my room and stayed there. I never varied my routine. Most of my evenings were spent reading books from the library, for I had missed more than ten years of literature, and I was anxious to fill this void. Other than that, I treated myself to an occasional movie, and during the summer I enjoyed my Sundays by taking long solitary walks along the coast.

I lived and worked under the name Frances Anderson and never broke my vow of silence by writing or contacting anyone from the area of Seattle. No one knew where I was. I had severed the past, and to my reasoning, I had not deserted my parents. Before vanishing, I did what I could to reestablish them. We had finished our course together, and I saw no reason to rekindle an already-dead flame.

I had been in Eureka nearly two years when I was tracked down through the local Social Security office. I received a letter telling me that both my parents were gone. Mamma had died at Rita's the first day of March, 1955, and Papa died in Seattle on July 16, 1956.

In order to settle the estate, legal efforts had been instigated to find me. At the end, deciding I should be her sole heir, Mamma had endowed me with all her worldly goods—namely, the old house in Seattle. The house was eventually sold on contract for five thousand dollars, and with it, the last page was written.

My taproots, already decayed, finally withered and died.

My main regret, in it all, was that my secret life had been uncovered, for only in guaranteed solitude had I been able to heal many of the old wounds from the past.

I had become a functioning part of the photography studio and fanatically relished my oblivion. No one had ever recognized me, and with little wonder, for I had been away from the public eye for over a decade. And since I had not become personally involved with anyone in Eureka, there was no one close enough to question me about who I was or where I was from.

This is not to say that I lived without anguish, for most of my nights were spent fighting a constant fear and the recurring nightmares. I was afraid of the past. It snapped at my heels until, with the thought of somehow easing the tension, I began stopping at the liquor store on my way home from work to buy a bottle of wine.

It was a harmless and rather comforting repast, at first. I would cook supper on my two-burner hot plate and enjoy a glass or two of wine as I ate. A dangerous game, and I knew it, but I had lost my sense of security and privacy, and the tensions began to mount.

I gave serious thought to disappearing again but realized that it would be useless, for sooner or later something would come up and I would be tracked down again. The disquieting knowledge that I was no longer alone in my own universe caused all the ancient suspicions and anger to surface.

During the day, while at work, I would busy myself with the picayune details required of me, but I kept a hawkeye on the clock, growing more and more anxious for quitting time to come. On my lunch hour, I would hurry to my room, but rather than eating, I would substitute the meal with a glass of vodka. My main intake was still wine, for it was cheaper, but I had enough sense to know that if I showed up at work with a drink on my breath, my boss would fire me on the spot.

Without realizing the insidious hold it was taking, my noon meal was vodka, and at night, rather than having the glass or two of wine, I was drinking until I fell across the bed stupefied. During my stay in Eureka I had managed to save four hundred dollars—one hundred for each year—and nothing could tempt me to use the money. To make up for the growing expense my drinking was creating, I decided to move into an even shoddier room and started buying the cheapest wine.

Eureka was a small town, and I knew that if I kept buying at one place, word would soon reach my boss. Twice a week, I would spend most of the evening going to different liquor stores and bars, buying a bottle here and a bottle there in order to keep my secret. And since I had no social life whatsoever, the surliness and antagonisms that invariably surfaced when I drank were also kept secret.

On completing these treks I would hurry to my room with the shopping bag stuffed full of bottles. Not trusting the lock on my door, I kept my loot in my suitcase and went even further and bought a chain and a padlock to secure it to the bedsprings. If any of the other roomers came in to steal while I was at work, they would have to dismantle the bed before they could carry off my precious booze.

There was no concrete cause for my heightened sense of agitation, except that I no longer felt safe. I would hear a siren and try to hide. Or I would see a policeman and fear that he was coming for me. And as the weeks passed, I receded even more, afraid to speak except in stringent monosyllables, lest I offend and somehow trigger an adverse situation. I was a solitary drinker who caused no one any trouble. I, no doubt, became more tense at work and logically could not produce as well, but my behavior was reasonable and gave my boss no cause to complain. So life went on much as it had, except I crashed my way into sleep every night, totally and thoroughly drunk.

One evening, on one of my shopping sprees, I stopped in one of the sleezy bars on the waterfront and stood impatiently at the bar, waiting for someone to notice me. I had already made five stops that evening and my two shopping bags were almost full. But I had to make sure that I would not run out, so this was to be my last stop.

It was a dark smelly hole-in-the-wall, but I couldn't care less; all I wanted was a pint of vodka and a quart of wine. While I was standing at the bar, a man came up behind me and said, "You're Frances Farmer, aren't you?"

The shock of hearing my name spoken after all those years was palpitating. I turned around and saw a puffy middle-aged man staring at me. My initial instinct was to cut him short, but he spoke again before I had a chance to reply. "You *are* Frances Farmer, aren't you?"

For some reckless reason I replied, "Yes, how did you know?"

And he said simply, "I remember you."

To detail this relationship would be time-consuming and pointless. Suffice it to say, he told me he was a talent manager on his way to San Francisco, and he was a fast enough talker to convince me that I was wasting away and should "come back." He insisted that I let him handle my career and demanded that I quit my job and leave with him the next morning.

I was never a woman to act or react spontaneously, but this once I made a quick decision and abided by it. I left with him the following afternoon. I withdrew my four hundred dollars from the bank, quit my job, packed my suitcase (which had been emptied by our previous night's binge), and boarded a bus with him to San Francisco.

During the years I had been in Eureka, I had never thought of picking up my career. In the first place, I did not see how it would be possible. Having been away so long and having smashed up under such a scandalous cloud, it never occurred to me that I could resume it.

I suppose the fact that he remembered me was not only flattering but provocative. My job and life had grown pointless, so when a freewheeling, fast-talking con artist breezed by (and I recognized him for what he was), I decided that I had nothing to lose by gambling. We were both derelicts, and even though I did not give any credibility to his optimism, it was worth taking a chance. His having come to my room where we spent the night drinking together was also a factor. I suppose he rang a bell by showing up at the right time and the right place.

On the first of May, I arrived in San Francisco bleary-eyed from drinking and almost deaf from listening to his outlandish plans for my future and his. I knew he was down at the heels, but he had enough of a flair about him to prompt me to risk giving him a chance to prove himself. Other than that, he was someone to talk to.

When we arrived at the bus station, he said he had friends who would let us stay with them until I could get settled into an apartment of my own. We moved in as houseguests of a man and wife who were his devoted fans. They were also devoted drinkers, and for the next week we all stayed glued to the bottle.

Finally, I had the sense to move out. I took a small furnished apartment, and after searching through the want ads, I applied as Frances Anderson at the Park Sheraton Hotel and was hired as a reservation clerk. I was not disturbed at having to take this kind of work, for I had no illusions about a comeback. I was satisfied just to earn the seventy dollars a week the job offered.

After I was settled, I called the couple I had stayed with to thank them for their hospitality and told them where I was working, giving them my apartment address when they asked for it. That evening he showed up on my doorstep still peddling his plans for me and reassuring me of his contacts.

He was always on the verge of clinching a big deal, always a day away from signing some fantastic agreement. When I came home from work, he would be there and spend the night blowing about his connections. He was a heavy, determined drinker, and I was depending on liquor more and more to put me to sleep. It took him about a day to consume a fifth, but from the time I came home from work until I finally found the sleep that evaded me I would come close to equaling his capacity. To calm my stomach I now had to begin my day with a strong eye-opener, but I had foresight enough to form one advantageous habit. As soon as I would get home, I would set my alarm clock and put it on the table beside my glass and bottle. I never missed work, nor was I ever late. I managed my time on the reservation desk with total competency and functioned automatically. But at night, after a light supper, he and I would sit across the narrow room from each other, each with our own bottle, and I would drink until, more often than not, I spent the night slumped in my chair.

He became an immovable object, but I really wasn't interested enough in the situation to have him bodily evicted. He would curl up on the couch after making masculine noises and drunken advances, but that's about as far as the relationship went. Most of the time, whenever he had been sufficiently rebuked, he would stagger away berating himself and his impotence. "I'm washed up," he would groan. And I couldn't have cared less.

Since he was contributing nothing toward expenses, my four-hundred-dollar nest egg began to diminish rapidly. Then one day, after I'd been on the job about a month, the manager of the hotel brought over the new public relations director and introduced me. There were plans to spruce up the approach to any important person who booked through us. As we talked, I noticed the man kept eyeing me curiously, and he finally interrupted the conversation and said,

"You not only look familiar to me, but I've heard your voice somewhere."

Once again, for no logical reason, perhaps out of a warped curiosity to see his reaction, I replied, "I'm Frances Farmer."

A keen and talented pressman, he sensed he could wring some value out of a news story. Within an hour I was luxuriating in one of the hotel's most elegant suites. As he made plans for a press conference the next day, I was skeptically whisked up in the excitement. In the back of my mind, however, that old gnawing fear of the past drummed its ominous chord. But nothing I could say could dampen the plans, and I was warmly reassured that this would be the door that could open a whole new world for me.

I returned to my apartment quite late after spending the evening with the executive staff planning the press conference. As usual, he was there attacking a bottle of cheap whiskey. When I told him what had happened, he was livid. He accused me of cheating him out of his rightful commissions as agent/manager, even though no money had come in other than my seventy a week from the hotel. He shouted and ranted that he would drag me through every court in the country if I permitted the hotel to exploit me for its ends. Then began a long harangue that "I couldn't fool him," he knew I was getting paid for doing a publicity gig for the Sheraton chain. In short order he worked himself into a state of violence.

The situation was sick and absurd, so while he was belching fire, I packed my clothes and went back to the hotel. I slammed the door with his "I'll find a way to get even with you yet" ringing in my ears. But this was just another harmless, booze-induced plan.

Yet I must give him this point of credit, for had he

not ambled through Eureka and, by chance, recognized me, I might have spent the rest of my life within its confines and restrictions. Likely, I would have hobbled through the years, never discovering the joys that I have come to know.

When I checked into the hotel that night, I was apprehensive and on edge. Instincts formed over the past solitary months dictated a drink to soothe my fears, but without too great a struggle I didn't resort to alcohol. I was concerned and frightened to be on the verge of taking a step toward the world which had helped destroy me. But it was a move I had agreed to make, so there was no point in my condemning myself or my motives.

The whole thing was by chance anyway. I had not come to San Francisco on fire for a comeback or even with a tepid hope of resuming a career. To be ambitious requires a life spark, and there was none in me. I was rather like a zombie, I suppose. I seldom smiled, and when I did, only the facial muscles moved. Nothing came from within. I was curt in my manner and remote. There was no humor in me. There was nothing I wanted except to subsist until I died. Nothing really interested me. Brick by brick, I had erected a wall between me and the rest of the world. When I met people, my remote disposition kept them at arm's length. And if they made a slight effort to defrost my total frigidity, I stopped them in their tracks. I did not like people or trust them, and I refused to become entangled in any life other than my own. I had the well-earned right to take nothing and give nothing.

I thought about these things throughout the night. I knew who I was and what I had become. I was a dedicated loner intent on remaining unencumbered, and if, by some peculiar chance, the press responded to the invitation from the hotel and if anything inter-

esting happened as a result, I made up my mind to
take whatever was in store.

I knew that nothing could ever again defeat or disturb me. The once-potent pressures of my family
now lay dead, and even the personal complications
that accompany any artistic career were like harmless
gnats compared with the shocking years I had survived.

I did not coddle myself into dreaming of a story-
book comeback. I knew, if the press did respond, that
the ugliness of the past would be revived and I would,
sooner or later, have to face up to pointed questions
about it. I could not avoid it, nor could they, and I
wondered why I was doing it. What curiosity was di-
recting me to reenter a world that probably did not
even remember my name? Money, or its prospects, was
not a factor. Fame, or the desire for it, did not enter
the picture, nor was I smothering a strong desire to act
again. I was no longer young and I knew the public
tastes had changed from the days when I was accepted.
But the face that had intrigued my fans was still there
and held no visual evidence of the years of horror. I
was unlined and unmarked.

I planned on being cordial to the press, knowing
that nothing they might say or do could dent my ar-
mor-plated coat of steel, and even though there was
still a fiendish hostility that bubbled inside me, the violent years had been a stern teacher and I had learned
to keep a taut control.

But, despite all this, I was nervous. I had a long relaxing bath and washed my hair. I did my nails and
polished my shoes. I decided to wear an inexpensive
but well-chosen blue two-piece dress and steamed it in
the bathroom. With that done, I went to bed, sober,
and eventually fell asleep.

The management had set aside an impressive suite
in which I was to meet the press, and when I arrived

on time, it was bedecked with flowers and a well-stocked bar. I did not want a drink and I'm sure the PR man breathed a sigh of relief. I settled quietly in a chair for a while and watched the frantic last-minute preparation. I was doubtful that the name Frances Farmer could still produce sparks. However I was going along for the ride mainly, I think, to see what would happen.

Shortly after five the room began to fill, and when I came back in to meet the reporters something inside me screamed "Run." I saw face after face studying me in minute detail and I wanted to flee. After a long moment or two, as we eyed each other, the room relaxed and the questions began.

They came rapid-fire and were surprisingly civilized. For the most part the conference was conducted with a fair amount of decorum. One or two tossed impudent queries but I was able to answer calmly. It would be at later press conferences that the old familiar bombardment would come.

I was asked if I intended to resume my acting career and I gave a truthful answer: I had not had any offers. The old frankness that had alienated me in Hollywood now brought out a mutual exchange of respect. I was not trying to tout myself, and, in turn, the reported results were, for the most part, accurate and somewhat flattering.

The national response astonished me. When the story that I had been "discovered" working at a seventy-dollar-a-week job hit the wires, I began receiving calls and telegrams from all over the country. I was honestly puzzled that after years of oblivion, people still remembered me. Within days, letters came pouring into the hotel, and the curious made it impossible for me to continue with my job.

I moved into a smaller apartment, and the grim

facts boiled down to the uncomfortable reality that I had created an interesting ripple, but I had lost my job in the process.

For the most part the letters and calls were typical fan stuff, and after a week or so of going through the stacks, I was disgusted with myself for having agreed to the foolishness of a conference. I had enjoyed the work at the reservation desk and I did not relish the tedious search for another job. I had gained nothing.

When I was down to about thirty dollars, the hotel transferred a call from Ed Sullivan with an offer to appear on his Sunday night television show. That was all well and good, except that I did not have the fare to New York and a performer was not paid in advance for these appearances. I had to stall giving him an answer.

About this same time I received a letter from Michael Ellis, the director of the respected Bucks County Playhouse in New Hope, Pennsylvania, offering me an extended run during the summer season. Even more exciting was the wide scope of plays he submitted for my selection.

This offer, along with Sullivan's, made a trek to the East a little more solid, but I still did not have the money to get me there. It was then the manager of the hotel suggested that, if I wanted to borrow the money, he would co-sign the note for me. I was touched by this and I appreciated not only the businesslike approach but, even more, his belief that I was good for the debt.

I borrowed enough to take me East and I signed for two shows with Sullivan, one in June, the other in October. I booked in with Bucks County to do *The Chalk Garden* and *The Jamison Affair* in August.

I assumed I would do something dramatic on the Sullivan show; instead, I ended up singing "Aura Lee," my song from *Come and Get It*. It had a little more value to the public, for Elvis Presley had made a success of it under the title "Love Me Tender."

During the rehearsal I was given my first taste of the rough road that lay ahead of me. I was hounded by the scandal magazines and tabloids, and the accredited press began tagging me with most unpleasant adjectives. Old pictures were reprinted of me being hauled out of court between two policemen, and all the sordid details were given new life.

Some of the more bland comments that appeared in syndicated columns were (verbatim):

> . . . Frances Farmer, a beautiful actress who skidded out of Hollywood on a liquor slicked emotional breakdown fourteen years ago is climbing back up the stardust trail. Her tumble from filmland heights ended in the shadowland of mental institutions. She entered Hollywood in 1936, and from that point her screen rise was phenomenal. She starred opposite Cary Grant, Bing Crosby, Tyrone Power and other romantic lights. Then suddenly she fell apart. She was dragged screaming and kicking from court rooms. She fought police. She out-shouted a judge, and after eight years in and out of mental hospitals the actress who once earned two hundred thousand dollars a year was discovered working for seventy dollars a week in a San Francisco hotel.

Other reports went on to say (verbatim):

> An almost forgotten name, an almost forgotten face . . . Frances Farmer. Suddenly she's back looking once again for the fame and stardom she lost fourteen years ago. Suddenly there she is on the Ed Sullivan show singing "Aura Lee" in a

low, soft voice, looking as beautiful as ever.

It has been fourteen years between public appearances. These were, for her, years of trouble, alcoholism, public disturbances, institutions and disgrace.

She speaks softly, firmly. She seems a little tired, a little subdued, a little unemotional. But her smile, while infrequent, still radiates. She appears to be the picture of calmness. There have been many offers before and since the Sullivan appearance. Some want her to make records. Some to do plays. Many want her to write a book about her life.

"Probably I should write it," she mused. "There has been so much said about me that is wrong. So many stories that say I'm a terrible person. So, if I write a book I will do so to tell the truth. I won't gloss over any of the bad things, but I shall want to correct some of the wrong things that have been written. Is it selfish to want the truth known?"

And so, Frances Farmer is back, tall, blonde and lovely. Only a few worried lines around her eyes are there to testify to the past.

From the release of these two New York-based interviews, every article since written about me has always been prefaced with the alcoholic label and from there to speculation that I was probably an addict.

The shell that surrounded me prior to the Sullivan show hardened, and I retaliated against the press by not allowing them ever again to invade my privacy. I gave interviews only when they related to a performance, and if any other questions were asked, I pretended deafness.

The night of the Sullivan show, my voice faltered as

I began the song, but then something inside me, that other person, saw past the cameras and technicians, on into the audience that filled the darkened theater. Contact was made, and I drew strength from the power that I was once more standing in my rightful place, giving the only part of myself that was still alive. Giving, to the millions beyond.

I have never been an exceptional singer, and I would have preferred to appear as an actress, but the effect was satisfactory and I was content in knowing that I would be able to retest my dramatic skills during the run at Bucks County.

I remained in the East during July and decided to begin divorce proceedings via deposition. I made contact with a lawyer in Seattle who arranged for me to give written notarized answers to questions he had prepared. The marriage had served its purpose, but it was nearly a year later, on March 7, 1958, that the divorce was finally granted.

My first appearance as an actress or, better, my rebirth as one, came on August 12 at Bucks County. I was indeed pleased when I broke all box office records for the nineteen-year history of the Playhouse. And my reviews were strong, even though laced with the weary recounting of my smashup. While I yearned to forget it, people seemed to grow more anxious to dredge it up.

I was well aware that whenever I was forced into a social or business meeting, my drinks were counted. If I laughed, which was seldom, eyes turned and I could read the looks that said "Ah-ha . . . she's hitting the bottle again."

For my own private dignity, I put a governor on my drinks and held them down to never more than three in public. In private, it was another matter. Once again, as I had in Eureka, when I was finished with my work, I would go to my apartment or room and drink myself to sleep.

I was able to cope with the responsibilities of my career, but I yearned for an escape alley, I suppose, for the privacy I had known as an incognito in Eureka. I knew my thoughts and reasonings were muddled and I was finding it ever more difficult to understand myself. I was emotionally hung over and I continued to drink, but I never suffered the pangs of withdrawal. I was not fooling myself, for I knew something incongruous was taking hold of me.

I had always used liquor, perhaps at times I had misused it, but I was always capable of stopping its control over my behavior before it could interfere with my life.

The amount I had drunk in Eureka was excessive, but I never missed work because of it, nor did drinking hamper my ability to perform on the job.

The bouts I had in San Francisco had been equally as heavy, but also as uncomplicated. I was still able to control the rapid-growing problem.

But, suddenly, something was incubating, and I was reaching a place where I resented anything that interfered with my private drinking. My will was strong enough never to drink when I was working, but I gave up all the frills that come with success. I went to parties or gave interviews only when they were a definite requirement. I made an appearance but left quickly for my private quarters, and there, alone, I would drink.

I was miserable and dissatisfied. Even though I was earning a modest income, there was nothing to spare. I had to cut back in order to hold out until the next job came along, and this only served to increase my insecurity.

Minor irritations loomed in my mind as major issues. Unimportant details became overwhelming in their importance. I was growing more unpleasant, often rude with people.

I believe the main cause of my difficulties, now that I can contemplate it, stemmed from the panic I tried to bury at being alone. There was no one I needed and certainly there was no one I trusted. I cajoled myself into believing that I had the life I wanted. No strings. But there is a human tension that spouts like a stubborn weed when a life is not shared.

This prolonged emptiness, I believe, was the cause of all my difficulties, but years were to pass before I could objectively realize it. At that particular point, when success was again standing in front of me, I was deliberately slamming the door in its face. The inner conflicts were building up and some of the old familiar devils were beginning to run amok. But to all outer appearances, all was well.

I did the second Sullivan show in October and then went to Hollywood to appear on *Playhouse 90,* opposite Hugh O'Brian. Thank God, nothing of the old town remained, except the name. The star system was gone. The major studios, suffering from the impact of television, had lost their stronghold, and what could have been a traumatic experience for me failed to open a wound. The scab had healed. I was intact until I agreed to become involved in a show that I consider the most distasteful episode of my life. Nothing ever cheapened me in my own sight as did my appearance on *This Is Your Life.*

Due to my notoriety, the show had contacted me a few times. The gimmick of the program was to surprise the guest celebrity, but it seems they could not risk taking the tempestuous id of Frances Farmer unaware. I believe only two or three other appearances have been prearranged. I'm not sure why I finally ac-

cepted the show. I've asked myself that question countless times and never found the answer.

There was no dignity attached to my name, but
when I was asked, before millions of viewers, if I was
an alcoholic, or had I ever been an addict, or had I
ever really been mentally ill, I felt degraded and filthy.
What in God's name was I doing there? I could only
reply with curt noes to every question. I came across
as a frigid harpie, and indeed, I put up my coldest defenses. I had never sold myself for so shoddy a price.

And it also seemed that Hollywood still had a bad
taste in its mouth where I was concerned. Many people were asked to appear on the show, people with
whom I had worked and even those who had claimed
to be close friends, but, without exception, not one of
them appeared. It was a dismal affair.

And the impact of the show was far-reaching. What
is said or even implied on television unfortunately be-
comes fact. To the public at large, I was a drunk addict who had gone nuts. These are not the imaginings
of a persecution complex. People to whom I was introduced after that show would sooner or later come up
with, "Oh yes, I saw you on *This Is Your Life.*" A
cocked eyebrow and an all-knowing expression reveal-
ing more than words. I live with so many regrets, but
none as sincere as that ill-timed appearance, and from
that point on I insulated myself further.

After I made a quick movie at the old Paramount
lot called *Party Crashers,* I did a television drama
with Margaret O'Brien called *Tongues of Angels.* There
was also a role on *Treasury Agent* with Lloyd Nolan
and Forrest Tucker.

Summer was coming on and I welcomed the change
of pace it offered. I signed with the Legion Star Playhouse in Ephrata, Pennsylvania, to do *Yes, My Darling
Daughter,* and since the theater had a reciprocal ar-

rangement with Avondale Playhouse in Indianapolis, I was booked there to repeat my role in *The Chalk Garden.* I split these engagements with an appearance in Traverse City, Michigan, thus ending the summer in Indiana.

When I arrived at Avondale Playhouse, I had been back at my profession about a year and wondered what in God's world I was doing and why. Weary, sullen and unnerved, I was becoming increasingly critical of myself and my surroundings. I was skittish, almost on the verge of panic. With the end of the season in sight, I knew I would have to return to New York and wait around for casting calls. The novelty of my "comeback" had worn off and nothing concrete was in the offing. Although my agent kept assuring me that something would turn up, my desperation was mounting.

I was as broke as I had been during my working days at Eureka. It took everything I earned to keep going. I had been able to buy three or four good outfits, but other than that, the money I made went for traveling and living expenses. What was left over I spent on my "survival kit." And I survived simply because I was able to block out my thoughts and fears by ending each day in a solitary, liquor-saturated stupor.

I was playing the old catch-me-if-you-can game, never buying whiskey where I might be recognized, driving ten or fifteen miles to another town to restock my larder. I humored myself into thinking that my secret was secure. And, in some respects, it was. No complaints ever reached me that I was not doing a good job. I performed well enough to earn good reviews and that was what I was being paid to do. My personal problems did not affect my professional life.

But this double life had drawbacks and I became increasingly irritated and hostile.

My contract with Avondale called for a week's rehearsal and a six-day run of the play. I was able to handle the rehearsal well enough, but from opening night on, throughout the rest of the week, I was stuck in a gluelike substance the native Hoosier calls hospitality. For the most part, I had an attentive audience and the critics were an interesting lot who gave rather sharp but fair reviews. This made for good box office.

Most small theater groups however are always in need of money to sustain the losses that seem to be built in. The Indianapolis patrons were generous in their support, but the big-money people, in exchange for their checks, expected to mingle with the "stars" during their appearances, and every night, after the curtain, I was expected to attend some sort of party.

I had cut ribbons at supermarkets, given press interviews or radio talks every day, and I had met half the distaff population at luncheons and teas. I was on television daily. I carried flowers to the Veterans' Hospital. I posed, for no earthly reason, with Ernie Ford, who was also appearing in town, and I had shown up at every theater party without too loud a complaint. The management expected this attendance to soften overstuffed wallets.

Midweek, I dug in my heels and refused to put up with any further social activities, but the management firmly insisted that it was necessary for me to make a showing, especially that evening.

And once more my life was to change course, except this time it would be an original turning and lead me into a rewarding involvement.

After the show that evening, I was tired and ill-tempered. I fooled around in my dressing room, hoping against hope that something would come up and relieve me of the chore that lay ahead. In no mood to meet people, I decided to try and slip away, but when I opened my dressing-room door, the assistant director was posted there to escort me to the party. I grumbled but followed after him.

What I had envisioned as a dull, boring evening turned out to be the most important one of my life.

I made a friend!

It would be trivial and insignificant to detail the introduction. What was said, or why, is not important. What matters is that I felt a sincere hand being offered to me, and, awkwardly, I took it.

16

The word "rehabilitation" means to restore a degraded person, and perhaps at birth I first tasted the despondent cup of degradation, for I came unwanted, and the weight of this burden is a bitter load for any child to bear.

It is not a temporary millstone that is laid aside when the age of maturity comes; instead, it grows even heavier and causes a gall to seep into every area. "Unwanted" is a word of true sorrow.

I was subject to a spiritual weakness, strangely coupled with an indomitable will, and only through this will was I able to survive. I survived, but my life was shallow and graceless. I knew nothing of kindness. I had never received it or given it. To be gentle was to be weak. To me, strength lay only in overpowering violence. Never having come across it, I had no way of understanding the word "love." I did not understand the meaning of loyalty, devotion, tenderness or friendship. The framework of my personality was barren and the frills of sentiment had no place in the hard structure of my survival.

I had run the gamut of life. I had laid in the whore's bed. I had rolled in human waste, and I had lived in such a brutish and physical world that salvation or, if you will, rehabilitation, could never have touched me had it required a physical involvement. My body had been stripped of its needs, and it was nothing more than a coat of flesh that housed a damaged soul. My physical self was spent and beyond all hopes of restoration, but the part of me leashed to the Hound of Heaven, to the spirit of God that dwells in all living things, cried out for recognition, and that silent cry for help, the cry I was unaware of uttering, was answered and carried with it the power that changed my life. Loving and being loved in return was the motivating strength that altered my life.

But the true face of love, defined in its purest sense, is, in today's world, almost drowned in specialized interpretation. It is fashionable to misspell it or to achieve contemporary artistic fame by printing it on two lines with a tilted *o*. It is blinded by psychedelic lights, sought after in mind-blowing drugs, depicted as a warm blanket, mutilated in song, ignored in marriage, deformed in church, and perverted in sex.

It has been altered and overpowered, twisted and turned, until all that is left is a plastic substitute, but there had not been even a synthetic substitute in my life.

When I was sixteen, I had reached a bleak stability and wrote "God Dies," and perhaps this demise of God in my life thwarted all future involvements that came to me and left me emotionally shipwrecked.

Almost too late, but still in time, my redemption did come. It did not arrive in a whirlwind. In fact, it was hardly recognizable at all. Unlike Saint Paul, there was no "road to Damascus" for me to experience; instead a gentle and intelligent human being came into my life and brought the tools which enabled me to rebuild my world.

I was given a friend and finally a family, opposite me in every detail, who withstood the severe challenges I inflicted and who remained reasonable in every crisis I instigated. They were to walk with me and sometimes for me on the long and treacherous trail that led to my eventual restoration. On this journey, they taught me that one cannot compromise when building a foundation. Together we sought solid rock on which I could stand, and through their world I was brought all things.

Jeanira Victoria Ratcliffe was a young widow of thirty when we met. Tall, with acorn-brown hair, she is a free and infectiously cheerful woman, lacking all pretenses but blessed with that indescribable assurance that comes from a strong, established heritage. A Virginian by birth, steeped in the romantic traditions of the South, she bustles with curiosity and quixotic zeal. There is no aura of harassment about her, no evidence of strain. She is the first happy person I have ever met. Life has been gentle to her and she returns it as such. She is, I learned, not only interested in, but concerned about, everything and everyone around her, and the result is a flexible, broad-ranging mind. She is the eternal student, always seeking new and exciting knowledge. But, strangely enough, this quest does not isolate her from the rest of the world. She is as comfortable with the cleaning woman as she is with the governor.

Children adore her, even though she demands a stern and proper pattern of behavior from them in exchange for her interest and friendship. She will not condone bad manners in any form, and I have known her to dismiss a child from the table by saying, "I shall not dine at a trough with piglets." Then buy them a five-pound cake and let them eat it with their fingers, provided they are not messy about it.

Her relationship to God and her belief in Him is a paradox. Reared as a strict fundamentalist, she has no gray areas in her mind where good and evil are concerned. Either it is or it is not. On the other hand, she leans heavily to the mysticism of Eastern religions and is a devout student of metaphysics. She sees no cause, after blending these disciplines, to concern herself with the prospect of either heaven or hell. To her mind, omnipotent reward or punishment is not pertinent to a good life. Her faith in prayer is unshakable, and I have seen her walk through the most desperate and soul-shattering experiences without flinching, simply because she has the innate belief that life is an unfoldment for one's highest good. When our situation has been at its bleakest ebb and I saw no way out, I have turned to her and grown strong from her calm reassurance that patience and faith would carry us through, and it has. She believes in miracles and considers them an indisputable occurrence in her life.

At twenty-two she seriously considered becoming a missionary, but instead started a chain of ice-cream stores, building them into a successful enterprise, then selling out on the spur of the moment when, as she put it, "One day the sun was shining on both sides of the street, and there was I, locked up in a fancy office counting popsicles and drumsticks. Somehow it didn't seem fitting."

She is unreasonably stubborn, but her temper is well controlled. It is also remarkable in its volcanic power. She tolerates conditions that would wear an average person thin, but gives warning that if pushed too far, she would tear a house down, and I have seen her almost do it. She is perfectly capable of leveling anyone who challenges her opinion and does it with a power of a Sherman tank sheathed in velvet, but I have never known her to confront a weaker person with criticism or an "I told you so" attitude.

She can repair a watch with a paper clip, drive a nail in a brick wall with the heel of her shoe, and paint a room during the evening news. She can read a paper in fifteen minutes and will carry an ant from the house rather than kill it. She refuses to carry out garbage, wash windows, or hang clothes on a line but sees nothing demeaning in scrubbing floors or painting the outside of the house.

When she senses the need for something to be done, she will devote herself to it and remain immovable in her loyalty. This, then, is a brief profile of my most cherished friend, Jeanira Ratcliffe, who one day saw a need in me and who, in turn, did something about it.

And it is important to me that I relate some of her complexes and virtues, for they became the point of reference on which my future rested.

At our first meeting I found that Jean, as she is called by her friends, was a prominent interior designer in the Indianapolis area, and from our first introduction I felt a mood of comfortable companionship.

During the course of our conversation I learned that she was driving to an artist colony in the southern part of the state the next morning to buy antiques. I surprised myself by asking if I might go along, but when she picked me up at my hotel, as arranged, I was in a foul mood. I had drunk heavily the night before, and I had tossed and turned until the early hours of dawn. Since the sky was just turning light when I finally fell asleep, an early morning appointment was no longer my idea of a welcomed obligation. Nevertheless, I was only a few minutes late.

Jean was not particularly pretty but was rather interesting-looking, with great brown eyes and an almost childlike smile. At that time, she was going through a particularly painful attack of inflamed cartilages in her legs and was walking with a cane, but the handicap was nothing she belabored or even mentioned.

As we settled down for a leisurely drive, I was mainly interested in nursing my throbbing head. But I was quickly drawn into an easy conversation, touching on everything from books to favorite colors. I was surprisingly at ease and comfortable. And it was almost (and I risk sounding trite) as if we had known each other most of our lives.

Mrs. Miller, whom I learned was the family housekeeper, had packed us a picnic lunch, and after an easy walk through the art studios and antique shops in the village of Nashville, we drove to the nearby state park and spent a quiet lunch hour. I mentioned my book, and she listened as I gave all the reasons why I didn't want to have it written, and rather than challenging my opinion, she agreed.

"In the first place," she said, "I've always had qualms about autobiographies. At what point in a life can one decide they have lived a sufficient span to risk telling who they are and why? So you're probably right in feeling this is not the right time for yours. As long as you have questions about it, it's premature, and that would show in the book. You'll know when the time is right." With that, she dismissed the subject.

When I returned to my hotel, there was a message from the manager of a local television station, an NBC affiliate, who asked that I return his call before theater time that evening. I remembered having met him at one of the parties that had dotted my stay in the city, and when I phoned him, he asked if we might set up a meeting to discuss a new TV project he had in mind. By the end of the week I knew I would be signed as hostess of an afternoon movie program with a guaranteed contract of thirteen weeks and renewal options. The salary was two hundred and twenty-five dollars a week, which meant that I would be able to settle down, at least for a few weeks, and not be physically or financially drained by traveling.

This good fortune pleased me tremendously, and yet I had no one with whom to share it, no one in the world who could have cared less. Wanting to tell someone, I called Jean. She suggested I come to dinner to celebrate; she could easily work the time around my call at the theater.

I was forty-four years old before I had a family, but from the moment I was introduced to her mother and father, I knew that, if I desired it, I had found a place with these gentle, well-bred Southern people. There was a joy and a compatibility among them that surpasses my description. Her father, Lunda, is a handsome and alert man who is known by reputation to have more friends than anyone else in the city. Newsboys and United States Senators both call him by his first name, and Jean gets her straightforward and capable approach to life from him.

Her mother, Lucy, is a delightfully feminine woman, with beautiful bright-green eyes and dark soft hair. Vague and charming, she seems to beguile life.

I took a cab to their home, and before I could ring, the door was opened by Mrs. Miller, Ethel, an intelligent and generous black woman who had for years ruled the family with an iron hand. They did as she pleased and adored her for it.

None of the Ratcliffes drink, not due to any religious or prudish reasons, but simply because their lives are so full that extra stimulus isn't needed. But their bar was well-stocked and Lunda proved a generous host. We dined in a rather hectic fashion with poodles running under the table and friends popping in, who, insisting they were not hungry, sat down and ate just the same. Lunda, having heard of my good fortune with the

TV contract, said that I was to come and stay with them until I could find a house to buy. I protested that I would have no need of property, but he shushed me by saying, "Good God, woman, if you do a good job, you'll probably be here the rest of your life, so why pay rent? You should own your own place."

Jean had been on the phone during this conversation, and when I mentioned that her father had invited me to stay with them, I expected astonishment. Instead, she said, "Well, if you can put up with us, we would be delighted."

Lunda insisted that he and Ethel check me out of the hotel while Jean drove me to the theater. I was so drawn to the Ratcliffes that I, who literally hated people, was moving in with a family who thrived on them.

Lunda is the first man I have ever known who takes hold of a situation and decides what should be done about it. And he is masculine enough that no woman can find any logical reason not to go along with his decisions. Lucy, delighted with the social prospects of a new houseguest, decided that I would have Jean's room and began making plans accordingly.

By the time we left for the theater everything had been arranged. One of the friends who had pulled up a chair and joined us for dinner said he would ride with them to the hotel and drive my car back to the house. Ethel asked how many suitcases I had, and Lunda took the key to my room. I mentioned that I would have to settle my bill, but he fluffed that problem aside by saying he would take care of it, and we would work it out later. It was never mentioned to me again. I was to learn in the years to come that this man was staunch in his belief that women were meant to be spoiled and he could find no cause for them ever to pay their way, as long as he was around. They were made to be cared for, and he had been brought up in the strict biblical dictum to help the "widows and orphans." On Sunday mornings, during the summer, he had a regular route of mowing the lawns for ladies in the neighborhood who were elderly or alone. And I learned, as time passed, that many fatherless families, black and white alike, lived in their apartments rent-free—with groceries mysteriously made available whenever the pantries were bare.

It was difficult to cope with pure giving when I had lived so long in absolute selfishness. It was hard to recognize tenderness without being suspicious, but the true kindness of this family was so inbred that it drew me in close, in spite of myself.

That night, after the play closed, I drove home with Jean, and my next three years with them were spent learning how to accept love. I use the term "learning" in its purest sense, for I had never been exposed to kindness before, and I had to "learn" how to live with it.

On October 1, 1958, I began my television show completely relaxed and at ease. I appeared every afternoon from five till seven on WFBM-TV, as hostess of a movie theater called *Frances Farmer Presents*. And, from the premiere showing, the ratings were excellent and were never to fall from the top of the chart. The station went all-out on promotion, and for a local program, it was expensively produced.

During the breaks I would discuss the motion picture I was presenting in what I hoped was an intelligent and informative manner, and within two or three weeks after the show was under way, name guests began joining me for chats and interviews. I was hostess of the program for six productive years, during which time I had as my guests a wide scope of celebrities, including Ginger Rogers, Barbra Streisand, Sophie Tucker, Kathy Crosby, Chet Huntley, Rory Calhoun, Hildegarde, Sylvia Sidney, Helen Hayes, Vivian Vance, and so many others that I cannot begin to name them all. Oh, yes, and lest I forget, Leif Erickson.

For the most part it was the most rewarding job I had ever had, but as time passed, it naturally became tedious. From the beginning, Lunda advised that I not do commercials. His feeling was that I should be identified only with the format of the show and not with any product. I recognized the logic in his thinking and had it written into my contract that I would never be required to do a lead into a product or handle a commercial. This was an intelligent decision insofar as it gave me a friendlier, more intimate relationship with my viewers.

When I began the show, I was a neophyte in television, but I was able to handle the demanding responsibility of a six-day-a-week program, and I seriously devoted myself to building a substantial audience. However, had it not been for the Ratcliffes and their easygoing assurance that I could do it, I would never have made it through the first week. Living with them during this period was the foothold I needed, and their involvement in my personal life and work never left the realm of good taste. I was made a part of the family but allowed total privacy. If I wanted to sleep until midafternoon, there was no one rapping on my door seeing why I was not up. Whatever I decided to do never seemed to complicate their flexible lives.

As the popularity of my show increased and I began meeting local people, I found that Indianapolis was much like any other city its size, and as I came to know the family better, I experienced the first joy of belonging and of knowing I was cared for. I took a chance and put my trust in them, a little at a time, and they never let me down. This is not to say that they failed, each in their own way, to recognize my shortcomings or imperfections. Rather, they were able to see them as temporary and perhaps necessary traits that needed the right of expression.

I began a new life. I learned to rely on Lunda and his judgments. I heeded his advice, and although Jean was fifteen years my junior, there was never a time gulf between us—at least not from my point of view. Lucy delighted me as the woman of the house, and she was shamefully spoiled. Delicate and blithe, she brought with her, in every situation, the ease and beauty of a contented woman. And Ethel adopted me with the devotion she had for the Ratcliffes.

I became a second daughter, sharing the same stronghold in their hearts, as did Farrell, Jean's cousin, whom she called "almost-sister." When Lunda would say, "Frances, you're my almost-daughter," I was as proud as I could be. I accepted this role and tried to live up to it. I wanted them to love me and I was almost infantile in my attachment.

However I was puzzled as to why they had accepted me so readily. I never found the courage to question them about it, and Ethel had told me I was not the first person to have lived with them.

I knew Lunda sensed this questioning in me, and one morning when he was working in the yard, I took him a cup of coffee and we sat down on the back stoop and talked. He brought up the subject head on, telling me he was well aware of my public reputation. He, too, had seen *This Is Your Life,* but unlike other people I had met, he looked past the Peeping Tom and saw, instead, a woman publicly stripped of her dignity. He compared it to an unjustified tar and feathering. Then, when he learned that Jean was going to spend the day with me, he checked into what I had been up to in Indianapolis, and it was not difficult for him to get a rather dismal report of my general disposition. But when Jean had come home and told him that I seemed so sad, so remote and so unhappy, he was pleased that we had been together. She went on to tell him that underneath it all, she thought I just might be a lady. We both chuckled over this. He was sophisticated enough to know that, in its purest sense, I could never be called that.

He added that when we met, he saw a woman almost ready to break and simply had to do something about it. It was that cut and dried. He didn't consider himself or his family saviors of any sort. He claimed that anyone else would have done the same thing, but the fact remains that they are the only people who ever did.

We sat together for an hour or so, and it was a sharing and acceptance of experiences. We spoke openly about my drinking and he was pleased that I felt I was whipping it. We talked about my years in the asylum and he held my hand tightly and listened. We talked about my family, and he flinched when I related some of the incidents that had happened between us. And we talked of my future and what it held for me.

In years, he was barely old enough to be my father, but he treated me as his own, and I reveled in the joy of having a family. To compare them and my own blood family was to list antonyms. They loved. Mine hated. They believed. Mine destroyed. They respected. Mine mocked. They repaired. Mine tore asunder.

When I told him I thought I had all my problems licked, he cuffed me under the chin and laughed. "Don't be too sure, old girl," he said, half teasing. "We've all got a long way to go, and things have a habit of jumping up at us when we least expect them.

Just don't be too hard on yourself, and don't worry about 'licking everything.' Just learn to take it easy and things will work out."

I lived, as one of them, sharing all their joys and loves for nearly three years, and during this time Lunda always kept a careful eye on my progress. Then, one evening at dinner, he mentioned a small house for sale on the north side of the city and suggested that we look at it the coming Sunday. He went on to say that since my contract had been renewed for another year, I should start thinking of investing my income, and a good piece of property, he felt, was a solid move in the right direction.

I was not being "moved out" and I knew it. Although I was lax to admit it to myself, I had reached a point of wanting to have a place of my own. I signed for the house about the same time Jean bought into an exclusive decorating studio located a block or two from my new home.

Jean had become my friend and sister as well as my mentor, and I did not want to be away from her, so one evening I asked if she would share the house with me. It was selfish and almost unthinkable to suggest that she leave her own home and act as a buffer in mine. But I who had always prided myself on my total independence panicked at the thought of being alone.

Jean thought about it for a long moment and then said, "Frances, this is something you need to do for yourself, but I'll help you in every way I can. And of course, I'll come and stay, off and on. But right now it's important that you dig your teeth into something and hold onto it . . . so I'll have to say no, conditionally. In time, when you're really settled within yourself, we'll talk about it again.

"If you find that owning your own place is too much for you to handle, emotionally, I mean, then we will do something about it, but, I feel, down deep, that you're really going to make it. It's a big step but at least you're taking it."

During the time I had lived with the Ratcliffes I had told Jean in brutal detail about the nightmare years in the asylum and my parents. She had been reared never doubting she was loved, while I had existed always knowing that I was not. Though opposites, we were somehow able to understand and respect each other. Perhaps because she had an attribute I had not yet acquired. Wisdom.

Taken up with buying furniture and picking out all the necessary things that go with setting up housekeeping, I kept pushing the realization that I soon would be leaving them to the back of my mind. The house was small, old and charming, with a bit of the English country look about it. It was built over the foundation of a log cabin and was tucked back on a quiet, tree-lined street. In front was a high hedge and a giant maple tree. An old, uneven brick walk led up to the front stoop. Across the back of the property, fencing in a deep, lush lawn, were giant pines that stood erect and tall.

The evening I was to move to my house, Jean came home with a shepherd puppy tucked under her arm. It was their housewarming gift to me, and although I had no wish for a dog, it was such a happy hooligan that I couldn't resist it. I named it Sport. It was soon to be joined by Willie, an injured stray kitten, which grew into a marvelous, cantankerous cat.

Lunda sensed that I did not want to be left alone that night and suggested that Jean stay with me until I got used to the place. I could tell that she had not intended to do so, especially after our talk, but she agreed and it was settled.

With a new puppy snuggling close to me, and my dear friend in a nearby room, I slept well that night under my own roof.

17

It was an exciting time for me. My program was gaining national attention and several good articles were written about me in important television and trade papers. My yearly contract was renewed, agreeably on both sides, with a modest pay increase.

My personal and private life was serene. Most of the old fears lay dormant and seldom seemed to surface. There were times when I felt uneasy, which was natural, but most often I was able to manipulate very well. But to say that I took on a whole new personality or outlook would be untrue.

When I was with the family, which was often, I was always as lighthearted as they and never felt tight or on edge. And when I was in my home, I was comfortable, but my public life was something else. I was never warm to my co-workers, but I'm sure they took my standoffish attitude as something left over from Hollywood. And I never made other friends. People approached me, I suppose, with a sincere desire to know me better, but I always shut the door in their faces. I did not want any part of the outside world.

The Ratcliffes entertained constantly, but their guests never tried to pry into my business or even appeared to notice that I was on television. I was simply a member of the Ratcliffe family. There were times when I would drink too much and no one seemed to think anything about it. But there were also times when I would start to mouth off and Lunda would quickly silence me. I took it from him and shut up. Lucy never seemed to notice when I was especially bad-mannered at parties, but Ethel would give me dark looks and cluck her tongue. Jean cringed at my "disgraceful behavior," as she put it, but it was always Lunda, as the man of the house, who would make no bones about my shaping up. And when the guest had gone, he would really land into me. He was firm but loving. He never rode me about my drinking, only about my manners.

I was a social misfit with no desire to be otherwise, escept with them. Public appearances connected with my program were handled well, but I shunned all social events that did not pertain to my work, or did not revolve around the Ratcliffes. All in all, things were going well. There was still inner torment, but it did not swim to the surface too often to hamper me. I was functioning better than I ever had.

That summer, during my vacation, I made my first of many visits with the Ratcliffes to their family home in Virginia, and I learned to love that gentle land almost as devoutly as did the native-born.

I was well aware that Jean had come from an elite heritage, but I was still surprised at the gracious home of her birth. Looking for all the world like a Tara, with the threadbare elegance that befits only the gentry, the house rested in a long, rolling valley. Surrounding it were the majestic foothills of the Blue Ridge, and in the distance, the rugged rim of the Cumberlands slashed the horizon. It was breathtaking, and I was puzzled why the family was content to leave it in the hands of a caretaker.

Their Indianapolis home was modest, though well

furnished, but in no way compared to the antebellum charm of their homeplace. I pressed Lunda for an explanation, and standing beside me on the long veranda, he said, "There is no way people like us can make a living down here, Frances. The life, as we knew it, is gone. The timberland is all worked out and the small mines are stripped, so all we can do is come back once in a while and dream a little of how things used to be. I suppose sooner or later we'll sell the house, because it's wrong to let it stand like this. But, for now, we'll just drop in once in a while and let it know we're still in the world."

Standing there with that strong, tender man, I felt the power of honorable taproots and I could not help envying Jean her heritage. I went back often, sometimes with them, sometimes with only Jean, until several years later it was sold for a pittance and turned into a hotel.

After that, we never went back.

I remained ever amazed how intimate a medium television is. During the life of my program people kept up a regular correspondence with me, despite the fact that I never replied to their letters. Letters came from schoolchildren asking outlandish questions, and there were proposals from all sorts of oddball men. There were countless letters from students wanting advice on how to get into show business, and from teachers asking me to conduct their drama classes. There were gifts of handmade doilies from elderly ladies who thought kindly of me and packets of flower seeds from retired gentlemen who had heard me mention starting a garden at home. There were untold letters asking me for my "old" clothes, and people would show up at the station, declaring themselves to be long-lost relatives, based on no other evidence than similar last names.

To be a personality on a local level is difficult. You possess the glamor of show business and the disadvantage of being a neighbor, so to speak. It was as if living in a fishbowl, and whether I went to the market or to the symphony, I was always surrounded by autograph seekers and the "stand off and stare at her" curious. This made me uncomfortable, but I felt I handled it all rather well. I assumed I was not making too many enemies. I was not making friends, that was certain, but I felt I was no longer alienating anyone.

For the most part, the public was kind to me and I became an accepted factor in the community. I never mixed with my neighbors, though I lived on a typical middle-class street. They seemed sensitive enough to recognize my need for privacy. Probably because I insisted on it. I would give them curt nods but never paused to chat. I contributed to the floral collection if one of them died, but, for the most part, I remained aloof and unattainable.

My drinking had almost subsided during the years I had lived with the Ratcliffes, and even though living alone had had its setbacks, I had not come to rely on liquor to the extent I once had. I drank more, in solitude, but it was not a problem. At least, nothing critical was developing from it. But I did notice that each month my bill from the liquor store increased on an average of twenty dollars. This, I reasoned, was not too bad; it meant only that I was drinking about a fifth more a week. Dividing that into days, I diagnosed that, overall, I was handling the situation very well.

I had fallen into the habit of calling home (the Ratcliffes') several times a day, and every night I would talk with Jean for an hour or two. Although I was not with them as much as I once had been, I was still connected and relatively satisfied.

But deep inside, there was still loneliness.

My first Christmas in my new home, in 1961, I spent drunk.

The Ratcliffes had planned on my being with them as usual, and I was anxious to share in the traditional, trim-the-tree open house that began on Christmas Eve afternoon and continued well into Christmas night.

I had to work on Christmas Eve, but I planned to go to their house as soon as my program was over. I had only a skeleton crew, but all went well on the show. During one of the longer runs I started reading the day's delivery of Christmas cards, and there, tucked in among the sincere and thoughtful greetings of countless people, was the first of many poison-pen letters I would receive over the next several years. I read it and sickened. It rambled with vile and gutter filth, accusing me of a lesbian relationship with Jean. I was horrified and hardly able to finish the show, for the evil words flushed everything else out of my mind. I went to my dressing room and threw up. The boys on the crew knew something was wrong, and when we signed off, one of them asked me if I was sick. The old, snarling anger came up. "You're goddamned right I'm sick . . . sick of this whole rotten town and every asshole in it."

I stormed out of the studio and almost stripped the gears on my car driving away. And for the first time in many months, I ran to the bottle. I picked up a full supply at the neighborhood liquor store and locked myself in the house. But before I started drinking, I called the Ratcliffes, hoping to talk with Jean. Lunda answered and he knew something was wrong. I told him curtly that I would not be out, and he didn't press me for an explanation.

"You know we want you with us," he said. "But we'll go along with whatever you say. If you change your mind, come on out . . . and you know, don't you, that if you need me, I'll be there."

My contract with the station called for me to do a special Christmas Day program, and I told Lunda I'd be at their house as soon as it was over. After an all-night bout with the bottle, I was unable to make either appearance. I was replaced on the Christmas show with a last-minute substitute, and when this was announced, Lunda and Jean immediately came to the house. For the first time, they saw me drunk, stumbling, and disheveled. The crude, filthy Frances Farmer had returned, but they didn't draw away.

Although I had consumed three fifths, I was still able to wobble around, but I had thrown up on myself, on the floor, in the bed, all over the bathroom, on the walls, in the sink. The house was a stinking shambles, and I had almost wrecked everything in it. I had wanted to tear up something, and in a fit of drunken violence, I had almost destroyed my home.

Jean looked around at the wreck while I tottered in front of them, mumbling, and with her brown eyes wide she said lightly, "Lord have mercy, Frances, you sure do know how to throw a shoe."

Then I began a wild tirade, screaming and shouting until I crumpled in a heap on the floor, sobbing. All the while she and her dad sat calmly on the couch and watched. They didn't try pouring hot coffee down me but tucked a pillow under my head and covered me with a blanket. Lunda built a fire in the fireplace and told Jean, "Stay with her until she gets on her feet."

When he left, Jean turned off the lights and curled

up on the couch. The last thing I remember was hearing her say, good-naturedly, "If you ever do a thing like this again, Frances, so help me, I'll sic old Willie on you."

In spite of my misery, I had to smile.

She stayed on, and for the next three days I drank incessantly. I had my supply delivered, and I don't know how much I consumed. She never tried to force me to eat or talk me out of ordering more when my supply started to diminish, but I knew her well enough to know that, at the right time and in her own particular way, she would flatten me with both barrels. She had the common sense to realize that the peak of a binge was no time for a lecture, but I knew that sooner or later it would come. Obviously, Lunda was leaving it up to her, for he called only to check how I was.

He covered me with the station by calling a doctor friend to verify that I was "quite ill" and unable to work for several days. Then, on the fourth day, when I was convinced I was sick enough to die, Jean called the doctor and asked if he would stop by at the end of his office hours. This physician, young and capable, was to make many similar visits during the next years, but I can never forget the first time he came. There was no whispering behind the door. Jean told him point-blank that I had been on a spree, which was evident, for she had made no effort to clean up my room. He had to step over broken glass and vomit to get to me. And after he had given me a vitamin shot, he said simply, "Well, you'll be all right if you lay off the booze. You're flirting with the dangers of low blood pressure, and if you keep on, you're going to end up in the hospital. I might as well tell you, straight from the shoulder, that, if you go, everyone in town will know why you're there. So your best bet is to sober up or take the consequences."

I was hardly able to move. I was sprawled out in soiled, sweaty pajamas, and after he left, she sat in a chair opposite me and asked politely: "Can you drink any more? Or is this it?"

The thought of a drink made me gag.

"Well, then," she drawled, "if you're through, I'll change your bed."

She helped me undress, for I was beyond doing anything for myself. But when I lay back, I began vomiting again. Dry, hard spasms hit me until I rolled and screamed in anguish and humiliation. I was sobbing and groaning, begging God to let me die while she washed my face and body in cool water. She sat on the side of the bed, keeping my face cool and eased with the moist cloth, until I fell asleep.

But it was fitful. I would wake up screaming and in panic, until I saw her sitting in the chair beside my bed. Alcoholic nightmares and fits are sometimes beyond human help, and screaming hysterically, I violently fought off Jean's attempts to settle me down. How long I battled, I cannot say. I do know that I remained desperately ill and disturbed for the rest of the week. The new year came and went, and she never left. I could see the strain was telling on her, and when the doctor stopped by again, both of us were near exhaustion.

During the week of my "bout," as she called it, I had only gone the short distance from my bed to the bathroom. When I told Jean one afternoon that I thought I'd like to get up and perhaps have something solid to eat, I walked into the wreckage I had created on Christmas Eve. Everything was as I had left it.

I picked my way through the revolting mess and

slumped into a chair in the family room, letting out a groan of dismay. She made a place for herself on the couch and said calmly, "In so many words, dear friend, you did it . . . and you clean it up."

"What day is it?" I mumbled.

"Forget it," she said. "I called Lorraine [my house-keeper] and told her not to come this week. Listen, Frances, you can do anything you want, but I'm damned if you're going to pass this off by paying somebody else to come in here and clean up your mess. This is your dirty linen, and it's going to stay dirty until you wash it. Nobody else is going to do it for you."

"You go to hell," I yelled. "This is my house, and I'll damn well do as I please."

"Not this time, you won't," she shouted back. She jumped from the couch and charged over to me, her face flushed with anger. I had never seen her as anything but a properly behaved gentlewoman. I was startled by her hot-blooded temper.

"I don't give a damn if you want to get drunk a dozen times a week," she stormed. "That's your business, but so long as we're friends you're never going to push your trash off on somebody else. I'll tolerate anything out of you except slovenliness, and you'd be purely sloven if you were low-down enough to pay somebody to mop up after you."

Although she was shocked at my drinking, she was even more horrified to think that I would let someone pick up the remnants of my binge.

"Okay! Okay!" I grumbled. "When I feel like it . . . but leave me alone, will you? You and your god-damned boarding school crap. Just leave me alone."

I spent another two or three days recuperating, seeing if I could wait her out, and from it I learned to respect yet another trait. What she said, she meant, and she had no intentions of backing down. But when I finally started picking things up, she made every effort to help me, and it took us the better part of a day to put the house back in some sort of order and to air it out. It smelled like a rotting brewery.

That evening, while I took a bath (my first in days), she scrambled some eggs and we ate together, also for the first time in days. I was still wobbly and my hands shook, but I knew that when dinner was finished, she would expect to have some explanation of my behavior. What could I gell her? How could I possibly confront her with the gossip that had triggered me off? But I knew I would have to say something. The basis of our relationship was too firmly grounded on honesty not to tell her the truth. And yet the truth would hurt, not only her, but her family. I had grown accustomed to having things said about me and evil gossip was no stranger in my life. My reputation had been wrung through the wringer a long time ago. But now, because of me, good and decent people would be soiled, and I cared too much to let it happen.

Over my second cup of coffee, she said, "Now, Frances, I want you to tell me what happened. I don't want to pry in your business, but I think we'd better talk this out, now. Don't you?"

I had the letter in my purse. I found it and handed it to her. I watched as she read, cocking her head from time to time and pursing her lips, and when she'd finished she looked at me and said, "Is this what upset you?"

"Is that all you have to say? Did it upset me? Jesus Christ!"

"Well, for heaven's sake! I thought it was something important. I had no idea junk like this could get to you."

I slapped down my coffee cup, exasperated. "Well,

what the hell's the matter with you? You and your goddamned pious blue-blood upbringing, you throw up your hands if the wrong fork is used, but let some filthy bastard call you a queer and you don't even bat an eye. Christ, you're nuts. Plain damn nuts."

"I can't do a thing about gossip. I can about table manners. And I have no plans to get myself worked up over something like this." She tossed the letter on the coffee table. "There is no way to fight or stop gossip. If tongues want to wag, there's no way to bridle them. Frances, grow up. I've heard this stuff for months."

"You've known this was going on for months and never told me?"

"What was there to tell? What did you expect me to do? Come up and say, 'Oh, by the way, Frances, people think we're sleeping together.' Is that what you expected? Really!"

"Does Lunda know?"

"I suppose so. He knows everything else that's going on in town, so he's probably heard it. But I've never asked him. Why should I?"

"And you don't care?"

"Of course I care. But what can I do to stop it, except use my head? I've thought all along that it had to begin somewhere, and the logical place was with someone we've known. But who? So the only thing to do in a case like this is cut off all the casuals . . . cut them off and forget them. And that's what I've done. The bad thing is, once something like this starts, especially where it concerns someone in the public eye, it spreads like wildfire and gets all out of hand. I'm only sorry you've had to put up with it."

"How could anyone think such a thing?"

"Who knows? Maybe, in a way, we've asked for it. I don't know. But it seems like in this day and time people have forgotten what friendship is. They see a man with a male friend or a woman with a female friend and, right away, their minds start thinking, 'Oh, ho, there's hanky-panky there.' So the way I figure it, as long as we know who we are, I couldn't care less what other people think. But don't ask me to give you any pat answers, because I don't have any. The best thing to do is let it burn itself out."

I listened to this friend and noticed, for the first time, the tired, new lines around her eyes. She had given me so much and in return had been slandered by lies.

This girl, young and talented, had not given way as I had. She had held it within herself and had gone on as though nothing had ever happened. Would to God that I had had the same bearing.

I knew then that I would have to make a move to protect her from herself. Notoriety had never stopped dogging my heels, but I could not let it bring additional harm to her or her family. They meant too much to me, and the thought of the lies made me shudder. I had to fight to keep from crying.

I stood up, haughty and swaggering, and gave the performance of my life. "If you think I'm going to risk what I've got going for me, you'd better think again. Listen, you dim-witted rebel, you haul your ass out of my house, right now, and don't you ever come back. I don't need you. I never have. And I'm damned if I'm going to sit around and have a queer badge hung around my neck. Not on your life. So, stay away from me. Once and for all, stay away."

She sat motionless for a long moment, then said, "Do you mean all that?"

"You bet your sweet ass, I mean it. Wise up. You've been a port in a storm. Nothing more. You've been something I could use, only it backfired on me. Christ! I've been called a lot of things in my life, but never a dike!"

The old, insulting talent came back and I was able to berate her until she was almost in shock. I mocked the family. I made fun of her mother. I laughed at her father. I called her a sucker and stooge. I ripped our friendship apart and tore up everything I held dear. I ended screaming at her to get out of my house.

She stood at the side door, ashen, then turned and said, "Maybe this is the best way to handle it, Frances. I'm not one to say. But if you ever need anything, and you will, I guess you know that I'll do whatever I can."

"Get out!" I screamed.

She left, closing the door quietly behind her, and I buried my face in my hands and wept. I was forty-six years old before I had had anything in life I felt worth protecting, and I had driven it away.

The house was empty now, and I sat alone.

Life became suddenly very bitter.

Lunda did not call me or make any effort to "solve" my problems or change my mind. That was the marvelous thing about the family; they each had an insight that told them when to make a move and when to stand still. And they sensed, perhaps rightly so, that this was my time of personal evaluation. Also, there was the strong point, inbred in Jean, that would have gone against everything in her to have come back to the house without my asking. I knew this and I counted on it to solidify the severance.

But was the letter an excuse? I asked myself that question so many times during the months that followed. Was it a crutch I grabbed to carry me back to the bottle? I knew that a drunk hunted for reasons to drink and then consoled himself or herself into believing that his plight was unique and his drinking was, therefore, justified.

It has been called "demon rum" by the hot-eyed evangelists, and there is much truth in this primitive label. All the devils that had lain quietly within me swung free and badgered me almost to death. Liquor became my sole companion and drinking my most passionate pleasure. It was my friend. My family. My salvation. And I would sit alone, looking into a half-empty bottle, talking to it as though it were alive.

I continued to breathe, but with each breath came the consolation that I was coming closer to the grave. That was my purpose, I told myself, to live till I died, and like all those who clutch the bottle to their breast, I rolled in self-pity.

There have been many sides to me, sides I do not understand, and one of the primary ones has been that perplexing factor that permits me to function while all the time I am cracking into a million pieces inside. I can stand erect when I am inwardly crawling. I can smile when my mind is screaming in agony. I can react when all spiritual action has ceased.

And this is the me that surfaced during that lonely period.

I did not see Jean again for more than two years. I continued doing a satisfactory job on television. I was named Business Woman of the Year for Indiana. I was honorary chairman of the Red Cross drive. I moderated fashion shows. I spoke before clubs and at student assemblies. I handled my public life well, but I did so in a suspended haze. I was never completely sober, and as the weeks passed, I grew tight-lipped and sour.

I was earning a living, but I was not saving any

money. I spent recklessly on clothes and trips. I would take time off and go to outlandishly expensive places. I made my house payments on time but spoiled myself with a full-time maid. I hired a secretary to take care of my mail and speaking schedules and in no way prepared for that inevitable rainy day. I simply didn't care.

At night, sitting alone and morose, I once again fell into the habit of drinking myself into a stupor. I was home by seven thirty every evening, and "out" in an hour or two. I would sleep, drugged with liquor, sometimes fifteen hours. I would get up, bathe, and make myself ready for the show. This routine went on day after day, week after week, month after month.

During this time I hardened against the gossip that peppered me on every side. Why and how it started, and by whom, I would learn much later but would not venture to detail the unspeakable things that were said. Things that chilled me to the bone. Hollywood had never been as dreadful.

Despite all this, I was kept on by the station, but for one reason only: My show remained at the top of the rating charts and I was money in the bank. Sponsors waited, sometimes for weeks, to get a spot on the show, and I became, I suppose, something of a household joke with the viewers. Is she drunk? Is she really living with a black man? Is she crazy? I hear she is on dope. Is she a nympho? Is she a lesbian? Is she? Is she? Is she?

And the despicable letters poured in, accusing me of every foul thing imaginable. Almost from that first letter everything snowballed, and all the choice tidbits reached my ears. And yet, not once was anyone in my house. Not one person could truthfully say he had had any personal contact with me. I minded my own business, and, unfortunately, so did everyone else.

Then, early in the spring of '64, I received a personal call from the *Today Show,* asking if I would be interested in letting them do an hour profile on me. Since this was not arranged through the local station, I explained that I would have to talk it over with the management. Needless to say, the front office was excited with the prospects, and plans were made for the *Today* crew to come from New York and film me for several days in my own environment.

I can't say I was especially excited over it, but there was personal satisfaction. The local gossip having almost torn me down, it was good to know that nationally I was gaining back some respect. The *Today Show* was prestige.

After the film had been taken and edited, I went to New York to appear in person on a segment. John Daly, the substitute host, was a charming, sensitive man, who gracefully skirted the old Hollywood difficulties and mentioned my smashup only in passing. He geared the interview to the current me. There were film clips of Sport and Willie and shots taken inside the house. And as far as the program was concerned, all went well.

However, I was personally furious. A cortege of executives from the local station had decided to make the trip with me, and I resented their cashing in. The appearance had not come about from any of their efforts, and I was especially livid when they brought along the station mascot, a lumbering Saint Bernard named WoofBoom, which contributed nothing except tons of slobber.

I stayed on in New York for a week to attend the World's Fair, but while I was there, I began to suffer dizzy spells, which made it difficult for me to keep my balance. I knew the effects were something more than the results of drinking, which I was still doing in deadly earnest.

At times my speech would slur and it was obvious to me that something was wrong. When I returned to Indianapolis, I described the symptoms to my doctor in detail. I learned, after three days in the hospital, that I was bordering on seriously low blood pressure aggravated, of course, by excessive drinking. He told me to cut down. But this was as if telling a rock to crumble. I lived to drink and drank to live, so there was nothing I could do except listen to his lecture and take his pills.

At this point, I believe the desperate strain of being alone took its toll. I had never been lonelier or so lonesome. I had nothing to rely on. After I went back to work, I was disgusted with my job and I wanted out of the whole thing. But it was money in the cookie jar, and I kept up a tired pretense.

My show suffered from this, but I no longer cared. Then, one afternoon in late March, 1964, I showed up as sober as I usually was but completely out of control. I could not walk a straight line. My eyes would not focus and my tongue was thick. I gave every indication of being falling-down drunk, and I was replaced for the rest of the show. But not until they had shot the opening segment with me squinting at the camera and not being able to find it, muttering something about "Frances Farmer prevents." My blood pressure had dropped to a critical low, but to the public at large, I had appeared on camera bombed out of my mind.

The story that I had been replaced made front-page news. It was reported that I had been fired on the spot, but the station denied the rift and said it was all a misunderstanding. We finally patched it up at a news conference, and all was sugar and cream.

To save face for all concerned, I agreed to go back to work and stand up before the camera as though nothing had happened. And my ratings shot higher, for the public has a distorted curiosity and wanted to see what was going to happen next. Nothing did, at least for a time.

That fall my self-esteem was partially restored when I received an invitation from the Purdue University Drama Department, inviting me to appear in a production of *Look Homeward, Angel* as actress-in-residence.

University theater was an original passion of mine, and I immediately accepted the invitation. The play was to be directed by Dr. Joseph Stockdale, a talented theatrical scholar whom I sincerely respect and admire. He also directed me in two other plays at Purdue, *The Sea Gull* and *The Visit*. Brave and experimental in his direction, Joe brought out a thread of my original talent, and under his guidance I came to life as an actress. In all my experiences on Broadway and in Hollywood, I was never as deeply touched or influenced as I was by him. My work at Purdue stands high in my memory as a valuable and cherished experience.

While I was in rehearsal for the play and during the run, I did not rely on liquor. I was too stimulated with my work. But when it was over and I had to return to the old routine of television fluff, the drinking cycle began all over again. The doctor kept warning me to stop or at least cut down, but I plowed on determined to do-or-die as I pleased. Not only was I suffering all the expected reactions of low blood pressure, but also I was magnifying them by bringing on super or abnormal reactions with my drinking.

All this, along with the trying problems of menopause and the days and nights of deep loneliness, brought me to a critical point in my life. For the first time I was suffering not only from emotional strain and defeat but from physical problems as well. And ever constant, ever present were the dreadful letters and obscene gossip. It was all more than I could handle.

Late in the fall of that year, we were scheduled to do a remote series of telecasts, and on this particular morning I felt too ill to appear on the show and, this time, not from drinking. I started to call my director to tell him I would not be in, then changed my mind. I wanted to make the effort, but by the time I arrived at the location site I was staggering and unable to hold my balance. I could hardly talk. I had great difficulty in parking my car and had run over the curb in doing so. I simply could not function.

The program director met me before I reached the set and told me I was being replaced. It was all over. That afternoon I released the station from my contract with no cash settlement and made a clean break. When I took inventory of myself, I found I had three hundred dollars in the bank, an extensive wardrobe I no longer needed, a home that was not paid for, a dog and a cat, and nothing else, except an unquenchable thirst.

The next morning a modest announcement appeared in the local papers to the effect that the station had canceled my contract. This time the report did not speculate on a possible reconciliation and concluded with the statement, "Miss Farmer was not available for comment." The subject died with hardly a flutter, and a new host was assigned to carry on the show. As for me, I was out of a job, but had one been offered (which it was not), I could not have accepted it. I was incapable of handling the most minor responsibilities. I had reached a desperate state.

That evening, after the announcement appeared, after I had had a day to mull over the situation, I came to the conclusion that I was not terribly disturbed over losing the job. The show had run its course and I had said all I knew about old movies and local PTA meetings. Naturally I would miss the income, but a six-day-a-week show spread over nearly six years can weave a net of total exhaustion, even under the most desirable conditions. And most certainly, I had not lived under an easy cloud.

I was in no shape to go out and look for another job straight off. My mind was almost refusing to function properly. The pressures from all sides, coupled with the flood of gossip and the ever-nagging question as to why, served as a constant shock treatment. I was numb and terribly confused.

Physically I was finding it more and more difficult to manipulate. I was having hot, searing pains in my stomach, pains that would almost knock me out, and I was also under heavy medication for the low blood pressure that constantly plagued me. I learned I had the beginning of an ulcer, and then a wild, horrible rash broke out all over my body. I was told this was due to nerves and "the change."

I had been so long by myself that all the old devils had climbed out of my submind and pranced in front of me. I relieved the years in the asylum. I would rattle through the house, talking to myself or the animals, my only living attachments.

And there was always the liquor, the coward's way out. It is a slow and messy road to suicide. And although I drank constantly, I hated myself and my cowardice for submitting to the weakness. And so, laboring under all these handicaps, I found myself at a total standstill. But if I were to consider all the factors that damaged me the most, I would have to name, without reservation, gossip. The filth that was spread never made sense, for it was all unfounded. And it disturbed me to the point of driving me to a breaking point. But that night, to my absolute horror, the puzzle was unraveled.

The man who had recognized me in Eureka and who had taken me to San Francisco to handle my "comeback" showed up at my house about ten thirty. The same man on whom I had walked out, in spite of his threats of "I'll find some way of getting even with you," stood on my front porch yelling for me to open the door. He kept his finger on the bell without letup and kicked the door with his foot. I was not only startled at seeing him after all these years but also annoyed at the fracas he was creating. Sport was in the house, looking for all the world like an honorably discharged canine veteran, and I grabbed onto his collar, pretending to hold him back from attacking. I barely opened the door, and for a moment or two I thought the man was going to force his way in, but instead, he stood on the porch and laughed at me, rocking back and forth on his heels, like a swaggering warlord. And then he began to rant and brag about what he had done.

When he had learned where I was, he had moved to Indianapolis and got a job selling advertising throughout the state. And in each city or town where he stopped to make calls, he would hang around the local bars and, at every opportunity, would pass out his "inside information." He had a lot of snapshots of the two of us together, taken that week we had stayed

with his friends, and this added credibility to his tidbits. They must have been choice items, for he was a
first-class con artist and a great high-pressure salesman, and he sold his product well. With the rumors he
started, it didn't take long for their poisonous juices
to spread in all directions. The fact that he traveled
the state accounted for the letters that had come from
so many areas.

So the filth that had been spread had not been con-
jured up from idle minds. Each foul and perverted story
had been carefully thought out and deliberately
planted. It was an insane plan set in motion by a man I
hardly remembered. Of course, the main tragedy is that
with each repeating, the lies became even more distorted, and he counted on it happening in just that
way.

When he finished telling me what he had done, and
it was all related to me in a jabbering, half-crazy kind
of way, he leveled his eyes at me and said that he
wasn't through yet. He was suddenly as hard and cold
as steel. He intended to kill me. I wouldn't know when
it would happen or how, but he promised that, sooner
or later, when I no longer expected it, he would kill
me.

I was terrified, and he knew it. I was well aware
that anyone who would carry a grudge to the point
he had was deranged enough to commit murder. He
would "see me rot in hell." He would hear me "beg
for mercy."

It was the most unearthly, bizarre episode in my
life. I had lived through many fiascoes, but this was
the most outlandish and the most insane. It was also
deadly serious, and I knew it. He walked slowly off
the porch and was still laughing at me as he drove
away. I stood frozen, watching after him.

I hardly remember what happened the rest of the night.

Trembling, I bolted the doors and checked all the windows. I left all the lights on, and then made a dummy of pillows in the bed. I let Sport run free in the house, and then I went to the basement and locked that door after me. There was a space under half the house, and I crawled into it and worked my way to one of the far corners. I spent the night stretched out flat on my stomach with my face in the dirt, terrified.

Later, much later the next day, I crawled out, knowing there was only one person who could help me.

I had not seen Jean or her family for nearly two years, but she had spoken her thoughts that last night we were together: "If there's ever anything I can do, let me know."

I managed to drive my car to her studio and parked it in a lot across the street. To phone would be wrong. I had to ask her face-to-face. I walked through the showroom, past a startled receptionist, through the outer offices, and straight to a door marked with her name. Without knocking, I pushed it open and saw her sitting at her desk.

Tear-stained and dirty, I begged, "Will you help me? Please? Will you help me?"

18

Five long, nerve-wracking years were to pass before I would be able to clear the troubled waters of my mind. It was almost as if hell were making one last violent effort to claim me. All the strings that had held me up suddenly snapped, and like a discarded puppet, I crumpled. I became little more than a fear-ridden robot. But from the moment I asked for help, the Ratcliffes once more established themselves as my family, and only through their grace did I survive.

Jean drove me home from her office and immediately called Lunda and Lucy. That evening, with the four of us gathered together, I asked Jean to move in with me. In spite of my confused state, I saw that she was not too anxious to assume the burden I was asking her to carry, and I could not blame her, especially with a madman running wild, making threats. But she put aside her own qualms and agreed to make the move.

Lunda's first thought was to call the police and let them handle the situation, or else bring charges against the man by putting him under a restraining order. I tried to explain, as best I could, my deep-rooted fear of the law, my terror of police, saying I'd rather take chances with a wild man than risk bringing in the law. Although Lunda could not accept my logic, he respected my right of decision.

The three spent the night at my house, and I slept secure. The next morning, Ethel and Lucy moved Jean's belongings and she became an actual part of the household. Without ever asking for or having a legal share in the house, she assumed total support and responsibility.

I had let the place run down, and for three or four months, Lunda saw to a great deal of repair work. An extra bedroom was added and new furniture was brought in. But no radical changes were made, except suddenly the house looked once more as if it belonged to civilized people.

I was not pushed into any activity, but in a week or so after Jean had settled in, I decided that I would like to take on some of the daily chores, especially since it was paramount that she return to her neglected decorating accounts. I offered to do the marketing and take care of the general errands involved in running a house. I was broke, for I had rapidly exhausted my three hundred dollars in the bank. My name was put on Jean's personal checking account, and with this act of faith I had access to what money was available.

I was still frightened about being alone, wondering if he would show up again, but I knew that sooner or later I would have to face the fact that I could not have another person stand guard over me all the time.

Jean went back to work, and for a week or so I managed to function. I went to the grocery and took care of the meals and did a fair job of keeping the house picked up. I wanted desperately to drink, or, rather, a side of me wanted the blackout security it could provide, but the other side of me wanted sincerely to make a go of my life. I wanted to deserve the faith that had been put in me, but it was almost as though a war between good and evil was being waged in me, and although the ice was thin, it was, at least, still holding me up.

One evening Jean phoned that she had a late appointment and suggested that, rather than cook dinner, I might like to drive by her studio and we would eat out after she closed. It was about nine o'clock when I left the house, and as I walked to the car, he sprang out from behind the high shrubs, slashing the air with a butcher knife.

In retrospect, I think he was probably more intent on frightening me than in doing me physical harm. As he yelled and pranced around, I was able to run to the car and drive off in my *This Is Your Life* Edsel. But he was right behind me, with his head sticking out his car window and his horn blowing. In desperation I screeched into the service station where we bought our gas. He zoomed past, yelling "I'll get you. I'll be back."

The station was run by Bob Jenkins, a slip of a man from Georgia, who, though short on stature, was long on chivalry. When I cried out that a crazy man was after me with a knife, he motioned for me to drive the car on the grease rack. When the villain swerved back into the station, I, in my car, was hydraulically lifted to the ceiling. I yelled down for Bob not to call the police, just as my pursuer jumped from his car and started shaking his fists at anyone in sight. Bob then raised himself to his full five feet two, took careful aim with his grease gun, and squirted the man from head to toe.

I was trembling, almost out of control, but when I saw this tiny little man hosing down my opponent, I buried my head against the steering wheel and fell apart, in relief, in hysterics, in laughter, and in panic.

He stumbled away to his car, gleaming like patent leather, and Bob called Jean at her studio, wanting to know what to do next. She told him to keep me up there until someone could come, and in a half hour or so, Lunda arrived.

By that time I had settled down somewhat and was playing the radio and eating a candy bar. Bob had devised a supply line by tying a basket on the end of a long pole, in which he put a Coke, a pack of cigarettes and a candy bar. All basic comforts were provided, except the most fundamental, and I thought during the long wait I would explode.

Tragedy is not without humor, except when one faces it alone. And that night, with my family around me, we laughed about the fiasco until we were drained. The more we talked about it, the funnier it became, and I could not resist comparing the way we faced that particular situation to the way my humorless blood family would have reacted.

I still would not agree to bringing in the police, and Lunda, as an irate father, stormed, "This stuff has gone on long enough." He would keep the police out of it, but he was going to take matters into his own hands. I'm sure, if he could have arranged it, he would have tarred and feathered the man; instead, he tracked him down through the license number Bob had thoughtfully taken, and within a week he told me that I would never be bothered again. To this day I don't know what transpired, but the man left town, knowing it would be best for him not to return, and I have not seen or heard from him since.

After that, I settled down, confident that whatever Lunda told me was dependable. It was then decided that I should go into the decorating business with Jean, and Lunda bought out her partner. He felt that in order for me to reestablish myself, it would be announced that I had always been a silent partner in the decorating studio, and with my severance from the television program, I had decided to become an active partner in the business. He believed that not only would this give me a new identity and career, but it might help silence some of the wild speculation going around about me.

The press responded generously and we received a great deal of publicity; but rather than help the business that Jean had built with hard work and imagination, I wrecked it in three months. I had started drinking again and would show up swacked. What customers we had knew it and were offended. And then I went through a phase of self-importance, and what can be worse than a cocky drunk? I would take it upon myself to fire employees without any provocation other than an imagined slight. I would insult the workmen and infuriate the decorators. Jean closed the studio but did not take it lying down. We had severe battles over my behavior that became a war of wills. It was at that point I think she became determined to win out and not let me sink. I suppose she saw me as a personal challenge and refused to allow it to whip her. The unique and marvelous thing about my relationship with Jean is that it never took on a patient/nurse attitude. Not one of the Ratcliffes pampered me or allowed me the luxury of feeling sorry for myself.

Needless to say, she suffered severe financial losses with the closing of the business and was left with only a small private income. This is what we lived on. She added to it with occasional free-lance jobs, and we managed quite well. I still couldn't work, and the Ratcliffes realized it. Lunda was masculine enough never to admit his mistake in letting me go into the business, and Lucy, in her delightfully vague way, "missed all the pretty things in the studio."

For several weeks, we spent a lot of time taking drives and long walks. Then Joe Stockdale, the director from Purdue University, came by the house and offered me the lead in *The Visit*. This was not to be the glamorized version as depicted by Lynn Fontanne or Ingrid Bergman, but was the grotesque interpretation originated by the author.

We all were excited and pleased, and then, to add to the occasion, the president of the university gave a reception in my honor for more than two thousand guests. It was all I could dream of as an actress, and once again caught up in my own involvement, I found no cause to drink.

I studied and planned and worked the role into perfection. I was playing an eighty-year-old woman, who was also the richest woman in the world. The woman was obsessed with the idea of buying the town of her birth and then hiring the populace to kill the man who had first tossed her aside. Friedrich Duerrenmatt's original version called for the woman to have a wooden leg and an artificial hand made of ivory. It took me three hours to apply the makeup, and I was so buried in the role that I found it difficult to separate myself from it. The opening reviews were excellent and the audience was most responsive. The play was scheduled for a two-week run, with Sunday, Monday and Tuesday closings. Jean stayed with me during the first week's run, but on Friday she felt she should go home and check on the animals. I stayed on in Lafayette until Sunday to attend a brunch given for me by the dean of the Drama Department.

I had one Bloody Mary with brunch and I was anxious to get home, for I was tired though inwardly relaxed. Driving the sixty miles from Lafayette to Indianapolis, I must have fallen asleep at the wheel, for I suddenly came to, driving down the median, out of control. I managed to brake the car, turn and land in a deep ditch. I hit my head on the steering wheel and was knocked out.

I came to with a town sheriff peering into the window asking if I was hurt. Rather than answering as Frances Farmer, I reverted to my role in the play and came out as the richest woman in the world, shouting to high heaven that I would buy his goddamned town. I got out stiff-legged and ivory-handed, quoting all the imperious lines I could remember, for in the play the first thing I had corrupted with my money was the police force, so I assumed he was on my payroll. Unfortunately, this did not set well with the local authorities, and a patrol car took me to jail.

On the ride into the little town I came to myself and was totally puzzled as to what was going on. I was horrified and offended, and I no doubt gave the trooper a difficult time, for his jaw was jutted out, and he told me if I opened my mouth, he'd bust me one. I believed him, so I huddled back in the corner and tried to figure out what had happened.

At the jailhouse, I was booked for drunk driving, finger-printed, and mugged front and profile. They would not let me use the phone, so I asked them to call Jean. The Sheriff called her, in my presence, and said that I had been in an accident and was in jail for drunk driving. He gave her no other information, stating only that I was not hurt, but that if I didn't keep my mouth shut, I would be.

It was Sunday and our lawyer could not be found, so the Ratcliffes showed up at the jail and were forced to wait outside for eight hours. I was finally let out of my cell, handcuffed to a trooper, and was taken across the town square, with a full audience lining the sidewalk, to be tried before the local justice of the peace. I was fined seventy-five dollars and my license was suspended for six months.

Since the incident had happened in a remote area, none of us thought the story would make the local papers, but the next night's news carried a full account. It is obvious one of the officers had called the Indianapolis papers and given them the details. I wanted to run out on the play. I couldn't face an audience, but Joe and his wife, Robin, showed up at the house and convinced me that I should not let it get me down. They wanted me to finish the run. They had been at the brunch, knew I wasn't drunk, and were ready to defend me in every way possible. But the honor Purdue had paid me was now soiled, and I did not see how I could possibly go back.

After Joe and Robin left, I asked Jean what she thought I should do, and she told me that it was something I would have to decide for myself. She said it had nothing to do with "the show going on" stuff, but it rested with my own personal feelings. The university would let me out of my contract without a penalty if I decided to quit, but Jean said that if I really wanted to finish the play, then I should. If Purdue did not feel hampered by the "disgrace," then I was free to make my own decision.

I asked her if she would stand in the wings during the rest of the run, and she said she'd be with me at all times. Sometime close to dawn, I decided to finish my job.

The second week's opening was a sellout, and while I was making up, I was consumed with anxiety. Jean sat in the dressing room and read while I painted my face and trembled. When my call came, I don't think I could have made it had she not given me a shove that sent me onstage. There was a long silent pause as I stood there, followed by the most thunderous applause of my career. It is not customary in university theater to acknowledge a "star," but the precedent was broken by that audience, and they swept the scandal under the rug with their ovation.

After the play closed, I knew I had reached a climax as an actress. It was my finest and final performance. I knew I would never need to act onstage again. I felt satisfied and rewarded.

We returned home, my car parked in the garage to await my six-month restriction, and for three or four weeks things went rather well. I feasted on the satisfaction of my work, and then I began to feel restless and morbid. I suffered a tremendous letdown; but for that matter, it seems that I lived in cycles, cycles of depression followed by even deeper remorse. During these times of black despair, my mind would almost cease functioning. I couldn't organize myself or maintain an interest in anything. Jean was also going through a dry run in her free-lance accounts but, in contrast, could always find something to keep her busy.

I lived through each hour feeling that my whole life was behind me, and during this phase I began drinking with a passion that frightened even me. I could not control it. I became more critical, more ill tempered, more despicable than in all the other years of my life. My behavior was so erratic that it would have driven any other person screaming away in disgust and panic, but Jean never left, and we lived in almost total seclusion.

After one terrible bout, Lunda came to the house and the three of us talked openly about my problem. No nice title was given to it. I was not ill or disturbed or an alcoholic. I was a drunk. Lunda asked me if I could quit, and I told him I didn't really know. He offered to put me in a hospital, but I ran from the idea. I was afraid the doctors would put me away. Even though he tried his best to assure me that no one could, that I was my own agent, still that constant fear was ever in my thoughts. Then he asked Jean what she thought about it, and this gentle woman, wise beyond her years, spoke words that I shall never forget.

"I don't see where it will solve anything for Frances just to stop drinking," she said. "It's more than that. Never to take another drink would prove nothing, or solve nothing, because the cause would still be there. She'd just be changing the effect and would probably take up something else as a substitute. She'll never understand the problem until she can handle liquor on a take-it-or-leave-it basis, and that day will come when she reaches a mental and emotional state of fully understanding herself."

She made it very clear that she intended to stand by me and suggested that we close up the house and rent a cabin in Brown County, the area where we had gone on our first day together. She felt this remote, sparsely populated district might help me more than anything else. Lunda was agreeable and suggested that we look for a place and then rent our home furnished.

Brown County is noted for its rolling hills and marvelous scenery, and the lodge we found to rent, about four miles from the little village of Nashville, had a magnificent view undisturbed by any other houses.

We read a great deal, watched television, and took long walks with Sport. I found myself retiring early and then being up before sunrise. I would sit on the porch with Willie on my lap and listen to the natural sounds that come with daybreak. Life was satisfying.

Jean and I would spend long hours talking about life and its involvements. There was liquor in the

house, if I wanted it, and there were many evenings
when I would have several drinks, then put it aside.

We were both pleased at my "progress," but Jean
warned me not to feel that I could ditch a lifetime of
grief in a week or two. She cautioned me to take things
a day at a time and not to make any commitments or
resolutions until they came about naturally.

After we had been there a couple of months, she
was offered a job handling the designs for remodeling an
old theater for a production company opening in Indianapolis. It was an attractive arrangement for her
that would not require a great deal of time, and we
both agreed that she should take it, even though it
meant that for two or three days a week I would be
left by myself. I felt I was secure enough to risk it,
and I told her that if things didn't work out, I'd tell
her, right off.

My driver's license had been reinstated and Lunda
had decided that the old Edsel had had its day, so he
bought me a new Oldsmobile. He thought it was necessary that I have a good car to rely on since Jean
would be away for a few days a week. Here, again, he
treated me as though I had been his own daughter,
and the car was titled in my name, even though he
paid all but two hundred dollars, the trade-in price of
the Edsel.

Everything was perfect, or so it appeared to be. I
was feeling better and more confident than I had in
years. I knew I had not undergone any radical mental
changes, but I was at ease. Then, one morning, I read
in the paper that Clifford Odets had died. I went to
pieces. Jean was due back that night and I dreaded
the day alone. Finally, around noon, I drove into Nashville and bought six bottles of scotch. When she came
home, I was roaring drunk. The lodge was a mess and
I was stretched out on the porch screaming. I was too

drunk to tell her what was wrong, but I had the paper clutched in my hand, and when she pulled it away from me, she read about his death.

She managed to get me inside and spent most of the night listening to my drunken ramblings about a man I had once loved but who had not loved me. I went into and through all sorts of things, and finally, when morning came, I was so exhausted that I fell asleep.

I could not sober up. It wasn't that I was so terribly grieved over Odets, for I really hadn't thought of him in years. It was shocking to me that a part of my life, my most intimate life, had passed. Death had never phased me before. I had buried my parents in my mind while they were still alive, and I had never known any other person who had died. I could not reason with death. It was unfair. Unjustified. I told Jean, sobbing and almost incoherent, that I wanted to die first. I could not bear her to go and leave me. And then I got hysterical thinking what if something happened to Lunda and Lucy. I then screamed my fear for Sport and Willie. Suddenly, and without warning, death loomed up in front of me and scared me within the inch of my life.

I had witnessed it in the asylum, but it had been impersonal, like a flood in Chile or an earthquake in some remote area that wipes out ten thousand people. The people in the asylum had been items. But Odets' dying had touched me. I had lived with him and, for a time, for him, and I could not imagine his genius stilled.

I wanted to call Lunda and Lucy on the phone. They might die and I'd never see them again. I begged Jean to have them come down and live with us. My antics had scared the animals away and I went screaming for them. Finally, I was in such a desperate state that she had to wrestle me back into the lodge, and the only way she could contain me was finally to tie me to the bed. She wept as she was doing it, but I was wild and had to be controlled for my own protection.

She was adamant about not bringing the family into it, and she screamed over and over that I was going to make it on my own. I was not going to drag them in.

It took a full week before I exhausted myself, and when I was finally calmed down, Jean said she'd go into Indianapolis, clear up her job, and spend the night there. I had never seen her so firm. Come hell or high water I was going to straighten up and face reality. She'd gone too far to let me dump everything now.

I begged her to take my name off the checking account, so I couldn't buy anything, but the thought of it made her angrier. "For God's sake, stand on your own two feet," she yelled. "If you're going to drink, I'd rather you use the money than roll in a gutter for it, and you would, wouldn't you?"

The truth of her words made me sob in remorse. After she left, I tried desperately to fight off the urge to get drunk again. Within an hour I was in the village buying a supply of scotch. I settled down into some concentrated all-night drinking. The next morning, still drunk, I went back to the village for more and created a to-do like the little town had never seen.

I drove in on a back road that ran behind the Nashville county jail and sheriff's office. Instead of making the wide turn in the road past the jail, I ran smack into it. I then backed up, bleary-eyed and double-visioned, and started out again. I made a mistake and hit the jail once more. Then the car zoomed back and I gunned it off across a vacant lot. On the way, I took a small outbuilding and ran over a pile of discarded tires behind a service station. How it happened, I don't know, but I retraced my tracks and the car finally stopped with a dull crash at the front door of the jail.

I screamed bloody murder as several deputies pulled me out of the car, held me under the arms, and scooted me down the hall on my heels. Unfortunately, my cell had a window looking out over the courthouse lawn. I spent the day turning the air blue by shouting obscenities at passersby. I shut up only when the sheriff threatened to gag me.

Poot Jean! Once again the same scene, only a different court and a different town. My license was taken away again, for a year, and the fines totaled more than three hundred dollars. The new car was battered beyond satisfactory repair, and although no one could understand how I came out of it uninjured, I never had a bruise except to my ego.

Once out of jail I sulked at the lodge for days. Jean was furious with me. And she had every right to be, but as time wore on, things eased out. Much later, we were to retell the story for its humor, and I marveled again that out of despair can come lightness, if you're not alone.

Lunda was unhappy about the car and told me firmly I had to settle down and face up to myself. If I didn't, I'd be a cheater. It hurt me to know that I had disappointed him but I still could not promise to quit. I begged them to dump me. Lucy was horrified and scolded Lunda for being "an awful old brute." Jean stayed out of it until her father asked what she wanted to do. I waited, knowing that whatever she answered would be her permanent decision.

"Well," she said, slowly. "I've gone this far, so I think I might as well go the rest of the way with her."

Lunda put his hand on my cheek. "All right, old girl." He grinned. "You're stuck with us."

After they had gone back to Indianapolis, I tried to thank Jean, to tell her how much I valued our friendship, but it sounded trivial. That night I accepted the fact that I had become a compulsive drinker and I was ashamed. I could never solve my problems, Jean told me, without first finding security. That's for the birds, I argued, for how can there be security where it has never before existed? "Well, if you haven't got any, then you'll just have to get yourself some." We were back on the merry-go-round.

But how can you get it? I argued. Where does it come from?

"You can't get," she said simply, "until you're willing to give. You've been a taker all your life, Frances. Maybe you grew up that way. Maybe you had to, but all I know is that you don't know how to give, even an inch."

It made me angry to hear the truth, but then I asked what I had never dared ask another human being. "Do you think I am crazy?"

She looked at me and smiled. "That would be the easy way out. Nothing could ever convince me that you are bonkers. All that's wrong with you is that you're plain damn mean. You got a mean streak in you a mile wide, and you don't know how to keep your mouth shut. You've got a lousy temper and one hell of an ego. But crazy? Never."

"But I was locked up for years," I cried.

"Sure you were, but did it ever occur to you that if, just once, you'd have kept your mouth shut, you might not have got into so much trouble? But not you. You had to mouth off."

"Why do you think my people did it to me?"

"That I can't answer. God knows why, but you never needed to be put away. You just needed somebody who cared about you to stand up and be counted. That's all. You lost a lot of years, but you can't bring them back by hanging onto the past. It's gone, but as long as you hold onto it, you won't have a future."

"You can't throw it away like a dress that doesn't fit anymore."

"Maybe you can't, Frances, but at least you can try."

19

I hope to relate in accurate detail the step-by-step progress we made, for by so doing there might be others who could benefit from our efforts. I use "our" and "we," for it was not a solo trip, and I could never have done it alone, nor can anyone. There might be people who have laid aside false appetites and have overcome habits, but the core cannot be pulled out alone. And yet in the world there are so few with the wisdom and understanding that Jean had. I have known and been known by thousands of people, but only one counted.

She ignored my edict that an insecure person has nothing to give and thus has no hope of receiving. "Everyone," she said, "has something, except maybe they're too selfish to give it." She set about to prove her theory. It was months before I realized what she had done, and through the strife and stress, I never recognized her motives.

When we moved back to Indianapolis, it all began by her slowly teaching me how to give of myself. I did not stop drinking, but it was in spurts, and one day, when I had been in bed for over a week with the dregs of a hangover and low blood pressure, when I was, indeed, feeling low and very sorry for myself, she brought home a tiny kitten, not more than six weeks old, whose four paws had been nearly burned off. The little creature had obviously been tortured and was unable to walk. She laid it on the bed and said, "I found this, Frances, and I thought maybe you'd know what to do about it." It looked almost like the cat in the asylum, and I panicked and screamed, "I don't want it. Get it out of here."

"You just shut that up," she stormed. "What do you expect me to do, throw it out in the street? Now, straighten yourself up. The least you can do is help this little thing."

I grumbled and groaned but finally reached down and stroked its tiny head.

We called our vet who prescribed an ointment to be applied every three hours, around the clock. It seems it is not uncommon for kittens to be mistreated in such a way, although I could never accept the reality of such horror.

Jean picked up the medicine, and after she was satisfied that the kitten and I had settled down, she decided to spend the night with her parents. I was furious that she would pull such a "dirty trick," but she left with me yelling after her that I wanted none of the responsibility. I was extremely angry at being left alone to care for a half-dead animal. It was not my forte, but having no choice, I did my best by the kitten. I settled it at the foot of my bed. I decided to call it Holly-go-lightly. I set the clock on a three-hour schedule, in case I happened to fall asleep and miss its medication, and by the next afternoon when Jean returned, Holly and I were fast becoming good friends. I would try, though not too hard, to keep it at the foot of my bed, but it would wiggle itself up, and despite the fact that it couldn't walk, it would somehow end up on my pillow . . . and I left it there beside me.

Jean did not embarrass me by commenting on my obvious care, and I declared gruffly that as soon as the damn thing got on its feet, out it would go.

I didn't mention to Jean that I had named it or that I set my clock to make sure it was treated on time, and long after it was well, I still grumbled about taking in strays.

Not long afterward Jean just happened to find another wounded kitten, a tiny gray-and-white one, which had been attacked by dogs. She carried it in, wrapped in a towel, and once more, over my objections, we had a new and helpless resident, which, of course, I had to care for. This one I named Clarence, after the cross-eyed lion, for obvious reasons. We could never tell which way the cat was looking.

Our household was growing. We now had three cats and a dog. Then Holly "got in a family way," as Jean put it. She seemed to have a sixth sense in such matters, for on the day the kittens were due, she conveniently decided to visit her parents and left me to face my first experience with motherhood alone.

Of course, Holly decided to have the babies in my bedroom, at about five in the morning. I was panic-stricken, and when I called Jean about an hour later to report on the delivery, I was gloriously drunk.

"I've got goddamned kittens spewing out all over the place. Now, you come on out here. I don't know what to do."

And she said. "Frances, *you* don't have to do anything. You'll see. Just sit back and watch life happening. Holly will take care of her own babies, and when they're all birthed, she'll let you hold them. You'll see."

"Don't hand me any more crap. I'm not going to be a damn midwife to a cat, and that's final. Now, you get out here."

But she laughed at my fears and hung up with nothing more than a promise to show up the next afternoon. So I poured a stiff drink and sat cross-legged in the middle of my bed and watched it happen. I saw her greet each one, turning it over and over, licking it with its tongue, biting the cord and tending it until it began to cry. Six times it washed and cleaned and brought them to life, then guided them to its breast.

I had always pictured birth as something of pain and labor, but to see the intricate and detailed care the mother cat gave its newborn shed a rewarding light, and by the time Jean came we had a household of eight cats and one dog.

I was determined that we would find homes for the kittens, and halfheartedly, she agreed. At the end of six charming weeks with them, I had them ready for well-respected homes and Holly made a quick trip to the vet to have her tubes tied.

Perhaps three or four months after the litter was adopted out, Jean found still another kitten; this one, we thought, had had its leg cut off. But after an examination by the doctor, we learned that it had probably been run over, and the leg had been shoved up into the shoulder socket. So once more I doffed my uniform and set up a feline hospital in my bedroom.

Deciding that kittens were all well and good, but that children were also a working part of this world, Jean brought her five nieces to visit. Before long, Betty Whitaker began stopping by with her youngest daughter, Carolyn, and Bezie Droege, a dear friend of Jean's, would show up with her two girls, Kay and Mary.

And there was I, a hard-bitten old dame, caught in the middle with kids running in and out, people dropping in, unannounced, and cats peeking at me from every corner. What had once been a dry, crusty house was suddenly coming alive. We were always busy, making plans for imaginative parties, giving cookouts for the children or planning special projects around the house. Something, it seems, was always happening, and without realizing it, I was drinking less.

Then, in the spring, when it was first beginning to turn warm, Jean decided that we needed to "redecorate" the backyard and put in a swimming pool. She made a deal with a local contractor to handle part of the costs by doing some advertising work for him, and almost overnight we had it done. With her planning we were able to turn the yard into a charming, carefully overgrown area that was private and green. I began getting up at dawn to work in the garden and would stay outside until well after dark, puttering around the flower beds.

It was common for us to have a group of twenty people sitting around the pool by the end of the day. We would grill hamburgers and sing cowboy songs and share good conversation. Without knowing it, I was planting roots and learning the pleasures that can come with responsibility.

That summer, on one of the rare quiet days at our house, sitting alone by the pool, I looked around me and saw a house that had somehow become a home. I saw Sport racing up and down his run and Old Willie snoozing on the patio. The other cats, all eleven of them, were tucked away in the lush bushes, and then I saw Jean stretched out in the hammock asleep. Lunda and Lucy were playing rum under the shade tree, and I knew the first stirrings of truth. I knew the security of love. I had given it, and I had received it.

There had been a gradual awakening within me. A strange and exciting stirring of self-dignity, almost like a rebirth. Though I was still anxious and on edge about many of the old inner complexes, there was a new complexion to my life. I was still supicious of most people, wary of their motives, and there was the ever-constant dread that some calamity might topple my newfound security, but, nonetheless, I was striding into a marvelous and unique universe.

Those whom I had come to call friends had been brought into my life because of Jean's hospitality and introduction, but in spite of my evident inexperience and shortcomings in such relationships, they had remained and encircled me in their warmth.

John and Rita Hobbs, precious friends, gave me a sense of glamor and importance. With John's great flair and charm, I was carried into a world of true sophistication. Rita, a talented sculptress, did my head in a fashion that pleased me, for she saw in me the pioneer spirit of my ancestors and brought it to life through clay.

Ellen Glessing, so young and gentle, came quietly into my world and offered me the understanding of friendship.

Joe and Robin Stockdale, always near in thought, kept me involved in the theater and became beloved companions.

Flo Garvin, a marvelous talent, brilliant in her singing, showed me that black is more than just beautiful.

Jim Gerrad, a tender and kind spirit, shouldered so much of the responsibility when I could not handle my program and went even further to defend my name and reputation.

Pat Flannigan, an artist, painted a picture of a sorrowing clown for me and, in so doing, said, "I understand."

Ethel Miller, a gentle and loyal woman, who often disapproved but always cared.

And Farrell Whitfield, Jean's "almost-sister," who came to be mine and brought with her all the pleasures of a near-kin. And her five daughters, charming little creatures, who, one by one, captured my heart and became, in fact, my nieces.

And Jim and Bezie Droege, devoted and so loyal, have added strength to my life and happiness to my memories.

Betty Whitaker, a woman whom I trust, overflowing with charm and humor, led me to understand that people, regardless of who they are or what they have done, deserve to be loved.

And Ed and Moselle Shaeffer, who became especially mine.

All these wonderful people, one by one, opened the door to my heart, and with love I remember them. And in gratitude, I call them each friend.

20

The years from 1964 have been complicated and challenging, but the rewards have been without measure.

Professionally, I had accomplished a peak with my work in *The Visit,* and I was more than satisfied as an actress, but I had always been curious to know how it would feel to hold an audience with a solo performance.

Carl Winehardt, the director of the Indianapolis Museum of Art, and his wife, Neta, had become my good friends, and they suggested that I might like to present an evening of poetry for the members. I was hesitant, but the more I considered the idea, the more it fascinated me. In May, 1968, I read Tennyson's "Enoch Arden" and other selections, including my own favorite, Emily Dickinson's "Will There Really Be a Morning?" to the museum's audience. The personal satisfaction from it filled me to capacity, and I knew my hunger for expression had been stilled.

How strange to compare the *The Visit* and "Enoch Arden," done not for monetary returns but only for their artistic merit, with the cold-cash epics of Hollywood. One had filled my purse, the other my soul.

All the loose ends of my life seemed to be coming together, and I remember the summer of 1968 as the season of my rebirth. And when I think on it, I am reminded of the Bible verse ". . . and a little child shall lead them."

I had never been around children until I formed an attachment for "my nieces." In fact, it was stamped on my mind to avoid any contact, and this I had accepted as the result of the guilt I felt about my Hollywood abortions. I simply did not have the gall to face a child, but the five little girls opened my heart and eased away my guilt.

On a particularly hot summer day, Farrell had brought them over to enjoy the pool, and Jean had kept them busy with food and activities. I had spent most of my time supervising the swimming, for we never left any child unguarded. Then, in midafternoon, amid their howls of disappointment, Farrell decided it was time to go. She gathered them up with the promise that there would be another day.

Children, so it seems to me, invariably arrive and depart in a hassle of excitement, and this day was no exception. They were all frantically hunting a towel or a lost shoe, and after much to-do, everything had been gathered up and they disappeared around the house to their car. When they were gone, the yard was suddenly naked in its silence, for when children leave they take something musical with them. As soon as the had left, Jean sighed with exhausted pleasure and went immediately into the house to lie down.

With the yard empty, I felt suddenly alone and pensive. It was terribly quiet, and the sun prancing on the water made the air almost unreal. I am not able to describe my thoughts, except to say they were privately haunting. I felt the warmth of love, and yet, suddenly, I knew the sorrow of unexpected solitude. I had an empty, lost feeling. Perhaps a blue mood would describe it.

And then I saw my "niece" Gina, who was twelve at the time, peek shyly around the corner of the house, and in the pure, simple voice of a child, she ran toward me, crying, "Aunt Frances, I didn't kiss you good-bye."

I held out my arms to her and felt her nestle her cheek against mine, and in my ear, almost with the whisper of a butterfly on wing, I heard, "I love you so much, because you're good."

And then she was gone. Skipping away, her long hair swinging behind her like a wind-tossed goldenrod. As she left, a dry sob caught in my throat. No one had ever said that to me before. No one had probably ever thought it, for that matter, and it was there, at that moment, that a heart chiseled of stone melted.

I could not hold back the floodgate of tears, not for being told that I was loved, or even good, but because my heart pounded with the joy and humility of belonging.

On that quiet summer day I felt the first thunderous movement of God in my life, and the soft voice of a child, the tender caress of her cheek against mine, had opened the door.

It was a terrible and marvelous experience, and I was aware of all the evil that had surrounded me being washed away. I was overpowered with a sense of forgiveness and change.

Life took on a new meaning. It was all-powerful. It flowed from me like a wellspring. I was reborn, and I knew that I would have to find a disciplined avenue of faith and worship. Without knowing how, without ever consciously seeking it, God had come into my life, and from that day forth, I began on a path to spiritual fulfillment.

I had changed, and Jean knew it without ever asking how or why. And others knew it. It showed.

I had never given great concern to organized religion, and I was like a wayfaring stranger until one day I found myself sitting in Saint Joan of Arc, the Catholic church of our neighborhood. I had passed the cathedral countless times, but that afternoon, as I was returning from marketing, I stopped and sat alone in the great hall. It was quiet and dark, and I studied the massive altar and understood, for the first time, the power and meaning of the Crucifixion.

I petitioned that very day to begin my instructions and was converted to the Catholic faith. But the conversion was not without personal crucifixion, for the good father who had instructed me suggested that I make my first confession to someone in another church. He wanted me to go where I was a stranger. He was a delightful old man, and I'm sure he pictured me a certain way and preferred to hold to his own thoughts. I went to a downtown church where I was not known, and I have never had such a soul-shattering experience.

I felt it necessary to purge myself in the confessional, but we started off on the wrong foot—he thought I was a man. I have a deep, theatrical voice, my so-called trademark, but to the father, I was someone in the confessional making fun. We finally settled down, and I think I sent him into shock with my confessions. By the time I started counting off the abortions, he was livid and not at all understanding. He reprimanded me so violently I went sobbing from the booth and fell facedown at the altar. I, in his eyes, was an unforgivable sevenfold murderer. My cries brought out the monsignor, who, though puzzled at the commotion, tried to comfort me. I sobbed out my story, and there at the altar that kind and gentle man gave me his blessings.

Horrified by the incident, I wore dark glasses day

and night for three weeks. Jean tried to reason that I was starting afresh. She was not of the faith, in fact had no understanding of it, but she realized that unless I was able to face up to and accept the dogmas of my church, of which forgiveness was one, I would be lost in a whirlpool of remorse.

Finally, after days of prayer and petitions, I took off the dark glasses and accepted myself and the world around me.

From the faith I have taken the security that there is a God who loves and directs all things. I have been able to lay aside the grinding hatred and guilts. I still suffer from the past and hope that in time I can better understand the ragged pitfalls into which I have fallen. And yet, if that understanding fails to come, there is a faith now abiding deep within me which promises that I can come through them all unharmed.

I do not choose to proselytize, for I hold strong to the belief that each of us must find our own salvation, and the fact that I did not choose the religion of my closest friends only confirms the freedom of choice and personal discernment that was allowed me. I found my way through their love and understanding, and I elected my faith, though far removed from theirs, of my own free will.

Jean would go to mass with me, and then I would attend her services at Unity, so our Sunday mornings were full of all good things, and though we were far distant in our methods of worship, we were able to bring them together in fellowship and understanding.

And so it was, in 1968, that I laid aside all false appetites. The compulsion to drink the past from my memory faded. The need to obliterate was gone. I was no longer chained. I understood the causes and savored the freedom this understanding brought me. I became positive and solid. My world and my spirit were secure. And my mind was, at last, free.

And I have learned that to have a good friend is the purest of all God's gifts, for it is a love that has no exchange of payment. It is not inherited, as with a family. It is not compelling, as with a child. And it has no means of physical pleasure, as with a mate. It is, therefore, an indescribable bond that brings with it a far deeper devotion than all the others.

So with gratitude I think of Jean, for she remained when others vanished. She believed when others doubted. And she gave when others received.

Through her, all good was brought into my life, and through the good, I came to know and believe in God.

21

That fall, when I was well and happy, I was able to appraise my life with sound logic. I had not worked in more than four years. It had taken all those months to resolve the wounds of a lifetime. No pressures had been brought to bear on me to contribute to the up-keep and support of the house, but now that I was, at last, solid and established, I told them at a family meeting that I was ready to do something with my life. We spent days thinking over what business Jean and I could share that would offer us a secure future.

I had long been fascinated with the art of makeup, and it was Lunda's suggestion that I should take this experience and knowledge and convert it into a beauty product. I knew nothing about the chemical com-pounds that went into creams and lotions, but I did know quality and its results. With Jean's business knowledge and my contribution to the partnership, we founded a cosmetic company. For more than a year we worked with a laboratory until I was convinced that we had a line of products that was not only unique in quality, but reasonably priced.

I became immersed in the pride of this accomplish-ment, for at last I was a necessary and contributing part of an undertaking. Jean was not carrying the whole load. We were sharing.

When we had successfully field-tested our products,

we formed a corporation and set out to raise the necessary monies required for national distribution. In order to finance the original development, we had mortgaged the house and Lunda had come into the partnership with the rest of the money. Now the time had come to set all our plans in motion, but the man involved in funding the corporation manipulated our investment portfolio until all the backup funds were exhausted. He appeared to be the epitome of honesty, but he was the greatest crook I had ever met. Our personal money was wiped out, and we had to lay the project aside. We had lost everything we had. Not only that, we owed Lunda an amount we could never repay. All this meant that the house and all other negotiable properties would have to go, and our standard of living would be drastically cut.

Both Jean and I felt the blow severely, but neither of us was shattered by it, as we might have been. As for me, I was overwhelmed with the joy that even though we faced a most serious loss, I had not felt the slightest urge to drink the troubles out of my system. I had lost a battle, but I had won the war.

Lunda and Lucy never complained or criticized us for having lost so much money; they only wanted us to have the courage to try again and felt it would be good if we would live with them until we could get back on our feet. But we were no longer free agents. We were owned by a troop of cats and an overgrown dog, and though neither of us wanted to admit it at first, we couldn't bear to break up the menagerie. We were hemmed in, and we loved it. It is, however, difficult to find living quarters for thirteen cats and a dog. A day or two before we had to give up possession of the house, Jean, while wildly scanning the rental ads in the paper, saw two lines listed under suburban property. We found a farmhouse for lease.

Everything fell into place. I called the listed number and talked with a delightful Irish lady, a Mrs. Sullivan, who said her daughter, Marie, owned the farm, but she gave us the address of the house and suggested that perhaps it would be best if we drove by and saw it. She apologized that it might be a little run-down for our tastes, but we were already smitten with the prospects of living in the country and would have taken it sight unseen. Ancient and Chekhovian in its tumble-down state, the house rested on a soft hill in the middle of a three-hundred-acre compound. The farmland was leased out to a commercial farmer, but the big old creaking house stood vacant and terribly alone. Under its many-gabled roofs were twelve high-ceilinged rooms, and as we peeked in through the dusty windows, both of us knew we had found our home.

We signed the lease on November 1, 1969, and within a month, on a budget that was barely sufficient to feed and warm us, imagination and sweat had turned it into a magic land. The cats, after exploring all nooks and corners, went out to become great hunters, and Sport was allowed to run free.

We were almost financially destitute, but that was unimportant, for the house overflowed with people we loved. Gina and her friends filled the rooms on weekends with slumber-party guests. We had an old-fashioned Thanksgiving dinner, with people arriving all day long, bringing covered dishes and good cheer.

And then Christmas came, blanketed in a heavy pure snow, and my heart was never so warmed as when I saw those I loved gathered around me. Lunda and Lucy. Jim and Bezie and their girls, Anne, Mary and Kay. Betty and her daughter, Carolyn. Farrell and her girls. All our other friends dropped by to say hello, and everything was perfect and exactly right.

There is a peace that comes with living in the country. We were only a few miles from town, but we seemed isolated, in a different world. I had reached a place where I could objectively see my life and I felt that it was time for me to begin to record my thoughts and feelings. I timidly approached Jean with the idea that I would like to begin writing my life story. I was at that point in my experiences where all the fears had been calmed. All the doubts had been stilled. My house was in order.

We were sitting in the big, comfortable kitchen when I brought it up, and she just smiled at me with pride.

It was strange, in the beginning, to settle into the past. I took it out almost as you would old souvenirs that had been tucked away in a long-forgotten box. I hunted through the attic of my mind to find the threads of my story, and I did so without vanity, for there was little of which I could be proud.

As I wrote and thought, I laid down the facts of a tattered and war-torn life. I had not lived as a good woman, but there was one factor to my credit. I never pretended to be what I was not.

I drew heavily on Jean, and in mutual trust we began to formulate a book. Whenever I was tempted to hedge or venture too much self-pity, she would pull me back. We wrote and rewrote, always together. When I became pontifical, she would edit me ruthlessly. When I felt I could not reenter the violent years, she listened through my screams and compiled the nightmare. She consoled me when I became guilt-ridden and conscience-stricken, and finally I was able to recount my years, facing them with honesty and self-understanding.

As the pages began to grow into a healthy mound, I was able, almost, to hold the past in my hand. And as I relived all the days that had affected me, retasting all the bitterness, remembering my youth, seeing my failures, knowing my sins, the agony seemed worth it, for every crooked twist had led me to the happiness I now possessed. I wrote, knowing that I had reached contentment and it was as actual as had been my misery. Both were extremes. Both were soul-shattering.

In April, after a cold, white winter, after days of soft pleasure and nights of gentle peace, I began to feel a tightening in my throat. I was working very hard at my writing and I would arise in the mornings rather tired. By midday I would have to go to my room and rest. Sometimes I could feel a catch in my throat, almost as if something had lodged there. I was having headaches, and I thought at first it was nothing but a sinus congestion.

And then the tightness took a stranglehold and I could not swallow without pain. I knew that something was wrong, and I tried to hide it from Jean. I was startled therefore when she said one day, "I think it's time you saw a doctor, Frances. There's probably nothing much wrong, but you'd better have a checkup."

But I faced one drastic problem. There was no money. Every cent was budgeted in careful expenditures, and a doctor's call was not included.

For a few days I went ahead and worked on the book, and then one morning I called Moselle and asked if I could have a talk with her and Ed. Ed is a prominent orthopedic surgeon, but I thought he might be able to prescribe something for me. Moselle invited us to dinner, but I begged off, not wanting to go through the difficulties of trying to swallow a solid meal, and suggested that we stop by later in the evening.

That night I told Ed the symptoms and admitted that I did not have the money to pay for a doctor's call. It might sound, to some, like a humiliating experience, but it was far from that, for these two people had become dear friends. We sat in their family room talking, and then Ed walked over to me and wrapped his arm around my shoulder. He bent down and kissed me on the forehead, like a big brother, and told me not to worry.

The next morning he called and said there was an appointment set up that afternoon with a specialist. When we left the office, Jean and I knew, without saying it, that I might have to face a serious diagnosis. The doctor wanted an immediate biopsy performed on the esophagus, and though the word was not said, we knew the danger signals were up.

A week later I was in the hospital, quartered in a pleasant room, and although I have no assurance of it, in my heart I know that Ed and Moselle provided the way for me. I received the very best care but never a bill, either from the hospital or from any attending doctor or surgeon. Somehow everything was handled without a disturbing thought.

The morning I left for the hospital, I awoke very early and I could hear Jean downstairs feeding the cats and Sport, talking to them as she always did, and as I lay there, thinking of what might lie ahead of me, I was comforted, for I knew I was not alone.

We had a long, quiet breakfast together and our talk was not strained or pretended. It was much like any other morning. We spoke about my book and how near I was to finishing it. And we wondered if Gypsy, one of our cats, was pregnant, and I admitted that it would be fun to have kittens at the farm. We talked about the weather and the signs of spring in the air.

It was, indeed, much like any other morning, except I felt I wanted to say something special to Jean.

But what does one say at such times?

Buds were just beginning to come on the trees, and through the window I could see the gentle rolling hill that ran up from behind the house. New calves, clinging to their mothers, dotted the fields, and it came to me that all the words I could possibly combine could be simply put into one brief sentence. And it was then, for the first time in my life, I spoke the words "I'm happy."

22

Cancer! Not real! Not true! Not at first! Even after I was told that a malignant tumor had diseased the esophagus and lay against the great artery, making an operation impossible, I still could not accept it.

X-ray therapy has been ineffective, and finally, after five weeks in the hospital, a plastic tube through which I am to be fed has been sutured into my stomach. I can never swallow again.

I have not been told, in so many words, that I will die, and when I faced Jean with the dreadful query "Is it hopeless?" she gave me the strength to know that faith is the only link we have with God.

And so, during all the days that have followed, through the pain and blood, through the nights of prolonged agony, when I have weakened, she has strengthened that link and renewed my faith.

In the still night, when I am suddenly frightened, she calms me. In the hard glare of day, when there is no hope to soften the dread reality, she teaches me to live without fear, or despair. I have walked through the shadow, and my friend has come with me, quietly and kind, and I am not alone!

I am home! Oh, God. After three weeks away, I am home and it is like springing to life again. Sport leaped and howled as we drove up, jumping the fence to get to me. And the cats were lined up at the window, waiting.

I have come home to mend.

I see the grass has turned green since I've been away and the trees are now in new leaf. In the yard, forsythia bushes hang heavy with bright-yellow blossoms.

And there is no sign of death. No thought of it. I am alert to the pleasures that come with all living things, and I must not gaze, even for a moment, on darkness.

I am so anxious to be well, and I sit on the porch, comforted to know that somehow my body might mend.

The July sun pelts the city, but on our hillside a stubborn breeze cools the air and causes the leaves to sing, even in the heat of the day.

At night, the quiet sounds of the country and the rustle of shy rabbits in the tall grass are all that invades our world.

All is well.

I find new strength inching its way, and I wait.

There is much, now, for me to write about. Things I would say, for there is poetry in life. It is important that I finish.

We have four new kittens today. They are born in my room. Soft and still blind, they cling to their mother and I hear her gentle purr telling them that she is near and ever aware of their needs. And I hear them cry when she ventures away.

I am like that with God, I think.

There are times now when my world is dark. Sometimes so dark that I cannot see or feel it, and then I hear the sounds of His being.

I feel the pulse of my heart singing in my ears.

I smell the heady breath of summer come softly through my window. And I see the face of my friend, drawn and tired, but always gentle . . . always somehow able to smile.

And then I know that God is nearby.

Blood! Violent, fierce hemorrhage! It strangles my heart with fear.

What is it? I cry. What's happening?

Sunday, late July. I hold onto her while blood spurts from my mouth in great waves and drenches us.

And then the shrill scream of a siren blocks out everything, and I am taken away.

It is hard to think.

I would keep my senses, for I fear oblivion. And I am carried back to the years of shock and the nightmare comes again to haunt me.

But this time it haunts with a reason and tells me that I have faced more of death than at this threshold on which I now stand. I have died by the hour, by rote almost. For years I died; every day, every hour, every movement of the clock was a death. And knowing it, I can face this strangulation with ease.

I know the terror of pain, as it now is, but locked away those years, forgotten in a madhouse, I suffered even more.

I have God here, but He was never there.

On the afternoon of August 1, 1970, at three Frances Farmer died. Alone.

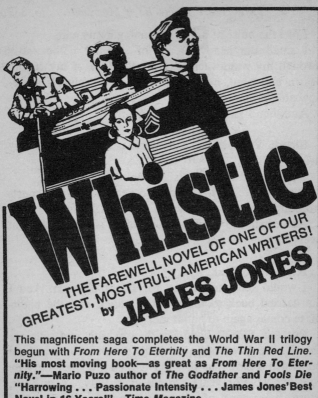

![Dell] Bestsellers

To be a powerful television event,
starring Ellen Burstyn.

STRANGERS

by Michael de Guzman

Abigail left home at 16. She did not return even for
her father's funeral. Now the years have passed and
42-year-old Abigail must come home, to face her
memories and her mother, Lucy. Although their hostility and long-smoldering jealousies gradually melt
away, the shattering moment is coming when Lucy
realizes that she is being betrayed again, and that
Abigail has come home to die!

A Dell Book $2.25